CHRISTIANITY AND DEMOCRACY

CAMBRIDGE STUDIES IN IDEOLOGY AND RELIGION

General Editors: DUNCAN FORRESTER *and* ALISTAIR KEE

Religion increasingly is seen as a renewed force, and is recognised as an important factor in the modern world in all aspects of life – cultural, economic, and political. It is no longer a matter of surprise to find religious factors at work in areas and situations of political tension. However, our information about these situations has tended to come from two main sources. The news-gathering agencies are well-placed to convey information, but are hampered by the fact that their representatives are not equipped to provide analysis of the religious forces involved. Alternatively, the movements generate their own accounts, which understandably seem less than objective to outside observers. There is no lack of information or factual material, but a real need for sound academic analysis. 'Cambridge Studies in Ideology and Religion' will meet this need. It will give an objective, balanced, and programmatic coverage to issues which – while of wide potential interest – have been largely neglected by analytical investigation, apart from the appearance of sporadic individual studies. Intended to enable debate to proceed at a higher level, the series should lead to a new phase in our understanding of the relationship between ideology and religion.

A list of titles in the series is given at the end of the book.

CHRISTIANITY AND DEMOCRACY

A theology for a just world order

JOHN W. DE GRUCHY

Robert Selby Taylor Professor of Christian Studies,
University of Cape Town

CAMBRIDGE
UNIVERSITY PRESS

Published by the Press Syndicate of the University of Cambridge
The Pitt Building, Trumpington Street, Cambridge CB2 1RP
40 West 20th Street, New York, NY 10011–4211, USA
10 Stamford Road, Oakleigh, Melbourne 3166, Australia

© Cambridge University Press 1995

First published 1995

Printed in Great Britain by Athenaeum Press Ltd, Gateshead

A catalogue record for this book is available from the British Library

Library of Congress cataloguing in publication data
De Gruchy, John W.
Christianity and democracy: a theology for a just world order / John W. de Gruchy.
p.   cm. – (Cambridge studies in ideology and religion)
Includes bibliographical references and index.
ISBN 0 521 45216 3 (hardback) – ISBN 0 521 45841 2 (paperback)
1. Democracy – Religious aspects – Christianity.
2. Democracy – Regilious aspects – Christianity – History – 20th century.
3. World politics – 20th century.
I. Title.   II. Series.
BR115.P7D34   1995
261.7 – dc20   95–29548   CIP

ISBN 0 521 45216 3 hardback
ISBN 0 521 45841 2 paperback

To Thea and David,
and to all the children of the
new democratic South Africa.

Contents

General editors' preface

Only twenty years ago it was widely assumed that religion had lost its previous place in western culture and that this pattern would spread throughout the world. Since then religion has become a renewed force, recognised as an important factor in the modern world in all aspects of life, cultural, economic and political. This is true not only of the Third World, but in Europe East and West, and in North America. It is no longer a surprise to find a religious factor at work in areas of political tension.

Religion and ideology form a mixture which can be of interest to the observer, but in practice dangerous and explosive. Our information about such matters comes for the most part from three types of sources. The first is the media which understandably tend to concentrate on newsworthy events, without taking the time to deal with the underlying issues of which they are but symptoms. The second source comprises studies by social scientists who often adopt a functionalist and reductionist view of the faith and beliefs which motivate those directly involved in such situations. Finally, there are the statements and writings of those committed to the religious or ideological movements themselves. We seldom lack information, but there is a need – often an urgent need – for sound objective analysis which can make use of the best contemporary approaches to both politics and religion. Cambridge Studies in Ideology and Religion is designed to meet this need.

The subject matter is global and this will be reflected in the choice both of topics and authors. The initial volumes will be concerned primarily with movements involving the Christian religion, but as the series becomes established movements involving other world religions will be subjected to the same objective critical analysis. In all cases it is our intention that an accurate and sensitive account of religion should be informed by an objective and sophisticated application of perspectives from the social sciences.

It is some considerable time since a major theological study of democracy has appeared. At one level, John de Gruchy's book is a 'tract for the times', addressing the situation following the collapse of the Marxist regimes of eastern Europe and the emergence of democracy in the wake of the apartheid regime in South Africa. Broad issues of the theological significance and the religious undergirding of democracy are addressed in the broad context of the end of the Cold War and the emergence of a so-called New World Order. This is an exciting, timely, and relevant book which is a major contribution to contemporary debate and a constructive endeavour to 'discern the signs of the times'.

DUNCAN FORRESTER AND ALISTAIR KEE
New College, University of Edinburgh

Acknowledgements

An invitation from Cambridge University Press to contribute to this series on *Ideology and Religion* and another, by Ripon College, Cuddesdon, to be the Karl Jaspers' Lecturer at the University of Oxford in the first half of 1993, provided the incentive to embark on this project and the possibility of a five-month sabbatical in Britain in which to pursue it. Half of this period was spent at Ripon College and the other at New College and the Centre for the Study of Christianity in the Non-Western World at the University of Edinburgh. At the outset, then, I wish to thank Alex Wright of CUP for his confidence in my endeavours and help along the way to their completion as well as Canon John Garton, Principal of Ripon College, Professor Duncan Forrester, Dean of New College, and Professor Andrew Walls, Director of the Centre for the Study of Christianity in the Non-Western World, for all they and their colleagues did to provide such hospitable and stimulating environments in which to live and work. I would also thank Jonathan Draper, rector of St Mary's, Putney, London, and formerly a lecturer at Ripon College, who initiated the process which took us to Oxford.

Much remained to be done on returning to Cape Town last July. The problem was not just trying to meet publishing deadlines amidst other responsibilities, but doing so at a moment in world history when many of the issues being considered were headline news virtually every day. A week seldom went by without new books, essays, and articles being published on the subject of democracy as well as on the role of the churches in the process of democratic transition. It was also a turbulent period in the history of South Africa's own political development as the country sought to overcome the fearful and violent legacy of apartheid and prepare itself for its first democratic election. The eyes of the world had become fixed on South Africa as the laboratory in which one of the most difficult yet remarkably hopeful experiments in the history of democratic transition was in progress.

The University of Cape Town was generous in its granting of study and research leave, and my colleagues in the Department of Religious Studies were willing to take on additional responsibilities to make it possible for me to be away. The Centre for Science Development (CSD) provided financial assistance to make the sabbatical a reality and, through the Research Institute on Christianity in South Africa (RICSA) and the Religion and Social Change Unit (RESCU) in the Department of Religious Studies, they also provided additional resources especially in the person of Noël Stott who helped track down important bibliographical material. My colleagues in RICSA, Charles Villa-Vicencio (whose own volume, *A Theology of Reconstruction*, initiated this series) and Barney Pityana were, as always, helpful in their encouragement and critical comments. I am also grateful to those who participated in my graduate seminar on Christianity and Democracy during the second semester of 1993 for their stimulating participation, and especially to Steve Martin for his editorial assistance and work on the index.

Alex Boraine, Executive Director of the Institute for Democracy in South Africa (Idasa) and a lifelong friend and colleague was helpful in a variety of ways, not least through inviting me to tour eastern Europe in May 1992 as part of a study group examining the problems of democratic transition in Germany, Czechoslovakia, and Hungary. Paul Gifford of the School of Oriental and African Studies at the University of London was instrumental in inviting me to participate in a Conference at the University of Leeds in September 1993 on 'The Christian Churches and Africa's Democratization', an event which was most helpful in providing resources and insights for chapter 6.

There are many others whom I wish to thank for their comments at various moments in the writing and revising of the manuscript. In particular I would mention Wolfgang Huber, André du Toit, Annette Seegers, Denise Ackermann, Larry Rasmussen, Mary Simons, Tom Ambrogio, Michael Pye, and Keith Clements. Of course, none can be held responsible for any of the blemishes in the book. As always, Nan Oosthuizen has been the very best of secretaries; Jane Perry an excellent editor; and Isobel a warm and supportive wife who has a growing appreciation for the biblical warning that 'there is no end to the writing of books'.

The book was completed during the week of the inauguration of Mr Nelson Mandela as the President of South Africa. In several of his speeches during those unforgettable days, notably in opening the first democratically elected parliament, Mr Mandela spoke with great passion about the importance of children in the building of a new nation. It is therefore appropriate that this book should be dedicated to our grandchildren, Thea and David, and all the children born into a reborn South Africa. May they not only enjoy the fruits of a truly just society, but also make their own contribution to its future success.

Introduction

Future generations will look back on the events which occurred in eastern Europe in 1989 as a watershed in world history. My wife and I were at Union Theological Seminary in New York at the time. For a few days in September we hosted the Director of the Marxist–Leninist Institute in Rostock, Dr Günther Hoffman. Hoffman was a member of a group of theologians and philosophers from the German Democratic Republic who were visiting the United States to experience life within a liberal democratic and capitalist society and compare it with their own. Together we watched the news on television each evening. It was the week during which many East Germans were fleeing across the border into Czechoslovakia and then to the West. On two occasions the television coverage of the events taking place in East Germany was juxtaposed with that of mass marches in Cape Town protesting against apartheid. These were the first such protests for many decades which were permitted by the authorities in South Africa.

As South Africans we found the marches no less remarkable than the events taking place in eastern Europe. As we watched their unfolding, we believed that this was the beginning of the end for apartheid; our guest, on the contrary, was confident that the German Democratic government would reform and survive. Yet, whatever our differences of perception, we sensed that the traumatic developments in eastern Europe were historically connected to what was happening in South Africa. This was, indeed, the case as it turned out. Moreover, the demolition of the Berlin Wall in 1989 and the first democratic election in South Africa in 1994 have been hailed as two miraculous events which have reshaped the global politics of the late twentieth century and ushered in a new world order.

If one looked closely at the television footage of the democracy protests in Leipzig, Dresden, and East Berlin, it was possible to recognize the presence of Protestant pastors, often within the leadership ranks. Some of the televised scenes took place within church buildings and even during church-services. In the case of South Africa one did not have to look quite as closely. Certain church leaders, Catholic and Protestant, were already international celebrities in the struggle against apartheid, and were prominent at the head of the protest marches. There were also many others within the crowds who would have professed that they were there out of Christian conviction and commitment. This introduces a major theme of our study, namely the role of the churches in contemporary struggles for a democratic and just world order, which we will examine in Part Three. There, specifically in chapter seven, we will also discuss more fully the role of the church in democratization in Germany and South Africa.

A new world order?

One way of understanding the dramatic events which have occurred in eastern Europe and South Africa is to see them as part of what has been called 'the third democratic transformation' of the world which began with the Lisbon coup in 1974.[1] Within a decade of the demise of the Salazar government in Portugal, one country after another formerly ruled by authoritarian regimes, embarked on a process of democratization. Once this process was underway there was a snowballing effect leading inexorably to the ending of the Soviet empire, which in turn altered the course of events in southern

[1] Robert A. Dahl, *Democracy and its Critics*, New Haven and London, Yale University Press, 1989, pp. 311f. For different analyses which reach the same conclusion with regard to the significance of the Lisbon coup in 1974 see Samuel P. Huntington, *The Third Wave: Democratization in the Late Twentieth Century*, Norman, Oklahoma: University of Oklahoma Press, 1991, and Phillippe Schmitter 'The International Contest for Contemporary Democratization,' draft paper, September 1991.

Africa and proved to be an even greater catalyst for further change than the Lisbon coup. 'Never before in history', it has been said, 'has awareness of popular struggles for democracy spread so rapidly and widely across national borders. Never have democrats worldwide seemed to have so much cause for rejoicing.'[2] Western political analysts and leaders began to talk about a new liberal democratic capitalist world order, and Francis Fukuyama, adapting G. W. F. Hegel's philosophy of history to support his argument, declared that we had arrived at the 'end of History', the 'end point of mankind's ideological evolution'.[3]

All democrats rejoiced in the collapse of Communist totalitarianism as they did at the ending of apartheid, but not all were as convinced or exuberant about the prospect of a victory for liberal democratic capitalism.[4] Certainly not all rejoiced at the extension of North American power and influence. As Noam Chomsky put it, 'the guardians of world order have sought to establish democracy in one sense of the term, while blocking it in a different sense.'[5] Thus the proclaimed victory of a new world order of liberal democratic capitalism raised again the question of the meaning of democracy and its global significance at the end of our millennium.

An irony of present world history is that western forms of liberal democracy are in trouble and even decay at precisely this moment when their triumph over totalitarianism is being

[2] Larry Diamond, 'Three Paradoxes of Democracy', *Journal of Democracy*, 1, 3, Summer 1990, 48.
[3] Francis Fukuyama, 'The End of History?', *The National Interest*, 16, Summer 1989, 4; *The End of History and the Last Man*, London: Hamish Hamilton and Penguin ; New York: The Free Press, 1992.
[4] See Jonathan R. Macey and Geoffrey P. Miller, 'The End of History and the New World Order: the Triumph of Capitalism and the Competition between Liberalism and Democracy', *Cornell International Law Journal*, 25, 1992, 279ff; Fred Halliday, 'An Encounter with Fukuyama'; Michael Rustin, 'No Exit from Capitalism?'; Ralph Miliband, 'Fukuyama and the Socialist Alternative,' *New Left Review*, 193, 1992; Krishan Kumar, 'The Revolutions of 1989: Socialism, Capitalism, and Democracy,' *Theory and Society*, 21, 3, June 1992; and the essays by David Held, Alex Callinicos, and Anthony Giddens, in *Theory and Society*, 22, 2, April 1993.
[5] Noam Chomsky, 'The Struggle for Democracy in a Changed World', a paper presented to the conference on Negotiating for Change, London; Catholic Institute for International Relations, 1991.

celebrated. Cynics also have reason to suspect that the western insistence on multi-party democracy in eastern Europe, Latin America, or sub-Saharan Africa is motivated more by economic self-interest than a concern for meaningful democratic participation in government and economic justice. Newly established democratic systems are already being severely qualified in some eastern European and African countries by presidential rule in the name of protecting democracy.[6] There is also the possibility that some well-established western democracies might regress and become more authoritarian in defending their own interests, even under the guise of protecting and extending democracy.[7] Some are certainly better advocates of democracy in faraway places than at home, and when they are struggling for power than when they achieve their goal, or when they are voted out of power. Understandably, many people living in the West have opted out of the political process, no longer believing that their vote makes any difference. This has long been true of the disadvantaged, the discriminated against, and the poor. As a result, a vacuum has been created which has been eagerly filled by those who seek to manage the system in such a way that it serves self and group interests rather than the good of society as a whole. Hence John Dunn's somewhat cynical reference to democratic theory as 'the public cant of the modern world'.[8]

Reinhold Niebuhr, writing on the eve of the allied victory in the Second World War, cautioned those who believed that the forces pushing towards world community could not be stopped or reversed.[9] In similar vein, Kitson Clark later remarked, in words which still retain their validity, that the 'most terrible lesson of this century is the ease and swiftness with which retro-

---

[6] Neal Ascherson, '1989 in Eastern Europe: Constitutional Representative Government as a "Return to Normality"', in John Dunn, ed., *Democracy: The Unfinished Journey 508BC to AD1993*, Oxford University Press, 1992, p. 227.

[7] Dahl, *Democracy and its Critics*, p. 79.

[8] John Dunn, *Western Political Theory in the Face of the Future*, Cambridge University Press, Canto edition, 1993, p. 2.

[9] Reinhold Niebuhr, *The Children of Light and the Children of Darkness*, New York: Charles Scribner's and Sons, 1944, new edition, 1960, p. 159.

gression can take place'.[10] However cogent democratic theories might be, they are not self-fulfilling;[11] there is no guarantee of inevitable democratic success. The very process which has brought us to this moment in history has revealed or created contradictions and tensions which have the potential for future and ongoing conflict, much of it violent, on a world-wide scale. Some analysts even suggest that we might be entering a new period of world disorder rather than order.[12] It is too early to tell. But it would be theoretically foolish, politically fatal, and theologically unsound to assume glibly that a new democratic order of world justice and peace is around the corner, and that all that is now required of us is some mopping up operation.

Nevertheless, there is reason to believe that present and anticipated traumas associated with democratic transition may well be the birth-pangs of a more just and democratic global society. We are living in an environment which is turbulent, traumatic and dislocating, yet it is also one which is potentially creative.[13] In other words, the fact that a new world order may not have arrived, and the further awareness that its arrival cannot be taken for granted as part of an evolutionary process, does not mean that the third democratic transformation is not underway. Like its predecessors, it may run out of steam, and the democratic transformation of the world might take some steps backwards before a fourth wave may take democratization further. But time probably is, as Samuel Huntington suggests, 'on the side of democracy',[14] even if it is not always on the side of present movements of transition. There is no reason then 'to replace an optimistic evolutionary view with a cynical and pessimistic cyclical alternative'.[15] Yet the critical question remains: what kind of democracy, and what kind of new world order, is – or should be – in the making?

---

[10] G. Kitson Clark, *The Kingdom of Free Men*, Cambridge University Press, 1957, p. 71.
[11] Dahl, *Democracy and its Critics*, p. 30.
[12] Ken Jowitt, 'The New World Disorder', *Journal of Democracy*, 2, 1, Winter 1991.
[13] *Ibid.*, pp. 15f.   [14] Huntington, 'Democracy's Third Wave', p. 33.
[15] John A. Hall, 'Consolidations of Democracy', in David Held, ed., *Prospects for Democracy*, Cambridge: Polity Press, 1992, p. 272.

Understanding democracy

The problem of defining democracy is notorious.[16] But it is essential to try and understand democracy if we are to consider meaningfully its relationship to Christianity and enter into the debate about the new world order. This is the task we have set ourselves in Part One of this volume. All democrats would affirm the classic words of Abraham Lincoln in his Gettysburg address in 1863, that democracy is 'rule of the people by the people for the people'.[17] But there is considerable disagreement on what this sovereignty of the people means, and on how 'popular power' should be structured politically. In response to a 1949 Unesco questionnaire on the subject, all those scholars selected to participate agreed that democracy was recognized as the ideal description 'of all systems of political and social organization advocated by influential proponents', yet they found it difficult to define precisely what it meant and the way in which it can be put into effect.[18]

Traditionally, discussions on democracy have distinguished between direct, participatory democracy, and representative democracy. Participatory democracy reminds us of the necessity of the involvement of the people as a whole in the democratic process, and of the importance of what is called civil society. Representative democracy, on the other hand, whereby the people elect others to make decisions and act on their behalf, has become necessary at the macro-level of the region, nation-state, and global arena, because of the demands of size.

The two competing ideological variants which have shaped the modern world, liberalism and socialism, have both determined the way in which democracy has developed. Hence the distinctions made between liberal democracy, social democ-

---

[16] See also C. B. Macpherson, *The Real World of Democracy*, Oxford: Clarendon Press, 1966.

[17] 'Address Delivered at the Dedication of the Cemetery at Gettysburg, November 19, 1863', in Abraham Lincoln, *Great Speeches*, New York: Dover Publications, 1991.

[18] *Democracy in a World of Tensions*, Unesco: Paris, 1951, appendix III, p. 527, in S. I. Benn and R. S. Peters, *Social Principles and the Democratic State*, London: George Allen and Unwin, 1971, p. 332.

racy, and democratic socialism. Contemporary struggles for democracy and the theoretical debates they have evoked, particularly with regard to gender, culture, and economic issues, have made it possible, however, for us to go beyond the arid confines of the debate between these contending ideologies. At the same time the globalization of democracy has injected a new range of issues of fundamental importance for the future of the world which have direct significance on local, grass-roots democracy. All of which makes us aware as never before that democracy is an open-ended process in constant need of broadening and deepening, and therefore of debate and clarification.

Fundamental to our discussion will be a distinction between the democratic *system* and the democratic *vision*. By democratic *system* we mean those constitutional principles and procedures, symbols and convictions, which have developed over the centuries and which have become an essential part of any genuine democracy whatever its precise historical form. When we speak about the democratic *vision* we refer to that hope for a society in which all people are truly equal and yet where difference is respected; a society in which all people are truly free, yet where social responsibility rather than individual self-interest prevails; and a society which is truly just, and therefore one in which the vast gulf between rich and poor has been overcome.

The democratic *vision* has its origins not so much in ancient Athens, the symbolic birthplace of the democratic *system*, as in the message of the ancient prophets of Israel, and especially in their messianic hope for a society in which the reign of God's *shalom* would become a reality. This we will discuss in chapter two. Undeniably, the religious custodians of the prophetic vision, whether Jewish or Christian, have often failed to witness faithfully to its demands. At the same time, the vision has been secularized in various ways, some of them revolutionary. Utopian as it may be, it is this vision which has been, and remains, the driving force behind the struggle for democratic transformation across the world, even if it can never be fully realized and embodied in democratic systems of government.

Christianity and democracy

As we will document in Part Two, the relationship between Christianity and democracy has been ambiguous for much of their respective histories, reflecting both the divergent tendencies in the Christian movement (conservative, reformist, radical) as well as those within the evolution of democracy (liberal and socialist). Wolfgang Huber rightly reminds us that the 'affinity of Christian faith to democratic values' has been severely compromised by 'the historical distance of churches towards democracy'.[19] At the same time western Christendom undoubtedly provided the womb within which the democratic *system*, as we now know it, gestated, and it also contributed decisively to the shaping of the democratic *vision* through its witness, albeit ambiguous and severely compromised, to the message of the Hebrew prophets.

Despite this, Christians have by no means always regarded democracy (the *system*) as the best form of government. While certain Protestant 'free churches' have had a close connection with the emergence of liberal democracy, mainstream Christianity on the whole, especially Roman Catholicism, has long resisted it. This was especially so from the time of the Enlightenment when democracy became equated with liberalism, which in turn was regarded as the handmaiden of revolution and seen as an onslaught upon traditional Christian faith and values (chapter four). Christianity, it was argued, does not proclaim that the voice of the people is the voice of God or that the majority is always right.[20] With this in mind, the contemporary theological ethicist Stanley Hauerwas insists that the 'church does not exist to provide an ethos for democracy or any other form of social organization'.[21] There is obviously a fundamental truth in this claim. Christianity, after

---

[19] Wolfgang Huber, 'Christianity and Democracy in Europe', *Emory International Law Journal*, 6, 1992, p. 35.

[20] John Howard Yoder, *The Priestly Kingdom: Social Ethics as Gospel*, University of Notre Dame Press, 1984, p. 168.

[21] Stanley Hauerwas, *A Community of Character: Toward a Constructive Christian Social Ethic*, University of Notre Dame Press, 1981, p. 12.

all, has no 'ideal political model written into its foundation charter',[22] and cannot be equated with any system of government.

But the fact that it is wrong to equate Christianity with a particular political system does not mean that all systems of government are equally acceptable to Christian faith. 'There is', wrote Dietrich Bonhoeffer, 'justification for asking which form of the state offers the best guarantee for the fulfillment of the mission of government and should, therefore, be promoted by the church'.[23] Reflecting on the task of the church in the aftermath of the Second World War, Karl Barth observed that Christianity, when faithful to the gospel, 'betrays a striking tendency to the side of what is generally called the "democratic" state'. Without equating democracy with any of its historic forms, he argued that there is 'an affinity between the Christian community and the civil communities of the free peoples'.[24] This affinity is now widely acknowledged within the ecumenical church as Pope John Paul II's *Centesimus Annus* and recent documents of the World Council of Churches indicate.[25] In passing, it is noteworthy that, while previously Anglo-Saxon Protestantism was the home of democratization, the 'third democratic transformation' began in predominantly Roman Catholic countries. Thus Christianity, especially after the twentieth-century experience of Nazi and Stalinist totalitarianism, now appears to be irrevocably committed to the retrieval of democracy as essential to its vision of a just world order.

In Part Three we will examine several case studies on the role of the churches in the struggle for democracy since the end of the Second World War: the struggle for civil rights in the United States and for democratic liberation in Nicaragua

---

[22] Adrian Hastings, *Church and State: The English Experience*, University of Exeter Press, 1991, p. 4.

[23] Dietrich Bonhoeffer, *Ethics*, New York: Macmillan, 1976, p. 352.

[24] Karl Barth, 'The Christian Community and the Civil Community', in Barth, *Community, State and Church*, Garden City, N.Y.: Doubleday, 1960, p. 181.

[25] See John Paul II, '*Centesimus Annus*', in David J. O'Brien and Thomas A. Shannon, *Catholic Social Thought: The Documentary Heritage*, Maryknoll, N.Y.: Orbis, 1992, pp. 474f.

(chapter five); the 'second liberation struggle' in sub-Saharan Africa (chapter six); and the transition to democracy and democratic reconstruction in East Germany and South Africa (chapter seven). These are all paradigmatic in understanding the relationship between Christian faith and the church in contemporary struggles for democracy.

Christianity and the church are complex phenomena. It is important, therefore, not to indulge in sweeping generalizations, nor to assume that there is Christian unanimity on the issues at hand. There are, in fact, different Christianities, and different ways in which the gospel is understood and related to the world. Confessional and denominational differences clearly affect the ways in which churches participate in the political arena. We must also avoid claiming too much credit for the churches. Their participation has often been ambivalent, and in some instances even today they have resisted rather than enabled liberation and democratization. Yet it is misleading when political analysts ignore the extent to which churches and church-groups have contributed to democratic struggle and change, whether they do so out of ideological antipathy, or because they do not include such matters within their purview. The involvement of churches in the struggle for democracy in the second half of our century has demonstrated that in many places the churches have become virtually indispensable in the process of transition. But is this merely a matter of pragmatic usefulness and perhaps ecclesiastical expediency, or is it something which is more deeply grounded in theological conviction?

A theology for a just world order

The reader should note that there is a clear structural link between Part One and Part Four, even though they are separated by the bulk of the book. In Part One we express our understanding of democracy and the prophetic vision; in Part Four we reflect on this from a critical theological perspective. It is our conviction that, in order to engage in the task of theological reflection, it is important that we first critically analyze and consider the historic relationship between Christianity and democracy (Part Two), and also consider the church's involvement in twentieth-century struggles for democracy, as well as the theologies which informed or emerged from that participation (Part Three).

It may be helpful, then, to consider briefly here at the outset the theological perspective which underlies the project as a whole and which will be developed more fully in the final chapter.[26] In doing so we would suggest that theology has to reclaim its place at the centre of political discourse, not on the terms which other disciplines may be willing to allow, but on its own terms.[27] In Niebuhr's trenchant words which in many ways express the motivation for this study: 'democracy has a more compelling justification and requires a more realistic vindication than is given it by the liberal culture with which it has been associated in modern history'.[28]

Two major interrelated theological themes are fundamental to this task. The first derives from the prophetic tradition, especially as expressed in the ministry of Jesus of Nazareth and his teaching about the reign of God (discussed in chapter two). The prophetic tradition is based on Israel's liberation from slavery in Egypt, and the awareness that Yahweh has a particular predilection for the poor, the oppressed, and for other victims of society. This divine partiality does not mean a lack of love for other people, but a concern to overcome social injustices and thus bring about a society in which all people are equally respected as bearer's of God's image. This alone is the basis for reconciliation and peace in the world, and therefore for the establishment and consolidation of democratic societies.

The second theological theme derives from the Christian conviction that the God revealed in Jesus Christ is triune (Father, Son, and Spirit). Reflection on the doctrine of the trinity provides us with the insights necessary to overcome the

---

[26] For a more detailed account of the author's own theological position see John W. de Gruchy, *Liberating Reformed Theology*, Grand Rapids: Eerdmans, 1991.

[27] John Milbank, *Theology and Social Theory: Beyond Secular Reason*, Oxford: Blackwell, 1990.

[28] Niebuhr, *The Children of Light*, p. xii.

way in which democracy has become a casualty of the contradictions of modernity, and therefore lost its spiritual foundations. The doctrine also enables us to transcend the split between individualism and collectivism which has bedeviled the debate between liberalism and socialism, and develop an understanding of human sociality in which both individual rights and the common good are complementary rather than conflictual. Trinitarian theology likewise relates directly to the debate about gender and cultural differentiation, about hierarchy and power relations, human sinfulness and transformation. It is also fundamental to our understanding of the nature of the Christian *ekklēsia* as an inclusive, participatory, local and universal fellowship, and therefore as a sign of a just world order embodied in different contexts.

On the basis of both the prophetic message of the reign of God and the doctrine of the trinity we are thus able to reflect theologically on human identity, freedom and responsibility, universal values and cultural plurality, the relationship between the Christian *ekklēsia* and democratic polities, national sovereignty, political accountability, and economic justice. In this way it becomes possible to give concreteness to the message of the ancient Hebrew prophets and the ministry of Jesus, as well as to the experience of Christian tradition, in relation to the contemporary debate about democracy and a new world order, and so contribute to the ecumenical discussion about 'justice, peace, and the integrity of creation' which so helpfully provides us with a modern definition of God's *shalom*.[29]

---

[29] *Now is the Time*, JPIC Final Document, Geneva: WCC, 1990.

PART I

The system and the vision

CHAPTER I

Democracy: an open-ended tradition

Contemporary transitions to democracy are part of a long historical process which began, at least symbolically for the western world, in fifth century BCE Athens.[1] Parallels to what occurred there can be found in other cultures outside the western tradition. What is important, however, is not so much the starting-point as the fact that democracy has evolved unevenly in fits and starts in a variety of different historical contexts, often with long gaps between one significant moment and the next. Many of the contributing factors and generating seams which have shaped its development, especially before the Enlightenment, were not labelled 'democratic' at the time. Some of them might be appropriately referred to as proto-democratic analogies and antecedents. But irrespective of how they are described they have been significant building-blocks in the erection of the edifice of modern democracy.

Since the eighteenth century the evolution of democracy has become exponential, as the present wave of democratic transformation indicates, but the democratic transitions of our time are not to be regarded as the final stage in the process of global democratization. For one thing, there is no inevitability about democratic transformation and, for another, the process of democratization varies considerably in character, scope, and speed from one country to another. The transition to democracy is, in fact, a permanent condition. Like all living traditions, democracy is a 'narrative of an argument'[2] which is open

[1] M. I. Finley, *Democracy Ancient and Modern*, London: Chatto and Windus, 1973.
[2] Charles Davis, *Religion and the Making of Society: Essays in Social Theology*, Cambridge University Press, 1994, p. 108.

to change and development, retrieval and renewal. Put differently, it is 'the constantly changing, provisional result of historical processes which consist of conflicts and compromises
and which depend on social, economic and cultural developments'.[3] Our task is to understand this narrative in relationship
to another, even more complex, tradition, that of Christianity,
and to locate both within the contemporary debate about a
new world order.

PARTICIPATION, REPRESENTATION, AND CIVIL SOCIETY

In ancient Athens, democracy meant direct participation by
the people in government, but such participation was strictly
limited to those who qualified as citizens. The Athenians 'did
not acknowledge the existence of *universal* claims to freedom,
equality, or rights, whether political rights or, more broadly,
human rights'.[4] The success of direct participatory democracy
was contingent upon the homogeneity of male householders
who spoke the same language, worshipped the same deities,
and were willing to serve in the army in defence of the city-
state. Women, slaves, and foreigners living within its boundaries were excluded from the rights and privileges of citizenship. The doctrine of individual human rights, or even the
notion of individual persons in the modern or Christian sense,
cannot be traced to Athens.[5] Whatever its merits, Athenian
democracy was a 'tyranny of citizens'.[6] Right from the outset,
then, the debate about democracy had to do with what it
means to be a citizen. Underlying that are more fundamental
anthropological and theological questions concerning human
identity and sociality, not least that of the possibility of forging
new identities and communities.

---

[3] Kurt Tudyka, 'The Meaning of Democracy Today', in James Provost and Knut
Walf, eds., *The Tabu of Democracy within the Church*, *Concilium*, vol. 5, London: SCM,
1992, p. 4.
[4] Dahl, *Democracy and its Critics*, p. 22.
[5] Peter Brown, *The Body and Society*, New York: Columbia University Press, 1988.
[6] David Held, *Models of Democracy*, Cambridge: Polity Press, 1992, p. 23.

Not all Athenians of that period had a high regard for democracy. The philosopher Plato saw it as a recipe for anarchy. He was convinced that democracy could not resolve the crises facing Athenian society and ensure good government because it was based on a faulty conception of human nature. People are not equal, Plato argued, and it is folly to believe that any but gifted elites can rule wisely and well.[7] Given the choice between government by a good monarch, an able aristocracy, or the people as a whole, Aristotle, Plato's distinguished student, had little doubt that 'democracy was the worst form of government' which, while it undoubtedly benefited the poor, did so at the expense of the broader public interest. Yet, when monarchy degenerated into tyranny, and aristocratic rule into oligarchy, democracy was 'the best of the three forms of bad government'.[8] Aristotle's preference was for a government in which all three played a role, providing the necessary checks and balances to ensure that the common interest was served.[9]

Like Aristotle, the Roman jurist Cicero found it hard to decide between monarchy, in which a king expresses love for the people; aristocracy, in which wisdom prevails in counsel; or democracy, for the freedom which it gives to the people.[10] But, even though he could not decide which was preferable, for Cicero, sovereignty resided in 'the people'. A rule which affects all should be approved by all.[11] Kings and princes did not rule by divine right according to custom and tradition, but according to laws which were made in the interests of the people. Power needed to be depersonalized.[12] Thus Cicero provided 'a strategic link between the state and liberty' and a basis in law for the protection of person and property against tyranny.[13]

[7] *The Republic of Plato*, vii. 557–61, Oxford: Clarendon Press, 1955, pp. 274f.
[8] *The Politics of Aristotle*, trans. by Ernest Barker, Oxford University Press, 1958, III.7.
[9] *Ibid.*, III, 1279a.
[10] Marcus Tullius Cicero, *On the Commonwealth*, in George H. Sabine and Stanley B. Smith, eds., Columbus, Ohio: Ohio State University Press, 1929, p. 140.
[11] A. P. d'Entrèves, *The Notion of the State: An Introduction to Political Theory*, Oxford: Clarendon, 1967, p. 90.
[12] *Ibid.*, p. 94.
[13] Antony Black, *Political Thought in Europe 1250–1450*, Cambridge University Press, 1992, p. 19.

Gradually the parameters for the debate on good government – one which maintained order but also protected rights and pursued justice – were being established.

Writing in the eighteenth century with direct participatory democracy in mind, Jean-Jacques Rousseau observed that there never had been 'a real democracy, and there never will be'.[14] But direct popular participation in government is not the only democratic option, especially where citizenship is larger and more heterogeneous than in ancient Athens. Hence the development of representative forms of democracy, which emerged first in the city-states of Renaissance Italy, and then more significantly with the rise of European nation-states in the centuries which followed. Given the size, ethnic diversity, and technological complexity of modern industrialized societies, direct democracy, as Max Weber argued, would inevitably mean an ineffective and inefficient administration as well as political instability.[15] Modernity requires representative parliamentary forms of government, but this certainly does not mean that participatory democracy is obsolete.

The democratic need to participate in the political process, including the right of individuals to choose their own representatives, has often come into conflict with the need to ensure competence and efficiency in government.[16] It is the essence of democracy, however, that elected representatives, as well as the bureaucrats and technocrats appointed by them (the civil service), should be held accountable to the people. They should not be allowed to supplant public discussion and participation in the public square, thereby becoming the arbiters of social and political destiny, controlling even the power of the people's deputies to implement policy.

Despite George Bernard Shaw's cynical maxim that 'democracy substitutes election by the incompetent many for appoint-

[14] Jean-Jacques Rousseau, *The Social Contract and Discourses*, London: J. M. Dent and Sons, 1947, p. 55.
[15] Max Weber, *Economy and Society*, 2, Berkeley: University of California Press, 1978, pp. 949f.
[16] Robert A. Dahl, *After the Revolution? Authority in a Good Society*, New Haven: Yale University Press, revised edition, 1990, chapter 1.

ment by the corrupt few',[17] a genuinely democratic tradition is guided by the conviction that ordinary people are competent to make political decisions. For this reason, the idea of an 'elitist democracy'[18] has to be treated with much caution even though democracy, like any other enterprise, does require people with particular skills and training if it is to work at all. The weakness of democracy, which is the danger of incompetent and inefficient government is, paradoxically, indicative of its strength,[19] namely, that such government is regarded as legitimate and remains accountable. Thus there is a fundamental difference between those who fear and want to restrict popular rule, and genuine democrats for whom, on the contrary, the rule of the few, an elite, has to be kept in check by the majority.[20]

The way in which representative democracy has been embodied in particular nation-states has varied a great deal, but all systems of government which have reasonable claim to the title today embody certain basic principles and procedures which comprise the democratic *system*. Generally they include: universal adult suffrage or the right to vote; free and fair elections; representation of a fair proportion of the electorate in a legislative body; decisions reached by a majority vote on all major questions of policy; equality before the law; an independent judiciary; equality of opportunity; freedom to organize political parties; freedom of speech, conscience, and dissent; the freedom of the press and of assembly; the rule of law and therefore freedom from arbitrary arrest or punishment ('due process'); the separation of church and state; the freedom of religion and individual liberty consonant with social requirements.

These key elements in the democratic system were developed piecemeal as a result of political struggle and conflict in many different contexts. For example, the question of franchisement has remained a burning issue well into the twentieth century

---

[17] George Bernard Shaw, *Man and Superman: A Comedy and a Philosophy*, London: Constable, 1931, p. 212.
[18] J. Schumpeter, *Capitalism, Socialism, and Democracy*, London: Allen and Unwin, 1976.
[19] Diamond, 'Three Paradoxes', pp. 48f.   [20] Dahl, *Democracy and its Critics*, p. 25.

even in established western democracies. The issue has usually
been dodged by those who have achieved the vote, but increasingly recognized by those who have not. Filled with an almost
insatiable desire for freedom, dignity, and justice, the disinher-
ited and disadvantaged have been inspired by a vision greater
than that of the more satisfied custodians of democratic institutions who have already achieved their goals of liberty and
equality. But, as the disenfranchised have, in turn, taken up
the cudgels in their struggle for rights and freedoms, they have
often found support in the constitutional documents themselves. This was notably the case in the struggle for emancipation from slavery, women's suffrage, and civil rights in the
United States. In this way the constitutions not only revealed
'the extent to which democratic principles remained in practice unapplied', but also became subversive of the exclusive
rights of those who had drafted them.[21] The democratic *vision*
of an equal, free, and just society which inspired the constitutions was often far greater than the limited interests which
interpreted and implemented them.[22] At the same time, as the
vision was pursued, so the *system* had to change and adapt to
embody new gains in the struggle for human rights.

Civil society is of key importance in relating representative
and participatory forms of democracy.[23] If political society
refers to the structures of government or the state, including
the civil service, then civil society is that network of non-
governmental organizations (NGOs), churches and other
religious communities, trade unions and voluntary associations, which, in modern societies provide the means whereby
people can participate in pursuing social goals and protecting
particular interests. When it is functioning best, 'civil society
provides an intermediate layer of governance between the
individual and the state that is capable of resolving conflicts
and controlling the behaviour of members without public

---

[21] Held, *Models of Democracy*, p. 71.
[22] Karl Mannheim, *Ideology and Utopia*, New York: Harcourt, Brace & World, 1936, p.
167.
[23] John Keane, *Democracy and Civil Society*, London: Verso, 1988, and Keane, ed., *Civil
Society and the State*, London: Verso, 1988.

coercion'.[24] A strong civil society is necessary if democratic transition from authoritarian rule is to be sustained, reversals resisted, and democratic transformation pursued.

Regular voting in order to elect representatives is an essential element in the democratic process, but democracy cannot be reduced to a visit to the polls every four years. This inevitably reduces democracy to an ideology manipulated by the state.[25] Democracy is rather an ongoing quest for justice, and therefore one whose success is contingent upon the development of moral people who are able to participate fully in the body politic, and of institutions which allow and foster such participation. Thus participatory democracy becomes a way of life, critically complementary and essential to representative government and the state, rather than simply a means to protect self-interest.

LIBERALS, SOCIALISTS, AND ECONOMIC DEMOCRACY

Modern democratic theory and praxis have developed along two well-defined ideological paths, the liberal and the socialist, with the latter ranging from social democracy to democratic socialism. Some would argue that only liberal democracy is true democracy. On the contrary, we will argue that the liberal and socialist forms of democracy are rather to be understood as '*differently* democratic'[26] and complementary. Nothing better illustrates this than the different ways in which these two democratic trajectories have understood the democratic *vision* of equality, freedom, and justice, and the way in which they have sought to embody it in democratic *systems*.

For liberals, equality means that all human beings are equal as individuals and therefore have a right to be treated as such.

---

[24] Philippe C. Schmitter and Terry Lynn Karl, 'What Democracy is ... and is Not', *Journal of Democracy*, 2,3, Summer 1991, p. 80.
[25] Jürgen Habermas, *Communication and the Evolution of Society*, Boston: Beacon Press, 1978; James F. Bohman, 'Communication, Ideology, and Democratic Theory,' *American Political Science Review*, 84,1, March 1990.
[26] Schmitter and Karl, 'What Democracy is ...', p. 77.

Socialists, on the other hand, insist that having the vote does not necessarily mean that all people are equal. Not all people have the same access to resources or the corridors of power because of the way in which society has been stratified by ethnicity, class, or gender. Many in the Third World, for example, regard liberal democracy as the means whereby the industrialized nations have sought to retain power at the expense of the victims and poor within society, as well as the environment.[27] The first step towards democratization is therefore the liberation and empowerment of the oppressed so that they can truly participate in the political process. Genuine democracy only becomes possible when those who belong to what Mannheim called the 'lower strata' of society 'confront the ideas of the dominant strata on the same level of validity'.[28] Only when the *demos* actually has control of the agenda does the process become fully democratic.[29]

From a liberal perspective, freedom refers primarily to personal liberty and the protection of human rights, whereas for socialists, freedom refers primarily to liberation from oppression and poverty. In the same way, whereas for liberals, justice means fairness, so that everyone is treated equally before the law, for socialists, justice means that everyone should have equal access to resources, education, housing, and health care. Justice is redistributive, especially where there has been a legacy of injustice. All this requires, socialists insist, that government should play a more active role in ensuring that justice is achieved even if this may result in the temporary curtailment of some individual freedoms.[30] In response, liberals see this as the dangerous first step on the slippery slope towards totalitarian rule.

Liberal democrats generally have more confidence than democratic socialists in the ability of traditional western parliamentary procedures to embody equality, ensure liberty,

---

[27] Noam Chomsky, *Deterring Democracy*, New York: Verso, 1991.
[28] Mannheim, *Ideology and Utopia*, p. 8.
[29] Dahl, *Democracy and its Critics*, p. 130.
[30] Gary J. Dorrien, *Reconstructing the Common Good: Theology and the Social Order*, Maryknoll, N.Y.: Orbis, 1990, p. 3.

and achieve social justice. This is partly because these principles and institutions have largely been won in the struggle between liberal democracy and authoritarian regimes. But liberal democrats are often guilty of turning the principles of western parliamentary democracy into an ideology which protects the interests and legitimates the political and economic domination of the middle and upper classes of society. After all, liberal democracy had its origins within the struggles of the bourgeoisie and the rise of capitalism. Hence built into liberal democracy is an elitism made possible through the inheritance of wealth and the ownership of property. For liberal democracy the right to own property is, in fact, 'inalienable'.[31] No issue has been more hotly contested by liberal democrats and democratic socialists,[32] and in many countries today, especially where people have been dispossessed of their land and other property rights, it is the most urgent issue that has to be resolved if democratization is to be successful.

A distinction clearly needs to be drawn between the reasonable and legitimate ownership of land and property, and the vast concentrations of private property in the hands of the few. The latter, reveals 'the limitations of an excessively individualized democracy'.[33] What was originally 'intended to guarantee the economic freedom of the individual' eventually, as Adam Smith noted, became the '"ideology" of vast corporate structures of a later period of capitalism, used by them, and still used, to prevent a proper political control of their power'.[34] However much this might be grounded in the claims of individual freedom, it made a mockery of the claim that democratic societies are governed by the consent of all the governed.[35] Instead of the cultivation of a vigorous civil society

[31] Niebuhr, *The Children of Light*, p. 90; see also Bob Goudzwaard, *Capitalism and Progress: A Diagnosis of Western Society*, Toronto, Canada: Wedge Publishing Foundation, 1979, pp. 115f.

[32] Robert Bellah, Richard Madsen, William M. Sullivan, Ann Swidler, Steven M. Tipton, *The Good Society*, New York: Alfred A. Knopf, 1991, p. 117; John A. Hall, 'Consolidations of Democracy', in David Held, ed., *Prospects for Democracy*, Cambridge: Polity Press, 1993, p. 278.

[33] Bellah, *The Good Society*, p. 75.   [34] Niebuhr, *The Children of Light*, p. 26.

[35] Bellah, *The Good Society*, p. 265.

in which economic initiative was complementary to public
spirit and concern, exploitation of others and of the environment became the norm. The converse, Niebuhr argued,
namely greater public involvement in the economy, is necessary if the inherent problems of an uncontrolled capitalism are
not to hinder further democratic transformation. As John
Dewey pointed out, democracy does not amount to much if it
does not mean a 'democracy of wealth'.[36]

Marxist–Leninism was a direct assault on bourgeois liberal
democracy precisely because of its link with the right to own
property and control the means of production. For Marx, it
was almost impossible to think of democracy other than in its
liberal form, and thus as the ideological basis for capitalism.[37]
Class-divided societies, he argued, are incapable of electing
governments which serve the interests of the workers. Yet he
was also sceptical of democracy within the socialist movement
itself. Lenin was even more disdainful, and it is noteworthy
that, within a few years of the Russian Revolution, the Communist Party had turned away from any direct democratic
involvement in its structures and begun to create a centralized
dictatorship which led inexorably to Stalinism and eastern
European Communism. In the end, the lack of democracy
within both the Party and eastern bloc countries was a major
reason for the discrediting and collapse of Communism.

For many people the demise of Communism has also meant
the end of socialism as a credible political credo – witness the
inability of social democratic or democratic socialist parties to
gain significant support in the elections in the early nineties.
But many democratic socialists, while influenced by the
Marxian tradition, regard Communism as 'an appalling defor-
mation of socialism'.[38] They have therefore welcomed its
collapse as a clearing of the way to the creation of truly

[36] John Dewey, 'The Ethics of Democracy', 1888, quoted by Cornel West, *American
Evasion of Philosophy*, Madison: University of Wisconsin, 1989, p. 80.
[37] *Writings of the Young Marx on Philosophy and Society*, Loyd D. Easton and Kurt H.
Guddat, New York: Anchor Books, 1967.
[38] Neal Ascherson, '1989 in Eastern Europe', in Dunn, *The Unfinished Journey*, p. 228;
Ralph Miliband and Leo Panitch, *The Socialist Register 1992*, London: The Merlin
Press, 1992, p. 4.

democratic societies within which a socialist agenda can be better pursued.[39] The concerns of socialist forms of democracy remain firmly on the political agenda. Indeed the victory of the Hungarian socialists in May 1994 may have already signalled a turning of the tide in the fortunes of democratic socialist parties. It would be wrong, however, to regard this as a return to Communism; it is, rather, an indication that there is already a growing disenchantment with the ability of liberal capitalism to solve the problems facing eastern Europe.

There is, clearly, no guarantee that liberal democratic capitalism will inevitably 'succeed where Marxist–Leninism has obviously failed and discredited itself'.[40] The fact of the matter is that both capitalism and socialism have failed to resolve the economic crises besetting the modern world. Adam Przeworski puts it bluntly: 'capitalism is irrational; socialism is unfeasible; in the real world people starve'.[41] The challenge facing those liberals who put their confidence in capitalism is how to make the free market system more just; the challenge for those who wish to make the economy more democratic is how to do this without expanding the role of state intervention, while ensuring that the economy functions efficiently.[42] How to achieve a just and an efficient economic order is the problem. But efficiency must be understood not only as the ability to generate wealth; it must also be understood as the ability to distribute it in a way which deals effectively with the problem of poverty. If the free market system is to help rather than hinder the flourishing of genuine democracy, then it has to become less the servant of greed and more the servant of social justice. The criterion for a good economic policy today is whether or not it can overcome massive poverty. But how does this relate to democracy?

Neo-conservatives such as Friedrich von Hayek and Milton

[39] Hall, in Held, *Prospects for Democracy*, p. 288.
[40] Neil Harding, 'The Marxist–Leninist Detour', in Dunn, *The Unfinished Journey*, p. 186.
[41] Adam Przeworski, *Democracy and the Market: Political and Economic Reforms in Eastern Europe and Latin America*, Cambridge University Press, 1992, p. 122.
[42] Dorrien, *Reconstructing the Common Good*, p. vii.

Friedman, and other proponents of the new world order such
as Francis Fukuyama, are adamant in their insistence on a
market free from any kind of social control. For this reason,
many advocates of the free market, such as Hayek, resist the
checks and balances of democracy, even while using the freedoms it offers to achieve their own goals.[43] This suggests that
democracy and capitalism are not as closely linked in theory
and in practice, as is widely assumed. Liberal democracy
'encompasses a number of principles which are either divergent from, or entirely inconsistent with many of the fundamental tenets of capitalism'.[44] As a result, genuinely liberal
democratic governments and big business often find themselves
in conflict over issues and priorities. Some liberal democrats
accept the need for the regulation of the market-place, just as
there are social democrats who recognize the need for the
market.[45]

The reassessment of the market's role by some democratic
socialists is significant, and mirrors the current development of
new forms of democratic politics which have the potential to
overcome the deficiencies of both liberalism and socialism and
thus chart new futures for humanity.[46] There does not seem to
be a viable alternative to the market itself both in terms of
democratization and in dealing with the economic crises facing
the modern world. But it has to be restructured in ways which
actually help overcome poverty.[47] As long as the free market
treats labour, land, and money as commodities separated from
the lives and needs of people, it impedes democratization
because it means great economic advantages for the few at the
cost of colossal social dislocations for the many.[48] The real

---

[43] See F. A. Hayek, *The Constitution of Liberty*, London: Routledge and Kegan Paul,
1960; Dunn, *The Unfinished Journey*, p. 251; Niebuhr, *Children of Light*, p. 79.

[44] Owen M. Fiss, 'Capitalism and Democracy', *Michigan Journal of International Law*,
13, Summer 1992, p. 911.

[45] *Ibid.*, p. 4; by way of contrast, see Alex Callinicos, 'Socialism and Democracy,' in
Held, *Prospects for Democracy*, pp. 200f.

[46] David Held, 'Liberalism, Marxism, and Democracy', *Theory and Society*, 22,2, April
1993; Dorrien, *Reconstructing the Common Good*, p. 3.

[47] Fiss, 'Capitalism and Democracy', p. 919.

[48] V. A. Demant, *Religion and the Decline of Capitalism*, London: Faber and Faber, 1952,
p. 23.

problem, then, is the market and its control. Yet as Prze-worski soberly reminds us, governments do not even have the will 'to organize efficient markets, tax those who can afford it, and use the revenue to ensure the material well-being of everyone'.[49]

Neither liberal democracy nor socialist democracy are adequate on their own for the world today. They certainly need to remain in critical tension with each other, but we also need to go beyond both. The liberal democratic system of procedures is necessary for ongoing democratic transformation, even though it needs constant revision, as many contemporary democratic socialists recognize.[50] At the same time, parties to the left are necessary in order to prevent liberal democratic governments from becoming elitist one-party affairs,[51] and to ensure that the question of the just distribution of wealth is undertaken. All of which resonates with Jürgen Moltmann's formulation that socialism symbolizes liberation from 'the vicious circles of poverty', while democracy symbolizes liberation 'from the vicious circle of force'.[52]

GENDER, CULTURAL PLURALISM, AND GLOBAL DEMOCRACY

Liberal democracy, Anne Phillips argues, 'has not served women well'.[53] From the beginning it has been patriarchal. The rights which it has protected have been the rights of men.[54] Identifying herself with other more progressive democrats, Phillips queries whether liberal democracy in its minimalist sense (a vote every few years) really has any claim to the

---

[49] Przeworski, *Democracy and the Market*, p. 134.

[50] Bhikhu Parekh, 'The Cultural Particularity of Liberal Democracy', *Political Studies*, 40, 1992, Special Issue, 169.

[51] Douglas E. Ashford, 'Democratic Dilemmas: What Future for the Left?', *Political Quarterly*, 63,1, 1992.

[52] Jürgen Moltmann, *The Crucified God*, London: SCM, 1974, pp. 332f.

[53] Anne Phillips, 'Must Feminists give up on Liberal Democracy?' in Held, *Prospects for Democracy*, p. 93.

[54] Carole Pateman, *The Sexual Contract*, Cambridge: Polity Press, 1988; *The Disorder of Women*, Cambridge: Polity Press, 1988.

democratic label seeing that it really excludes meaningful citizen participation.

At the heart of Phillips' critique is the tension between a universalizing theory of human equality, and the specificities of gender. Are there individuals who are unrelated to historical relations and culture? Does human equality mean that differences, such as those of gender, ethnicity, culture, and religion, are of no significance? Unless women are treated differently, is it possible to treat them as equals?[55] Is liberal democracy not irredeemably patriarchal? Liberal democracy's insistence on equality may be, at its best, 'a statement of profound egalitarianism that offers all citizens the same legal and political rights, regardless of their wealth, status, race or sex'. Yet, at its worst, 'it refuses the pertinence of continuing difference and inequality, pretending for the purposes of argument that we are all basically the same'.[56] Genuine equality cannot be attained if the significance of difference is minimized.[57] Justice rather than claims about equality is a better 'antidote to relations of domination'.[58]

Equality, freedom, and suffrage without the recognition of the validity of difference and the demands it makes on justice are clearly inadequate. Jean Bethke Elshtain goes to the heart of the matter, then, when she asks whether liberal principles on their own can sustain liberal democracy.[59] There are at least two interrelated issues at stake. The first is whether it is right and possible to universalize liberal democracy; the second concerns the relationship between universality on the one hand, and particularity and contextuality on the other.

The starting-point for liberalism is the individual, and therefore individual rights, rather than society and the common

---

[55] Anne Phillips, *Democracy and Difference*, Oxford: Polity Press, 1993.

[56] Phillips, in Held, *Prospects for Democracy*, p. 104.

[57] Susan Mendus, 'Losing the Faith: Feminism and Democracy', in Dunn, *The Unfinished Journey*, p. 21.

[58] Jane Flax, 'Beyond Equality: Gender, Justice, and Difference', in Gisela Bock and Susan James eds., *Beyond Equality and Difference: Citizenship, Feminist Politics, Female Subjectivity*, London: Routledge, 1992, p. 193.

[59] Jean Bethke Elshtain, *Meditations on Modern Political Thought*, New York: Praeger, 1986, p. 58.

good. But in many ways the individual posited by liberal democracy is an abstraction, and the universalities but western cultural specifics.[60] Any knowledge of non-western societies soon indicates that such individualism runs counter to their understanding of human identity and deeply rooted and cherished social, cultural, and religious values. The fact that democracy in the West developed on a liberal basis was, at least partly, historically and culturally determined. To suggest that all societies must accept a liberal worldview is, on this reckoning, a form of cultural imperialism which will lead to the destruction of those cultural niches and traditions which enrich many societies. Yet, paradoxically, while global democratization runs the danger of promoting universal cultural homogenization, it is also shattering what Phillips calls 'the myths of homogeneity' as people and nations become more aware of gender, ethnic, and cultural differences in their local struggles for democracy. Indeed, multi-cultural and other forms of pluralism have widened the base for resistance to the abuse of power, and contributed to the well-being of civil society.

There is a dangerous shadow side to this resurgence of particularity. As is painfully evident in eastern Europe today, old nationalist tensions and ethnic hatreds, sometimes aided and abetted by religious fundamentalism, were let loose as the structures of the previous unifying order crumbled. Movements of rage harnessed frustration and perplexity with tragic consequences.[61] Social volcanoes, dormant since eastern Europe came under the domination of the Soviet Union, 'spewed forth a lava of passions and conflicts'.[62] Indeed, the struggle for democracy in the late twentieth century has been accompanied by a remarkable renewal of national and ethnic identities and demands, often reinforced by the conservative ethos of the dominant religious traditions of eastern Europe, in

---

[60] Anne Phillips, *Engendering Democracy*, Pennsylvania State University Press, 1991, p. 168.

[61] Ken Jowitt, 'The New World Disorder', *Journal of Democracy*, 2,1, Winter 1991, p. 19.

[62] Misha Glenny, *The Rebirth of History: Eastern Europe in the Age of Democracy*, London: Penguin, new edition, 1993, p. 237.

a way which has been destructive of democracy. Even in the traditional homes of liberal democracy, the problems of ethnicity and nationalism are more evident today than at any time since the eighteenth century because of the multi-cultural social changes which have occurred.

In South Africa, the problems of ethnic particularity have been exacerbated by the way in which the ideology of apartheid abused race and culture in the interests of white domination. It is against this background, for example, that we have to understand the use of the universalist phrases 'non-racist' and 'non-sexist' as symbols of anti-apartheid and democratic protest and resistance by those within the Chartist tradition – as distinct from the Black Consciousness Movement[63] – even though neither terms as such are used in the Freedom Charter itself.[64] Although the terms remain widely in use in order to define what is meant by a just democracy in South Africa, they may be replaced eventually by more positive formulations which recognize the validity of difference, while rejecting racism and sexism at the same time.[65]

As elsewhere, in South Africa today cultural identities have to be positively affirmed and encouraged to interact creatively within the overall task of nation-building. Such ethnic plurality can certainly destroy democracy, especially when ethnicity is given special political status and privilege, but it also has the potential to enrich and help sustain it.[66] It is interesting to note in this regard that, while the Freedom Charter rejects discrimination on the basis of race and sex, it explicitly affirms the

[63] See N. Barney Pityana, Mamphela Ramphele, Malusi Mpumlwana and Lindy Wilson, eds., *Bounds of Possibility: The Legacy of Steve Biko and Black Consciousness*, Cape Town: David Philip, 1992, pp. 111ff.

[64] See Raymond Suttner and Jeremy Cronin, eds., *30 Years of the Freedom Charter*, Johannesburg: Ravan, 1986; Albert Luthuli, 'Our Vision is a Democratic Society', in *Luthuli: Speeches of Chief Albert John Luthuli*, compiled by E. S. Reddy, Durban: Madiba Publishers, 1991, pp. 98ff; Nelson Mandela, 'I am prepared to die', (1964), in Nelson Mandela, *The Struggle is My Life*, London: International Defence and Aid, 1978; and *Nelson Mandela Speaks: Forging a Democratic Nonracial South Africa*, Cape Town: David Philip, 1993.

[65] See 'The New South African Identity Crisis', in *Work in Progress*, November 1993; Robin Peterson, 'Towards a South African Theology of Non-Racialism', *Journal of Theology for Southern Africa*, 77, December 1991.

[66] Niebuhr, *The Children of Light*, p. 147.

rights and dignity of race, culture, and 'national pride'. But
this does not mean that the universal values embodied in the
terms non-racism and non-sexism, or the liberal insistence on
universal human rights, are compromised or relegated in terms
of their importance. Nationalism, ethnicity, group and religious rights, cannot be allowed to undermine a democratic
commitment to human equality, freedom, and social justice.

There has been an important shift in feminist and non-
western political thinking since the seventies and eighties
which relates to both participatory democracy and to the
question of difference and particularity. Previously feminist
thinking was more radical in its rejection of liberal democracy,
and more unequivocal in its affirmation of direct, participatory
forms of democracy within the women's movement. But feminism as a political force was 'immobilized by the futility of
utopian visions' as much as it was by 'the frustration of liberal
tokenism'.[67] There was a need to transcend the classic debates
about liberal and participatory forms of democracy, and begin
to work at pragmatic solutions.[68] Thus the feminist critique of
liberal democracy now includes a recognition of those principles and practices which have proved their importance in the
defence of human rights. Whatever criticism may be directed
against liberal democracy, its gains and potential must not be
denied. At the same time there is a need for a democracy which
is more substantial and stronger than the weak, minimalist
democracy on offer.[69]

Like its feminist critics, non-western critics of liberal democracy affirm some of its core values without espousing its possessive individualism. As Bhikhu Parekh argues, liberalism may
define human rights 'in narrowly, elitist and bourgeois terms',
but 'it gives democracy moral depth by insisting on the inviola-
bility of basic human rights and on the protection of minorities
and dissenting individuals'.[70] That liberal democracy is the
product of a bourgeois civilization does not necessarily negate

---

67 M. E. Hawkesworth, *Beyond Oppression: Feminist Theory and Political Strategy*, New
   York: Continuum, 1990, p. 173.
68 *Ibid.*, p. 167.   69 *Ibid.*, p. 108.
70 Parekh, 'The Cultural Particularity of Liberal Democracy', 168.

all its values. Individual human rights, for example, remain fundamental to any genuinely democratic society, and must challenge traditional norms, such as patriarchy, which deny them. It is fundamental to liberalism that the protection of one person's rights and freedoms must not be allowed to infringe on the rights and freedoms of others.[71] Thus what is required is a firm commitment to those elements within the liberal democratic tradition which protect human rights and freedoms and promote justice, while at the same time recognizing the need, within those limits, for the affirmation of gender, cultural, and ethnic particularities.

The embracing of universal liberal values need not imply the rejection of difference and diversity, then, or be an agent of western hegemony. On the contrary, as Held points out: 'global interconnectedness is already forming a dense web of relations linking cultures to one another'.[72] The issue is how to relate such cultures to each other within the democratic process in a mutually creative way. Put differently, how should democracy develop in cultures other than western, where liberalism is contrary to accepted social norms, and yet in a way which ensures that important liberal values and institutions are incorporated? Parekh rightly insists that the 'principles of good government can be genuinely universal (in their scope and content) and binding only if they are freely negotiated by all involved and grounded in a broad global consensus'.[73] Hence the importance yet again of participation in the process of democratization, this time at the global level. This can only be achieved if the democratic process is not imposed on countries and groups from without, but develops from within through commitment to, and participation in, the process.

There remain many issues which have to be resolved with

---

[71] The classic formulation is to be found in J. S. Mill's essay on 'Liberty'. J. S. Mill, *Utilitarianism, Liberty, and Representative Government*, London: J. M. Dent and Sons., 1948.
[72] Held, *Prospects for Democracy*, p. 44.
[73] Parekh, 'The Cultural Particularity of Liberal Democracy', p. 173.

regard to how democracy will function best in particular situations, and how meaningful citizen participation can be achieved and maintained. Hence the wide-ranging debates on issues such as federalism, proportional representation, and the role and rights of minority groups. But these issues can only be dealt with in terms of specific historical contexts.[74] The problems facing the future of humanity, however, cannot be tackled solely within the confines of national boundaries. In order to deal with them effectively they require international cooperation.

Just as the tension between individual and community interests is dealt with most satisfactorily and creatively through the democratic process, so the future of just and peaceful world politics requires, and is insisting on, the global spread of democracy. Held suggests three reasons why this is so. The first is the challenge presented to sovereign states 'from above' by 'economic, political, legal, and military interconnectedness'; the second is 'the way in which local groups, movements and nationalisms are questioning the nation-state from below as a representative and accountable power system'; and the third is the way in which 'global interconnectedness creates chains of interlocking political decisions and outcomes among states and their citizens, altering the nature and dynamics of national political systems themselves'.[75] A good example is the debt crisis which, 'in the long-term interest of most people in the world', requires norms of international financial transactions which are more democratic.[76]

Given the alternatives, the struggle for just global democratization is the only realism left if we are concerned about the future of the world. After all, the worst and most terrifying blunders of the twentieth century have been made by non-democratic totalitarian regimes.[77] Hence the importance of a new, but just, democratic world order.

---

[74] Dahl, *Democracy and its Critics*, p. 162. [75] Held, *Prospects for Democracy*, p. 39.
[76] Bellah et al., *The Good Society*, p. 248. [77] Dahl, *Democracy and its Critics*, p. 78.

DEMOCRATIC TRANSITION, CONSOLIDATION, AND TRANSFORMATION

After considering a variety of democratic transitions, G. O'Donnell and P. Schmitter[78] have argued that there is an 'identifiable process of (gradual and relatively peaceful) *transition*, which is not the same as that of (violent) *revolution*, from authoritarian to more democratic societies'.[79] By this they do not mean that 'there is a single and inevitable process of transition to democracy at work in history', for all such transitions are complex and uncertain, but that it is possible to distinguish analytically distinct stages in democratic transition: from liberalization through democratization to social transformation. Our discussion of this process provides the background to Part Three where we will consider the role of the churches in democratic transition in the twentieth century.

Liberalization is not democratization. Authoritarian rulers can sometimes afford to introduce liberal reforms without running the immediate risk of losing power. Invariably they do so under pressure from liberation movements or their equivalents, as well as on the advice of moderate voices within government who see the need for reform in order to prevent revolution and establish legitimacy. Such reformism characterized the early years of P. W. Botha's presidency in South Africa. It was not an attempt to bring about democratic change, but to introduce limited reforms which would enable the co-option of sufficient people of other races into the system to enable the white minority to retain power and gain some legitimacy. Inadequate as such reformism is, it nevertheless has the effect of opening up space for political action which may well trigger off what has been called a 'cycle of mobilisation'.[80] This is precisely what happened in the Soviet Union as a result

---

[78] G. O'Donnell and P. Schmitter, *Tentative Conclusions about Uncertain Democracies*, vol. 4 of O'Donnell, Schmitter, and L. Whitehead, eds., *Transitions from Authoritarian Rule*, Baltimore: Johns Hopkins, 1986. See also L. Diamond, J. Linz, and S. Lipset, *Democracy in Developing Countries*, 4 vols., Boulder, Colo.: Lynne Riener, 1988.

[79] André du Toit, in the Introduction to du Toit, ed., *Towards Democracy: Building a Culture of Accountability in South Africa*, Cape Town: Idasa, 1991 p. 9.

[80] *Ibid.*, p. 12.

of Mikhail Gorbachev's *perestroika*, and later in other eastern bloc countries as Communist leaders hurriedly tried to bring about reforms within the system. It also occurred in South Africa.

Liberalization can be checked, at least for a while, as it was by Botha, but his successor, F. W. de Klerk, soon recognized that this could not be done indefinitely, given the situation in the country. Much depends upon the social and economic circumstances at the time. Given the right congruence of such factors, if those engaged in democratic struggle now change tactics and make use of the spaces that have been opened up, then a more far-reaching transition to democracy becomes possible as 'the transitional process passes beyond the control of the regime'.[81] What follows is a period of negotiation during which pacts may be made and new players enter the process. But this period of flux and uncertainty is also the critical moment in which a reactionary coup becomes most likely.

Such 'reverse waves' of reaction followed the first two waves of modern democratization, so it is not unreasonable to antici-pate that the same could happen yet again. Several third-wave democracies have already begun to turn back to authoritarian rule[82] and the tactics employed by President Boris Yeltsin in Russia, in squashing opposition to his policies in September 1993, hovered on the edge of that slippery slope. This danger arises not only because there are always dictators waiting in the wings seeking an opportunity to take control but, as Erich Fromm observed with regard to the Weimar Republic, people fear freedom and they find it difficult to cope with uncertainty and change.[83] Even those who may be leading the change to democracy can lose nerve and pull back at the critical moment. This is especially so if the security forces, the military and the police, have reason to fear reprisals for crimes which they might have committed in repressing dissent.[84]

---

[81] *Ibid.*, p. 13.
[82] Samuel P. Huntington, 'Democracy's Third Wave', *Journal of Democracy*, 2,2, 1991, 15f.
[83] Erich Fromm, *The Fear of Freedom*, London: Routledge and Kegan Paul, 1942.
[84] See Lawrence Weschlar, *A Miracle, a Universe: Settling Accounts with Torturers*, New York: Penguin, 1990, pp. 173ff.

Another major cause of anxiety is economic uncertainty, and the fear of a deterioration in the standard of living. A 'benign nationalism can turn malignant very quickly' if the standard of living deteriorates and unemployment escalates.[85] It may not even be that the economic situation is much worse, or even as bad as previously, but simply that there is a growing gap between expectation and the possibility that it can be realized. As Przeworski wryly notes, when 'paradise turns into everyday life, disenchantment sets in', and that is when the temptation to revert to authoritarian rule is at its strongest.[86] The fact of the matter is that the process of liberalization, which has become the necessary harbinger of democratization in much of the world, often means economic pain and social strain in the short term. This can only be endured if there are indications that there will be medium to long-term gains for society as a whole. The secret of success is to ensure that sufficient economic and social progress is made, and order is maintained, during any period of transition, before deprivation and hardship bring public patience to an end. The critical issue is how to ensure that it is not in the interests of most people, not least the military and police, to turn the clock backwards.

The problem is exacerbated, however, if a deteriorating economy also has to deal with a legacy in which there is a marked class discrepancy. This inevitably means that the gap between rich and poor becomes even more intolerable. It is not surprising that in situations of grinding poverty there is a growing sense of alienation and anger which is fuelled by the media-projected vision of the 'good life' which only a few enjoy – particularly if those few are known to be advocates of democracy. Massive inequality must undermine democracy. Poverty, and all its attendant problems with regard to health, housing, and education, especially in rural areas, breeds political apathy or revolution rather than informed citizens able to participate in the democratic process.

Thus there is the danger that previously deprived or

---

[85] Glenny, *The Rebirth of History*, p. 245.
[86] Przeworski, *Democracy and the Market*, p. 94.

oppressed people can expect too much from democracy, trusting that it will right all previous wrongs with speed and finality. Not all human problems can be solved, and often the best which democracy can offer is to find some proximate solution.[87] In any case, the problems which democracy is required to solve are seldom of its making. Just as a newly elected government has to try and remedy the failures of the previous incumbents in office, so emerging democracies in eastern Europe and elsewhere have to overcome decades of bad totalitarian rule and failed economic policy. Democracy may be far better than its alternatives, but this does not necessarily mean a more efficient, economic, nor stable form of government *in the short term*. The evidence suggests that democracies do not *inherently* perform more efficiently than dictatorships.[88] The fundamental difference is that of legitimacy and accountability.

The economic factor is clearly of paramount importance not only in the transitional phase, but also in consolidating the formation of a new democracy. Whether or not such democracies are able to endure beyond the first flush of their celebrated formation will depend not simply on the quality of the constitution agreed to, nor the strength of its ideological convictions, but on economic performance, and therefore on the creation of those social and political conditions which make a sound economy possible.

Nevertheless, central to all else is the creation of a democratic culture of tolerance and trust. This means, *inter alia*, that those who were in power as well as those previously engaged in protest and resistance have to learn how to change both their political strategies and ways of organization in keeping with their stated democratic commitment.[89] It is not easy to switch from authoritarian rule or resistance politics to those of democratic change. The whole climate of politics has to change. Democracy means accepting the necessity for dissent, opposing views and political parties. Such co-operation is essential in

---

[87] Niebuhr, *The Children of Light*, p. 118.   [88] Diamond, 'Three Paradoxes', p. 53.
[89] du Toit, *Towards Democracy*, p. 117.

order to make the system work. Hence it has been rightly stated that democracy requires settled and dependable institutions, and especially a 'loyal opposition' which 'refuses to entertain plans to change the system and to exterminate its rivals'.[90] In other words, opposition takes place on the basis of consent and cohesion within the political arena.[91]

Nothing illustrates this better than the fundamentally different ways in which governments change hands in democracies as compared with military dictatorships or totalitarian regimes. A British prime minister may be concerned about losing office as a result of an election, but dictators fear the firing squad.[92] Although the transition to democracy in South Africa was preceded by a long, bitter, and often violent struggle, when the change to democratic rule was finally made, those who had previously been in power handed over the reigns of office and became the 'loyal opposition' within a government of national unity. Nothing symbolized this more than the acknowledgement of Nelson Mandela as president by the armed forces at his inauguration on 10 May 1994. Thus it can be argued that the threshold from authoritarian to democratic rule is crossed when the outcome of free and fair elections is accepted by those voted out of power, and the due process of constitutional law is acknowledged by all. Even though the transition to democracy may be but the beginning of a long struggle for social transformation, the only permissible means to that end now become those consonant with the democratic process.

None the less, the democracy of tomorrow will not, and cannot, be precisely the same as the democracy of today or the past – though it will embody many of the same principles.[93] What occurred in ancient Athens was only the first step into an unknown future in pursuit of a vision of a transformed society in which all people are equal and their differences respected; free and responsible as citizens, but also liberated from oppression and poverty and therefore living in a society where justice

---

[90] Hall, in Held, *Prospects for Democracy*, p. 272.
[91] Diamond, 'Three Paradoxes', p. 56.
[92] Benn and Peters, *Social Principles*, p. 346.   [93] *Ibid.*, p. 340.

prevails. This vision, as we will argue in the next chapter, derives as much, if not far more, from the prophets of ancient Israel than it does from Athens, the Enlightenment, or the French Revolution.

Just as some ancient Greek political theorists recognized that a good political order could foster human development,[94] so a truly democratic transformation of society today, especially where democracy does not exist, carries with it new possibilities for the development of a genuinely human life. With this in mind, we can understand democracy finally as a way of being in the world which is continually enriching those who participate, and expanding their horizons. The 'task of democracy' Dewey wrote, 'is one that can have no end till experience itself comes to an end, the task of democracy is forever that of the creation of a freer and more human experience in which all share and to which all contribute'.[95] That is the democratic vision which democratic systems should seek to serve.

[94] Cynthia Farrar, 'Ancient Greek Political Theory and Democracy', in Dunn, *The Unfinished Journey*, p. 24. See also p. 34.
[95] John Dewey, 'Creative Democracy – The Task Before Us', in Max Fisch, *Classic American Philosophers*, New York: Appleton-Century-Croft, 1951, p. 394.

CHAPTER 2

The prophetic vision

Two distinct political trajectories may be traced in the Hebrew Bible, namely the Mosaic or prophetic, and the Davidic or royal.[1] These reveal different paradigmatic ways in which God was understood within Israelite religion, the consequences which this had for the organization of society, and the way in which social structure and political economy in turn shaped Israelite theology.[2] These two trajectories coexist in Scripture in critical tension with each other. This reflects a tension within ancient Israelite society itself, between a more universal and a more nationalist understanding of its vocation, as well as a more radical and open-ended interpretation of the Torah, and one which was conservative and closed. A similar tension is evident in other historical contexts where the message of the Hebrew prophets has been proclaimed. For the word of the prophets has always challenged unjust social structures, and in so doing has been formative in the development of the western democratic tradition.

'LET JUSTICE ROLL DOWN'

The prophetic trajectory perceived Yahweh primarily as the God who had liberated slaves from bondage in Egypt and entered into a covenant with them at Sinai. This act of liber-

---

[1] Walter Brueggemann, 'Trajectories in Old Testament Literature and the Sociology of Ancient Israel', in Norman K. Gottwald, ed., *The Bible and Liberation: Political and Social Hermeneutics*, Maryknoll, N.Y.: Orbis, 1983, pp. 308f., 322.

[2] Norman K. Gottwald, 'Sociology (Ancient Israel)', *Anchor Bible Dictionary*, vol. 6, New York: Doubleday, 1992, pp. 79ff.

ation and subsequent covenantal relationship was the foundation of all else. Yahweh, the liberator of slaves, was also
biased in favour of the poor and oppressed in Canaan, and
therefore concerned about social justice and the building of a
communitarian society. By way of contrast, the royal trajectory, which surfaced with the rise of the Davidic monarchy in
Jerusalem, and came to full flower in the post-exilic period, was
primarily concerned about cultic and social order, ritual
purity, and the maintenance of the exclusive identity of Israel
as God's chosen people. This provided divine legitimation for
the hierarchical structuring of society over which the king and
the temple priesthood in Jerusalem ruled.

The prophetic struggle against Baalism in the early period of
the Israelite settlement in Canaan was against more than the
idolatries of Canaanite religion. It was also against an autocratic social order sanctioned and maintained by the worship of
Baal. Norman Gottwald perceptively argues: 'the novelty and
threat of early Israel was not the introduction of new religious
ideas and practices as such but the conjunction of previously
separated and contradictory social groups in a united and
mutually supportive network of egalitarian relations'.[3] Yet the
religion of Yahweh had brought together disparate social
groups and welded them into one covenanted society.[4] In
attacking idolatry the prophets were rejecting the legitimation
of a social order which undermined obedience to Yahweh,
economically oppressed the peasantry, and destroyed the
freedom of Yahweh's people.[5] What was at stake was the very
basis of Israel's existence, its covenantal relationship with
Yahweh in and through which its freedom as the people of God
could be affirmed. The way in which the nation was structured
and governed reflected its commitments, values, and therefore,
its theology.

---

[3] Norman K. Gottwald, *The Tribes of Yahweh: A Sociology of the Religion of Liberated Israel, 1250–1050 BCE*, Mary Knoll, NY: Orbis, 1985, p. 645.
[4] Norman K. Gottwald, *The Hebrew Bible: A Socio-Literary Introduction*, Philadelphia: Fortress, 1985, pp. 285f.
[5] Gunther Wittenberg, 'Authoritarian and Participatory Decision-Making in the Old Testament,' in Klaus Nürnberger, ed., *A Democratic Vision for South Africa: Political*

In the light of this, the prophets perceived that the populist demand in Israel for monarchy was 'a revolt against God'.[6] None the less, contrary to what might have been expected given the situation which prevailed in the surrounding Canaanite city-states, it was remarkable that Israel avoided monarchic institutions as long as it did.[7] Internal pressures pushed Israel towards monarchy, a process accelerated by the need for a united Israel to counter the threat of a Philistine invasion, but the prophets remained adamant in their rejection of the monarchical style and absolutism which characterized the institution in surrounding nations. As a result the prophetic egalitarian ideal, and the prophetic resistance to monarchical encroachment on the rights and interests of the community as a whole, are reflected in the reformist Deuteronomic code which was probably drafted, shortly before the exile, by priests or Levites in the northern kingdom who were influenced by the prophetic tradition. While the Deuteronomic code was primarily concerned about cultic reforms, the theocratic nature of Israelite society meant that such reforms affected the whole of society and played a pivotal role in subsequent social and religious developments.[8]

Inter alia, the Deuteronomists insisted that the people should elect their king as guided by Yahweh, and decreed further that the person chosen not use his office for personal aggrandizement, nor regard himself as 'above his brethren' (Deuteronomy 17:14–20). Unlike the notion of the surrounding nations that only the king was divine, the prophets insisted that all human beings were created in the image of God. Yahweh's reign over Israel excluded any monarchical absolutism or hereditary claims. The ideal king was the servant of God's

---

Realism and Christian Responsibility, Pietermaritzburg: Encounter Publications, 1991, p. 95.

[6] James Barr, 'The Bible as a Political Document', *Bulletin of the John Rylands University Library of Manchester*, 62, 2, 1980, p. 273.

[7] Gottwald, *Tribes of Yahweh*, p. 430.

[8] Gerhard von Rad, *Old Testament Theology*, vol. 1, Edinburgh: Oliver and Boyd, 1973, pp. 71f., 219ff.; N. Lohfink, 'The Cult Reform of Josiah of Judah: 2 Kings 22–23 as a Source for the History of Israelite Religion', in P. D. Miller, P. D. Hanson, and S. D. McBride, eds., *Ancient Israelite Religion*, Philadelphia: Fortress, 1987.

righteousness and the people. That this model rule was often rejected *de facto* by the kings of Israel was regarded by the prophets as the reason for the woes which afflicted the nation.

In many respects the Deuteronomic reforms can be compared to those initiated by Cleisthenes in Athens a century later, which we now regard as the symbolic birth of democracy in the western world. In Athens and in Israel, political privilege and responsibility were patriarchical and excluded foreigners, but both Greek citizens in fifth century BCE Athens, and their Israelite counterparts, as envisaged by the Deuteronomist, had civic rights and responsibilities, and the well-being of the people depended on fulfilling them properly.[9] In both the Athenian *ekklēsia* and the Israelite tribal *qāhāl* (the regular assembly of Israel) people participated in the decision-making processes of society. However unlike Athens, where direct democracy eventually collapsed, within Israel, as the population grew and a settled agricultural society developed under the monarchy, the egalitarian participation of its nomadic period was replaced by a more representative form of government within the *qāhāl* (Deuteronomy 16:16–20), not unlike that mixture of monarchy, aristocracy, and democracy, proposed by Aristotle.[10] Future generations of Christian political philosophers had little difficulty in mingling together the insights of ancient Israel as expressed in the Deuteronomic code with those derived from classical sources.

Central to the Deuteronomic reforms were economic concerns. Under the monarchy, the egalitarian social ideals of the prophets were continually threatened, not least through burdensome taxation and the confiscation of land in lieu of the repayment of debts. Thus the Deuteronomic code called on Israel to emulate Yahweh's concern for the poor, oppressed, widows, orphans, and other victims of society. Even foreigners were to be treated fairly and with respect for their rights. The administration of the law (*mishpāt*) with regard to a plethora of

---

[9] Robert Gordis, *Poets, Prophets, and Sages: Essays in Biblical Interpretation*, Indiana University Press, 1971, pp. 45f.; Ludwig Kohler, *Hebrew Man*, London: SCM, 1973, pp. 152f.; Robert Banks, *Paul's Idea of Community*, Exeter: Paternoster, 1980, p. 15.

[10] Gordis, *Poets, Prophets, and Sages*, pp. 55f.

personal and interpersonal matters had to be exercised in terms of the covenantal obligation to pursue God's righteousness (*tsedākah*), Yahweh's 'burning compassion for the oppressed'.[11] *Tsedākah*, social righteousness or justice, was 'the barometer of the health of society'.[12] This meant that wrongs and social inequities were to be regularly redressed, as prescribed, for example, in the teaching on the Year of Jubilee (Leviticus 17). Concomitantly, the power of the privileged was to be kept under control. Laws and their administration were subject to the higher law of social righteousness, which meant, in effect, ensuring that the structures of society were themselves just. Hence the prophetic vision of a future transformed society in which human beings live together in peace with themselves and in harmony with the whole of creation (*shalom*), and in which the glory of Yahweh would be revealed.

Nothing better expresses the prophetic vision than *shalom*.[13] Its translation as 'peace' fails to convey its full complex of interrelated meaning. In its essence, *shalom* refers to the healing and wholeness of human relationships, of the well-being of creation, and of the covenantal relationship between Yahweh and Israel. *Shalom*, a synonym for salvation, also carries with it an eschatological dimension, pointing beyond the present to what God will yet do for the world. But *shalom* is also inseparable from the doing of justice. False prophets are those who proclaim *shalom* without justice (Jeremiah 14:13); *shalom*, on the other hand, is God's gift to those who do justice.

This prophetic vision of an egalitarian society in which 'justice rolled down like a mighty stream' (Amos 5:24) has contributed more than simply ideas to the struggle for political equality, freedom, and social justice in the course of human history. For, irrespective of what the textual critics may say about the historical veracity of the Exodus story, or whether Israel actually functioned as required by the Deuteronomic

---

[11] Abraham J. Heschel, *The Prophets*, New York: Harper and Row, 1969, p. 201.

[12] Jeffries M. Hamilton, *Social Justice and Deuteronomy: The Case of Deuteronomy* 15, Atlanta, Georgia: Scholars Press, 1992, p. 153.

[13] Gerhard von Rad, 'Shalom', in Gerhard Kittel, ed., *Theological Dictionary of the New Testament*, vol. 2, Grand Rapids: Eerdmans, 1964, pp. 402ff.

code, or practiced the prescriptions for the Year of Jubilee, such texts have provided the basis for an ongoing radical critique of social domination and its legitimating ideologies. They have also inspired and legitimated social protest, resistance, and transformation through the centuries.[14] The prophetic vision, in fact, has provided much of the substance and inspiration for the democratic vision even amongst those who reject its theological foundations.

In post-exilic Judaism, both proto-democratic and authoritarian styles of leadership emerged in Israel, the former as in the case of Ezra, the latter as exemplified by Nehemiah.[15] Certainly, with the ending of the monarchy and the loss of political power, a new political dispensation began in which there was clearly tension between those who were open to political reform, and those who sought to protect their own identity and interests in a defensive and exclusive way. Though it is true that in both instances, the 'people of the land' were generally excluded from political power.

Josephus referred to Jerusalem as a *polis*, but neither Jerusalem nor any other Jewish controlled town within the Roman empire functioned as a civil society. This was despite the fact that city-states were, as Gerd Theissen remarks, 'thickly clustered around Jewish territory' and 'governed by an assembly of all the citizens (the *ekklēsia*), and a group of magistrates elected by it (the *boulē*)'.[16] Two centuries before the Christian era, an Hellenistic reform movement within Judaism tried to bring Jerusalem within the orbit of these states, but failed due to a conservative Jewish backlash which discredited the very idea of the *polis*. After the defeat of the Maccabees, the Romans tried yet again to set up decentralized local forms of government, but the gulf between Judaism and the city-states and their institutions was too great on religious grounds alone. The

---

[14] See, for example, Michael Walzer, *Exodus and Revolution*, New York: Basic Books, 1986.

[15] Tamara Cohn Eskenazi, *In an Age of Prose: A Literary Approach to Ezra-Nehemiah*, Atlanta, Ga.: Scholars Press, 1988, p. 141.

[16] Gerd Theissen, *Sociology of Early Palestinian Christianity*, Philadelphia: Fortress, 1978, p. 69.

major opposition derived from the realization that, within the *polis*, Jews and 'foreigners' would have become fellow-citizens, culture would have been liberalized, and the centralized position of Jerusalem weakened. In Jerusalem Gentiles had no civic rights. This was the historical context for the life and ministry of Jesus.

JESUS AND THE REIGN OF GOD

Long before sociology became an accepted tool of biblical research, Ernst Troeltsch observed that Jesus addressed himself to the needs of the oppressed, considered wealth a danger to the soul, and 'opposed the Jewish priestly aristocracy which represented the dominant ecclesiastical forces of his day'.[17] This much was clear from a straightforward reading of the gospels. Since Troeltsch, an enormous amount of research has deepened and broadened our knowledge of Jesus and Christian origins,[18] demonstrating the extent to which the 'Jesus movement' must be located within the prophetic trajectory.[19] The prophetic understanding of social justice and the hope for a transformed world undoubtedly cast its long shadow into the New Testament.[20]

Jesus identified with the prophetic tradition[21] both as one who proclaimed God's righteousness against the injustices of his day, and as one who actively sought to bring about social renewal on the basis of God's reign.[22] Luke's gospel (4:18f.) portrays Jesus as identifying his mission from the outset in

---

[17] Ernst Troeltsch, *The Social Teaching of the Christian Churches*, vol. 1, London: George Allen and Unwin, 1956, p. 39.

[18] Christopher Rowland, *Christian Origins*, London: SPCK, 1986.

[19] See, for example, Richard Cassidy, *Jesus, Politics, and Society: A Study of Luke's Gospel*, Maryknoll, N.Y.; Orbis, 1978; Hugo Echegaray, *The Practice of Jesus*, Maryknoll, N.Y.; Orbis, 1984; Albert Nolan, *Jesus Before Christianity*, Cape Town: David Philip, 1978.

[20] Hamilton, *Social Justice and Deuteronomy*, pp. 2f.

[21] David E. Aune, *Prophecy in Early Christianity and the Ancient Mediterranean World*, Grand Rapids: Eerdmans, 1983, pp. 153ff.

[22] Richard A. Horsley, *Jesus and the Spiral of Violence: Popular Jewish Resistance in Roman Palestine*, San Francisco: Harper and Row, 1987, p. 207; Richard A. Horsley and John S. Hanson, *Bandits, Prophets, and Messiahs*, Minneapolis, Minn.; Winston Press, 1985, pp. 135ff.

terms of the words of a post-exilic prophet as good news to the poor, release for prisoners, healing for the blind, freedom for social victims, and the heralding of the Year of Jubilee in which the renewal of society and the environment as a whole is put into effect (Isaiah 61:1f.) – a profound expression of the meaning of *shalom*.

Several interrelated aspects may be mentioned to demonstrate the political significance of Jesus as a prophet. The first is the way in which he turned social relations upside down and sought to re-establish them along egalitarian lines. Jesus demonstrated this in his own interpersonal relations, and implemented it in creating his community of disciples. He disregarded those social and hierarchical barriers of gender or class, ritual cleanliness or piety, which traditionally separated people from each other. Moreover, Jesus challenged the authoritarian and patriarchal[23] patterns of leadership within contemporary Judaism and the surrounding cultures. In short, he 'insisted that the renewed covenantal community avoid the patriarchal social-economic-political hierarchy that constituted the chain of domination maintaining institutionalized injustice'.[24]

Secondly, as demonstrated in his exorcisms of demonic power and his healing ministry, Jesus was concerned about the wholeness of individual people, and therefore their freedom from the various forms of bondage which destroy the quality of life as God intends it. Ernst Käsemann's description of Jesus as a 'liberal' because of the way in which he opposed the strict legalisms and orthodoxies of his day and affirmed the human desire for freedom,[25] is misleading. But Jesus did liberate people from the bondage of dehumanizing powers, and enabled them to discover their God-given dignity, just as he also empowered them to live life more responsibly for others. Jesus' exorcisms and healing miracles were powerful symbolic acts, witnessing to the reign of God and the promise of *shalom*,

---

[23] Ched Myers, *Binding the Strong Man: A Political Reading of Mark's Story of Jesus*, Maryknoll, N.Y.: Orbis, 1988, pp. 279f.

[24] Horsley, *Jesus and the Spiral of Violence*, p. 244.

[25] Ernst Käsemann, *Jesus Means Freedom*, London: SCM, 1969, pp. 16ff.

'not because they challenged the laws of nature, but because they challenged the very structures of social existence'.[26]

Thirdly, Jesus strongly challenged social and economic injustices. This comes out in many different ways, not least in his teaching on wealth and poverty. Jesus' teaching was such that for centuries after the church found it difficult to sanction usury or even the ownership of private property without strict conditions and qualifications. His admonition to 'seek first God's righteousness' (*tsedākah*) was a clear prophetic challenge to pursue justice, especially for the poor, as the foundation of social life (Matthew 6:33). In pursuance of his mission to proclaim the advent of God's reign, Jesus confronted the religious and political authorities of his day, notably those who controlled the temple revenue in Jerusalem. This led to his crucifixion – a death brought about by religious interests, political complicity, and populist demands.

Many have recognized the 'impossible possibility' of Jesus' radical prophetic message, and have therefore regarded it as an interim ethic which Jesus taught in anticipation of the eschaton.[27] That is open to debate.[28] But there can be no denying that Jesus' prophetic witness to the reign of God provides an ongoing radical critique of all political systems in which people are dehumanized through the unjust domination of others.[29] In obedience to Jesus there have always been those who have sought to maintain this witness in society, often at great personal cost, and who in doing so have been instrumental in confronting tyranny and providing a radical critique of all unjust social systems.

Two themes in the development of primitive Christianity and its expansion in the Graeco-Roman world are particularly germane to our exploration of the Christian antecedents of democracy. The first is the way in which the Christian movement continued to witness publicly to the message of God's

---

[26] Myers, *Binding the Strong Man*, pp. 114, 147.

[27] Reinhold Niebuhr, *An Interpretation of Christian Ethics*, London: SCM, 1948.

[28] John H. Yoder, *The Politics of Jesus*, Grand Rapids: Eerdmans, 1972.

[29] See, for example, John H. Yoder, *The Priestly Kingdom: Social Ethics as Gospel*, University of Notre Dame Press, 1984, pp. 155f.

reign. The second is the way in which the Christian community (*ekklēsia*) understood and organized its own internal life and polity, and how this related to the broader society.

THE CHRISTIAN '*EKKLĒSIA*'

In continuity with Jesus, the first Christians sought to embody a form of egalitarian communitarianism within their own community (Acts 2:43–7), convinced that the death and resurrection of Jesus had brought the old order of human division, sin and enmity to its end.[30] Baptism was a sign of entry into the messianic community, which was the visible representation of God's new humanity; as such it was a radical rejection of all divisive social distinctions. A new age of universal righteousness, justice, equity, freedom, and therefore *shalom* was dawning, and would shortly be established once and for all when Jesus returned to establish his reign. Thus, built into Christianity from the beginning was a strong utopian dimension which gave the movement direction and hope.

As Christianity moved steadily beyond the parameters of Judaism and rural Palestine, and became an urbanized and Hellenized faith, its messianic expectations were subtly changed or else marginalized.[31] This is evident within the New Testament itself. For the Fourth Gospel as for Paul, the new *aeon* had begun for those who believed, and therefore they should not adapt to the norms of the present age. But clearly the old was not entirely gone, and somehow Christians had to be in the world though not of it. They had to work out what it meant to be a messianic community within society on a longer-term basis than originally anticipated.

Paul did not abandon the message of radical freedom and social equality which we find in his letter to the Galatians, and which documents his firm rejection of both the legalism of the conservative reactionaries of his day, and the compromises of his fellow apostle Peter.[32] But, as is already evident in his

---

[30] Christopher Rowland, *Christian Origins*, pp. 272ff.
[31] Christopher Rowland, *Radical Christianity*, Cambridge: Polity Press, 1988, p. 16.
[32] Richard N. Longenecker, *Galatians*, Dallas, Texas: Word Books, 1990, pp. 71ff.

Corinthian correspondence, freedom and equality had to be brought within the constraints of order within the church. Thus charisma was routinized in his theology just as it was in wider ecclesial practice. Ever since, radicals, reformists, and conservatives alike have found Pauline support for their opposing positions. While 'socially subversive' texts (for example, Galatians 3:28) have provided a basis for radical readings of the gospel, the 'house-tables' of the pastoral letters (for example, I Timothy 2–3) have often been appropriated for conservative interpretations in which patriarchy became the basis for participation within the church.[33] In terms of the latter reading, all Christians were equally respected within the *ekklēsia*, but were not of equal status.[34] The equality of women, for example, which was such a central theme in the ministry of Jesus, was down-played as counter-productive to Christian mission and apologetics within the Graeco-Roman world.[35]

The word *ekklēsia*, rather than *synagōgē*, was chosen by primitive Christianity to describe an assembly of God's people, chiefly because it was the preferred Septuagint translation of the Hebrew *qāhāl*. The word *ekklēsia* also distinguished the early Christians from the many voluntary clubs and private associations which existed in the Hellenistic world and which only permitted persons of the same status into their membership.[36] The church, on the other hand, did not regard itself as a voluntary society or private association, but as a universal community embodied in local congregations comprised of people drawn from every segment of society.[37] It exhibited a social plurality essential to the church's identity and mission as the new humanity within a new world order.[38] The way in which the various Christian *ekklēsiai* in different localities

---

[33] Banks, *Paul's Idea of Community*, p. 15.   [34] Rowland, *Radical Christianity*, p. 39.

[35] David L. Bach, '*Let Wives be Submissive . . .*': *The Origin, Form and Apologetic Function of the Household Duty Code (Haustafel) in I Peter*, Chico, Calif.: Scholars Press, 1981.

[36] Wayne A. Meeks, *The First Urban Christians: The Social World of the Apostle Paul*, New Haven: Yale University Press, 1983, pp. 79, 222, n.24.

[37] *Ekklēsia* is used in the New Testament to denote both the local congregation and the universal church. As such it is a term which denotes that the Christian community is intended to be both contextually specific as well as universal in its character and scope.

[38] *Ibid.*, pp. 78f.

originally organized themselves varied, though, at least in some, local leaders, both men and women, were democratically elected (Acts 6). Likewise, major issues facing the expanding church were dealt with in council and often by consensus (Acts 15). There was, as J. Christiaan Beker suggests with regard to the Pauline churches, a form of 'pnuematic democracy'.[39]

In its common Hellenistic usage, *ekklēsia* was a political rather than a cultic term, describing an assembly of citizens gathered to exercise their civic responsibilities. Ordinary Greeks may well have been puzzled by the theological way in which Christians used the word (*ekklēsia tou theou*). For Hellenistic Christians it would have suggested an analogy to the secular assembly of citizens, with the implication that Christians had a responsibility to ensure not only that their own community, but also wider society was well governed (cf. I Corinthians 6:2). The closest historical parallel to its meaning in relation to the Christian *ekklēsia* would be a New England town-meeting where civic and church affairs were often one and the same.[40] Even though we cannot build a theory on the basis of a word-study,[41] or assume that the first Christians chose *ekklēsia* with this consciously in mind, it was none the less 'a rather astonishing act of self-confidence' for a little group of people drawn largely from the underside of society to choose this word to describe themselves.[42]

The relationship between the Christian *ekklēsia* and political society became a matter of major concern to imperial authorities as Christianity expanded throughout the Roman empire. It was increasingly perceived as a rival socio-political institution, another centre of power, which made absolute and universal claims in the name of God.[43] Thus its mere existence was

[39] J. Christiaan Beker, *Paul the Apostle: The Triumph of God in Life and Thought*, Philadelphia: Fortress, 1982, p. 316.

[40] Meeks, *First Urban Christians*, pp. 108, 229, n. 159.

[41] Cf. K. L. Schmidt's discussion of *ekklēsia* which, however, predates significant developments in the sociological study of Christian origins, and is determined by confessional conflicts. Gerhard Kittel, ed., *Theological Dictionary of the New Testament*, vol. 3, Grand Rapids: Eerdmans, 1965, pp. 501–536.

[42] Wayne Meeks, *The Moral World of the First Christians*, London: SPCK, 1986, p. 20.

[43] Michael Mann, *The Sources of Social Power*, Cambridge University Press, 1986, p. 325.

politically and sometimes economically disturbing (Acts 19:23f.). This was recognized very early, when Christians refused to acknowledge local civic deities or worship Caesar as divine, or participate in the military on the grounds of conscience. Such civil disobedience injected a critical dualism into political society, and became an important milestone in the development of the notion of civil society. Not surprisingly, it took much effort on the part of Christian apologists to convince the authorities that Christians could be both devout believers and good citizens.[44]

Christians soon learnt to live obediently within Roman society, and even to regard its social structures as divinely ordained. At the same time, the development of Christian orthodoxy and the increasingly hierarchical structures of the church reinforced the socially conservative tendency already present within the Christian movement.[45] A single *episkopos* or bishop in each city, replaced the earlier looser organization in the second century, in order to maintain order and control heretical groups.[46] Those groups which were apocalyptic or millenarian in outlook, or within which women shared an equal status with men, found themselves outside the mainstream of the 'great church'. Christianity, in its dominant expression, came to stand 'for stability rather than change, hierarchy rather than egalitarianism, the rich rather than the poor, men rather than women'.[47] The foundations were well laid for that 'Christian-imperial political theology' which later found expression in post-Constantinian Christendom, a theology which would predominate in the centuries to come.[48]

Yet, throughout Christian history more radical groups have emerged which have retrieved those socially subversive texts within Scripture which demand liberation, justice, and equity

[44] W. H. C. Frend, *The Rise of Christianity*, Philadelphia: Fortress, 1984, pp. 131f.
[45] Eduard Schweizer, *Church Order in the New Testament*, London: SCM, 1961; H. von Campenhausen, *Ecclesiastical Authority and Spiritual Power in the Church of the First Three Centuries*, London: Collins, 1969; Beker, Paul the Apostle, pp. 322f.; Elisabeth Schüssler Fiorenza, *In Memory of Her: A Feminist Theological Reconstruction of Christian Origins*, London: SCM, 1983, pp. 8off.
[46] Meeks, *The Moral World*, p. 122.   [47] Rowland, *Radical Christianity*, p. 14.
[48] Jürgen Moltmann, *The Crucified God*, p. 325.

for the poor and oppressed, often combined with an apocalyptic millenarianism.[49] These groups on the left-wing of Christianity, usually regarded as heretics by the ecclesiastical establishment, have kept alive the utopian prophetic vision of an egalitarian and participatory society both in the church and the public arena. We shall note several examples in the next chapter. Others, inspired by the same prophetic vision, but less utopian in their expectations and usually less radical in their strategies, have likewise struggled for freedom and sought to establish just societies. In doing so they have helped to develop social structures which have found particular expression in representative forms of democracy. In some instances the radical and the reformist have co-operated in their pursuit of liberty and justice, joining forces in revolutionary endeavour to overthrow tyrants. At other times they have been strongly opposed to each other, representing different interests and pursuing different goals. Resisted by reactionary and conservative forces within church and society, their endeavours have none the less blended in the course of history in enabling the birth and nurturing of democracy.

[49] Norman Cohn, *The Pursuit of the Millennium*, New York: Oxford University Press, 1974.

PART II

Historical and theological connections

CHAPTER 3

The Christian matrix

Western democracy developed within the matrix of Christendom and the Enlightenment, and it can only be deciphered in relation to both. The relationship is, however, complex, multi-layered, and ambiguous. As Harold Berman reminds us: 'Liberal democracy was the first great secular religion in Western history – the first ideology which became divorced from traditional Christianity.'[1] Yet a divorce implies partners who were previously married, shared much in common, and who, even in their separation, cannot fully break with their past relationship. So, Berman continues, democracy took over from Christianity 'both its sense of the sacred and some of its major values'.

CHRISTENDOM: A NEW WORLD ORDER

The Edict of Milan in 313 was a turning-point in European history, 'the great charter of the *New Republic*', as Charles Norris Cochrane called it.[2] In terms derived from the priestly legitimation of Israelite monarchy, it provided much needed vindication of imperial authority,[3] and, while it did not make Christianity the Roman imperial religion immediately, it did give it the status and freedom for which earlier apologists had argued. The provisions of the Edict made possible, for the first

---

[1] Harold J. Berman, 'Religious Foundations of Law in the West: An Historical Perspective', *Journal of Law and Religion*, 1, 3, Summer 1983, p. 38. See also Harold J. Berman, *Law and Revolution: The Formation of the Western Legal Tradition*, Boston: Harvard University Press, 1983.

[2] Charles Norris Cochrane, *Christianity and Classical Culture: A Study of Thought and Action from Augustus to Augustine*, London: Oxford University Press, 1944, p. 180.

[3] *Ibid.*, p. 188.

time in antiquity, the separation of political and religious power, thus anticipating, though by no means achieving, the separation of powers and the distinction between political and civil society so fundamental to democracy.

Constantine was a transitional figure who initiated the 'project of a Christian commonwealth';[4] towards the end of the same century, Emperor Theodosius transformed what Constantine began into an Orthodox empire.[5] In pursuing his objectives Theodosius remained locked in an essentially pagan worldview despite his profession of Catholic faith, yet, as Augustine of Hippo later recognized, he was the prototype of 'the Christian Prince'.[6] Whereas Constantine regarded Christianity as a much needed tonic for an ailing society, Theodosius saw Christianity as providing a blood transfusion for a society nigh unto death. This was 'the only possible means of restoring to the *polis* something of the vitality which ... had passed from it to the *ekklēsia*'.[7] The *Pax Christi* and the *Pax Romana* were bound together, making Christianity the 'unitive religion of the unitary Roman state'.[8]

This remarkable reversal of historical fortune, in which a previously persecuted sect dethroned the traditional gods and became the imperial religion, determined both the way in which the church related to the state, and the way in which Christianity structured its own life. Gradually the lines between the Christian *ekklēsia* and the imperial *polis* were blurred. Clergy became a privileged class, immune from trial for criminal offences except in ecclesiastical courts. The state was now available to promote ecclesiastical interests, by coercion if necessary, and the rejection of the authority of the church was treasonable.[9] In exchange, the church was required to give its allegiance and support to emperor and empire. Despite this, strong counter-cultural currents prevailed in the church, protesting against the erosion of its commitment to the gospel.

[4] *Ibid.*, p. 179.   [5] *Ibid.*, p. 328.   [6] *Ibid.*, p. 324.   [7] *Ibid.*, p. 336.
[8] Moltmann, *The Crucified God*, p. 325.
[9] S. L. Greenslade, *Church and State from Constantine to Theodosius*, London: SCM, 1954, p. 33.

Even before the fourth century, monasticism had challenged the moral laxity which had begun to penetrate the life of the church. This opposition became even more crucial with the massive influx of people into the church. But monasticism was more than an ascetic counter-culture, it was also an example of participatory communal existence. Building on the earliest monastic rule, in the fourth century Basil of Caesarea designed a way of communal life which made the monastery 'a model, not so much of, as for, the *polis*'.[10] This provided the basis for the famous Rule developed by Benedict of Nursia in the sixth century, in which all class distinctions within the monastery were obliterated – in principle if not always in practice – in a society in which such distinctions were paramount.[11] Rank had little to do with wealth or ancestry.[12] As monasticism spread over much of Europe during the following centuries, it decisively influenced medieval society.[13] The Benedictine Rule provided a model for social organization in which the decision-making process was guided by both the wisdom of experience and the insight of youth, by consultation and consensus as well as by representation.

While monks took a vow of poverty, this was also an ideal held out to all Christians. Wealth was widely recognized as a problem for those who were seeking salvation, and generally regarded with suspicion.[14] Just as chapter thirty-three of the Rule of Benedict regarded private property as a vice, so there was much debate about the right to own property and to lend money at interest. Prominent church leaders, most of whom were of aristocratic parentage, voluntarily accepted poverty as a way of life.[15] Yet, for every radical statement on the subject,

[10] Cochrane, *Christianity and Classical Culture*, p. 341.
[11] Jean le Clerq, 'The Problem of Social Class and Christology', *Word and Spirit*, 2, 1981.
[12] Daniel Rees, *Consider Your Call: A Theology of Monastic Life Today*, London: SPCK, 1978, p. 69.
[13] Henry M. R. E. Mayr-Harting, *The Venerable Bede, the Rule of St Benedict, and Social Class*, Jarrow Lecture 1976.
[14] John Kenneth Galbraith, *A History of Economics: the Past as the Present*, London: Penguin, 1991, p. 21.
[15] Charles Kannengiesser, 'The Spiritual Message of the Great Fathers', in Bernard McGinn, John Meyendorff, and Jean Leclerq, eds., *Christian Spirituality: Origins to the Twelfth Century*, vol. 1, New York: Crossroad, 1989, p. 62.

there was one more cautious and qualified. The rich were not condemned for being rich, but for not sharing; both rich and poor needed each other, and both were included in the salvific economy of God.[16] The sharing of resources and the responsible use of money and possessions was taken as a measure of Christian commitment.

A struggle for sovereignty

Whereas monasticism was a protest against the compromise of Christian commitment, the protest of Ambrose, the celebrated fourth-century bishop of Milan, was against the abuse of state power. His excommunication of Emperor Theodosius after the infamous massacre at Thessalonika in 390,[17] marked a critical turning-point in the history of church–state relations and political accountability. It was the first time that a church leader claimed 'the power to judge, condemn, punish and finally pardon princes; and for the first time we find a monarch humbly submitting to a spiritual authority which he recognized and publicly acknowledged to be higher than his own'.[18] The church was not beholden to the state, but had the right to self-determination, and its representatives were free to speak and act according to their own convictions.[19] A lawyer by training, Ambrose used all his legal and rhetorical skills to ensure that political power was exercised for the common good.[20] Political authority did not depend upon might, but on doing what God required, ascertained from natural law[21] and understood in the light of the gospel. There was a clear distinction between auth-

---

[16] Boniface Ramsey, *Beginning to Read the Fathers*, London: Darton, Longman and Todd, 1987, pp. 182ff.

[17] F. Homes Dudden, *The Life and Times of St Ambrose*, Oxford: Clarendon Press, 1935, vol. 2, pp. 381ff.

[18] *Ibid.*, p. 391.   [19] Cochrane, *Christianity and Classical Culture*, p. 347.

[20] Gerard Watson, 'Pagan Philosophy and Christian Ethics', in J. P. Mackey, ed., *Morals, Law and Authority: Sources and Attitudes in the Church*, Dublin: Gill & Macmillan, 1969, pp. 49ff.

[21] The doctrine of natural law, which Cicero took over from the Stoics and made central to the development of Roman law, was introduced into the church through Ambrose and Augustine, and eventually significantly influenced the development of both canon and constitutional law. Watson, in Mackey, *Morals, Law and Authority*, p. 52.

ority as ordained by God and the way in which power was exercised. This meant that those in power could be challenged and resisted if they acted against the welfare of the people.[22]

Ambrose's claim that the church could intervene in political affairs had far-reaching and ambiguous implications. For good, it meant that the church had the right and responsibility to ensure that the state did not transgress the boundaries of morality in pursuing its policies. For ill, it meant an ecclesiastical triumphalism and authoritarianism in keeping with the character of imperial politics. At that historical moment, the strengthening of episcopal authority was probably the only realistic way in which the freedom of the church from political control could be maintained.[23] Yet, as the church increased in power and influence, so it was possible for it to use secular ordinances for its own purposes and goals.[24] Thus radical movements in the church which challenged the structures of society in any way were either brought under strict hierarchical control, or else were suppressed and punished by the state as heretical.

Whether Christianity was responsible for the fall of Rome in 410, as Niccolò Machiavelli and Edward Gibbon later argued,[25] or whether we assert with Augustine that imperial pride and avarice must bear the blame, is a matter of perspective. None the less, the contrast between republican virtues and imperial vices, paralleled by the contrast between the Christian virtue of humility and the hubris of fallen humanity, is a telling one. For Augustine, the collapse of Rome meant the triumph of Christianity over paganism, of truth over falsehood, of Christ over Caesar.[26] If the descendants of ancient Rome would only recognize the truth of Christianity, then those political virtues which had made republican Rome great would return in a new

[22] d'Entrèves, *The Notion of the State*, p. 185.
[23] Hastings, *Church and State*, p. 9.
[24] Ernst Troeltsch, *The Social Teaching of the Christian Churches*, vol. 2, London: George Allen and Unwin, 1956, p. 82.
[25] Quentin Skinner, *The Foundations of Modern Political Thought*, Cambridge University Press, 1978, vol. 1, p. 167.
[26] St Augustine, *City of God*, New York: Doubleday, 1958, pp. 39ff.

spirit.[27] For Augustine, Christian humility before God was as essential for the welfare of the *polis* as it was for the *ekklēsia*.

With its egalitarian character in mind, Cochrane describes Augustine's view of the church as 'profoundly democratic'.[28] Given Augustine's hierarchical world view and the way in which this influenced his ecclesiology, Cochrane's statement is something of an exaggeration. But even if Augustine's ecclesiology can be called democratic, there was little that was democratic about his politics. Augustine's view of human nature and the state was, in fact, as pessimistic as that of a Thomas Hobbes or Machiavelli.[29] For Augustine, political society was an emergency measure made necessary by human sin; it was an attempt to create order out of chaos.

Augustine's complex thought provided the rationale for the emerging, yet fragile, new order of western Christendom. It was a theology of transition in which the church was recognized as the only custodian of those values and virtues without which a genuinely human and social life would have been impossible following the fall of Rome. However, although Augustine's theology helped western civilization handle this extraordinary crisis, it also reinforced those developments in the history of the West which led to the exaltation of hierarchical structures, individualism, and rationalism. Indeed, Augustine not only laid the foundations for much of medieval Christianity, but also provided the ontological basis for that individualism which has so profoundly characterized modernity and its democratic polity.[30]

With the accession to power of the Emperor Justinian, who brought the Constantinian process to completion, Augustine's carefully constructed vision of two cities in which the secular kingdom is under the authority of the spiritual

[27] Hans von Campenhausen, 'Augustine and the Fall of Rome', in *Tradition and Life in the Church*, London: Collins, 1968, p. 211.

[28] Cochrane, *Christianity and Classical Culture*, p. 512. See Augustine, *City of God*, xix, 17–19.

[29] Herbert A. Deane, *The Political Philosophy and Social Ideas of St Augustine*, New York: Columbia University Press, 1963, p. 117.

[30] Colin, E. Gunton, *The Promise of Trinitarian Theology*, Edinburgh: T. & T. Clark, 1991, pp. 31ff.

was subverted.[31] Temporal and spiritual power were kept separate, but in a decisive turn towards the establishment of a theocracy, the emperor as 'vicar of Christ'[32] became the supreme ruler of *societas Christiana*. Thus the scene was set for a struggle between church and state for temporal sovereignty which would dominate the medieval period, and, in one form or another, remain a problem well into our own time. Indeed, the struggle for the freedom of the church from state control, or of the state from church control, eventually became essential aspects of the struggle for democracy.

The turning point in the medieval struggle to free the church from imperial and monarchical control came as a result of the 'investiture controversy', which began under the pontificate of Leo IX (1049–54).[33] Already by 1075 Pope Gregory VII had pronounced a papal victory and 'declared the absolute political and legal supremacy of the pope not only over all the bishops but also over all secular rulers'.[34] This was dramatically enacted in the submission of Emperor Henry IV at Canossa in January 1077,[35] even though the controversy was to continue for another fifty years before papal victory was assured. The papacy, now confessed to be uniquely the 'vicar of Christ' and having the 'plenitude of power', was sovereign within the church and, sometimes, as during the pontificate of Innocent III, within much of the secular realm as well.[36] In effect, power was concentrated in the hands of a centralized papal bureaucracy, the Roman *Curia*.[37]

The subsequent debates and the conflicts between the two

---

[31] Justinian's Code and related writings, which comprise the *Corpus Juris Civilis*, codified Roman law for the Middle Ages and significantly influenced the development of canon law.

[32] Berman, 'Religious Foundations of Law', p. 6.

[33] Gerd Tellenbach, *The Church in Western Europe from the Tenth to the Early Twelfth Century*, Cambridge University Press, 1993, pp. 185ff.

[34] Berman, 'Religious Foundations of Law', p. 6.

[35] Brian Tierney, *The Middle Ages: The Sources of Medieval History*, vol. 1, New York: Alfred A. Knopf, 1970, pp. 116f.

[36] Colin Morris, *The Papal Monarchy: the Western Church from 1050 to 1250*, Oxford: Clarendon Press, 1991, pp. 206ff.

[37] Michael Mullett, *Radical Religious Movements in Early Modern Europe*, London: George Allen and Unwin, 1980, p. 59.

centres of sovereignty were heated and drawn-out as the Middle Ages reached their climax.[38] The signing of the Magna Carta in England in 1215 was but one celebrated event in a long process. Such achievements may have been victories for feudal barons against kings and papacy, rather than victories for the common people, yet they were also critical turning-points in constitutional history. Sometimes, as in this instance, it was only because of the intervention of church leaders that they did not degenerate into victories for one faction, but became significant for society as a whole.[39] This is an early example of the mediating role of the church which has become commonplace in contemporary transitions to democracy.

As canon lawyers drafted legislation to relate papal supremacy to the rule of national princes and nobility, they made a formative contribution to the western legal tradition through the development of constitutional law.[40] Anticipating contemporary debates about universals and particulars, medieval political theory was worked out in relation to practical issues such as usury, war, property and land rights, the rights and limits of authority, tyranny and the right to engage in rebellion or tyrannicide. Thus far-reaching changes to social law and institutions were conceived within the ecclesial courts of Medieval Christendom, and key ideas developed which would impinge directly on the formulation of democratic theory in later centuries.

Organic society and subsidiarity

As before in the history of Christianity, classical thought provided the catalyst, this time through the rediscovery of Aristotle made possible by Muslim scholarship, and a renewed interest in Roman law. This prepared the way for Renaissance

---

[38] See M. J. Wilks, *The Problem of Sovereignty in the Later Middle Ages*, Cambridge University Press, 1963.

[39] Hastings, *Church and State*, pp. 13f.

[40] Berman, 'Religious Foundations of Law', pp. 9f.; Geoffrey King, 'Reception, Consensus and Church Law,' in James Provost and Knut Walf, eds., *The Tabu of Democracy*, pp. 42f.

republicanism[41] and the emergence of the modern secular state.[42] Contrary to the dominant Augustinian view that the state is divinely ordained as a means to maintain order amidst fallen humanity, Aristotle regarded the *polis* as a human creation. Structures of government were not divinely given, but had to be developed on the basis of reason with the purpose of serving the common good.

Following Aristotle, Thomas Aquinas, teacher of the greatest political philosophers of his generation, maintained that 'the best form of constitution', which is also to be found in the Bible itself, is 'a mixture of monarchy, in that one man is at the head, of aristocracy, in that many rule as specially qualified, and of democracy, in that the rulers can be chosen from the people and by them'.[43] At the same time, Thomas gave his unequivocal support to both papal and imperial absolutism.[44] Thomas believed monarchy mirrored the sovereignty of God and was undoubtedly the best form of government because it alone was able to maintain unity amidst diversity and so ensure peace.[45] Pluralistic regimes, Thomas argued, end up in tyranny more than monarchies, but if a monarch did become tyrannical, then those who elected him had every right to depose him.[46]

Thomas' political thought appears inconsistent if considered in terms of modern debates about absolutism and constitutional democracy.[47] It has coherence, however, when placed within the context of the medieval understanding of society as an organic whole in which church and state, pope and emperor, ruler and ruled, are bound together and related through mediating structures. Just as the church was, for Thomas, the 'body of Christ' in which everything was struc-

[41] Skinner, *Foundations*, vol. 1, pp. 49f.
[42] John B. Morrall, *Political Thought in Medieval Times*, London: Hutchinson, 1958, p. 59.
[43] Thomas Aquinas, *Summa Theologiae*, iaiiae, art. 105, q. l; see G. P. Gooch, *English Democratic Ideas in the Seventeenth Century*, second edition, Cambridge 1927, p. 18.
[44] A. P. d'Entrèves, *Aquinas: Selected Political Writings*, Oxford: Basil Blackwell, 1970, pp. 67ff.
[45] *Ibid.*, p. 107.   [46] *Ibid.*, pp. 32f; p. 186.
[47] Morrall, *Political Thought in Medieval Times*, p. 79.

tured hierarchically, so society was an organism within which every person has his or her rightful place. The head as well as the members of the body, whether *ekklēsia* or state, were subordinate 'to the needs of the other for the promotion of the common good' so that in effect there was 'no conflict between whole and parts', between the universal and the particular.[48] If there was a conflict of interests, justice, as the highest moral virtue, required that the common good, based on natural law, was primary.[49]

To what extent Thomas was influenced by the remarkably democratic ethos of the Dominican Order of which he was a member is difficult to tell, but it has been argued that the principles of Dominican government had some influence on the development of representative and constitutional democracy itself.[50] In any event, Thomas laid the foundation for what would later be called the principle of subsidiarity in Catholic social teaching, namely that 'social bodies exist for the sake of the person, so that what individuals are able to do, societies should not assume, and what smaller societies can do, larger societies should not take over'.[51] In due course this would provide the basis for a federal understanding of government in church and state, but it is also a principle fundamental to civil society. The idea of subsidiarity, it may be noted, has been used more recently in discussions on the structuring of the European Community.[52]

Popular sovereignty and Conciliarism

Jumping to the first half of the fourteenth century, and the thought of Marsilius of Padua, we find ourselves on the

[48] Wilks, *The Problem of Sovereignty*, p. 132.
[49] *Summa Theologiae*, 2a2ae 58.12; d'Entrèves, *The Notion of the State*, p. 223.
[50] Ernest Baker, *The Dominican Order and Convocation: A Study of the Growth of Representation in the Church during the Thirteenth Century*, Oxford, 1913; G. R. Galbraith, *The Constitution of the Dominican Order*, Manchester, 1925; Patricia Walter, 'Democracy in Dominican Government', in Provost and Walf, *The Tabu of Democracy*, pp. 59ff.
[51] 'Subsidiarity', Joseph A. Komonchak, Mary Collins, and Dermot A. Lane, *The New Dictionary of Theology*, Dublin: Gill & Macmillan, 1987, p. 986.
[52] Wolfgang Huber, 'Political Culture and the Future of Europe', *The Annual*, Society of Christian Ethics, 1993, p. 131.

threshold of a very different era in church–state relations. Arguing from the basis of natural law rather than a synthesis of reason and revelation, Marsilius provided a theoretical basis for the separation of temporal and spiritual power, the significance of which was far-reaching.[53] Although Marsilius sought to maintain the connection between Christianity and the political order, the logic of his thought led to the separation of church and state.[54] Popular sovereignty was made independent of church control, custom, or hereditary rule, and set within a republican framework where rulers were elected and accountable to the electorate.[55] This meant, following Cicero, the de-personalization of power,[56] a major step towards early modern constitutionalism.[57] Yet it must be noted that when political philosophers such as Marsilius spoke of the interests of the people, they did not have in mind individual self-interest, such as found expression later in liberal democracy. For them society was a corporation, not an aggregate of individuals, and government was about the maintenance of civic virtue and the common good.

As the Middle Ages reached their nadir, so curial corruption reached its zenith. The temporal claims of the papacy, financial extortion, simony, the wealth and extravagance of the papal court, the embroilment in political power struggles and warfare and, eventually, the Avignon exile and Great Schism in 1378, undermined the church's moral credibility. This gave urgent cause for the Conciliar Movement which found expression notably in the writings of Jean Gerson and later in those of Cardinal Nicholas of Cusa. Nicholas, the greatest German Christian humanist of the period, contributed significantly to the development of western constitutional law at a crucial stage in the period of transition from the medieval to the

[53] George H. Sabine, *A History of Political Theory*, London: George G. Harrap, 1954, pp. 251f; Marsilius of Padua, *The Defender of Peace*, (1324), New York: Columbia University Press, 1956.
[54] Morrall, *Political Thought in Medieval Times*, p. 118.
[55] d'Entrèves, *Notion of the State*, pp. 89f.
[56] *Ibid.*, p. 94.
[57] Quentin Skinner 'The Italian City-Republics', in Dunn, *The Unfinished Journey*, p. 65.

modern world.[58] Central to his thought was the distinction between the sacerdotal and temporal authority of the church, the one derived from above, the other from below. Hence, the need for popular representation and government by consent of the people.

The clash between conciliarists and the advocates of papal absolutism was eventually won by the *Curia*.[59] But conciliarism had a significant impact on the broader political scene. Princes could appeal to conciliar theory in their struggle for national independence from papal as well as imperial authority, and political philosophers could use the conciliar notion of the church as a corporation, to take further steps in the direction of representative government. Thus while conciliarism failed to curb papal absolutism, it did have a broader political significance.

The medieval controversy about the separation of spiritual and temporal powers was, in the main, not a denial of the moral authority of the church, but of its political claims and abuse of power. The English reformer John Wyclif not only insisted on the separation of spiritual and temporal power, but argued that the authority of both was contingent on the godliness of those who ruled.[60] But, for Machiavelli, the most astute and misrepresented political analyst of the Renaissance, established religion was necessary for more pragmatic reasons – to buttress the authority of political society.[61] By his day, the Italian city-states had begun to crumble. Everything to do with representative government and constitutionalism, so carefully constructed during the Middle Ages, was undermined by the rise of nation-states ruled by absolute princes.[62] From his own experience Machiavelli knew that leaving things in the

---

[58] See the Introduction to Nicholas of Cusa, in Paul E. Sigmund, ed., *The Catholic Concordance*, Cambridge University Press, 1991, pp. xxxivf.

[59] Brian Tierney, *Foundations of the Conciliar Theory: The Contribution of the Medieval Canonists from Gratian to the Great Schism*, Cambridge University Press, 1955, p. 1.

[60] Anthony Kenny, *Wyclif*, Oxford University Press, 1985, pp. 68ff.

[61] Skinner, in Dunn, *The Unfinished Journey*, p. 65; The classic statement is in Niccolò Machiavelli *The Prince and the Discourses*, New York: The Modern Library, 1950, book II.

[62] Sabine, *Political Theory*, p. 287.

hands of ruling individuals or groups inevitably meant that they ruled in their own, and not the broader community's, interests.[63]

Largely agreeing with Aristotle's views on mixed government, and looking back with appreciation to republican Rome, Machiavelli argued that politics was about power, about managing conflict, about using force to protect freedom and, above all, about keeping tyrants in check. Thus he anticipated a major dilemma which has since plagued democracies – how to preserve democratic values without resorting to means which deny and undermine them. For Machiavelli the only possible solution was to preserve society by whatever means were available and necessary.[64] Politics had its own laws, and these had little to do with morality. How to maintain a stable society in a world of irrational events and human corruption without divine sanction became *the* political problem. The importance of what J. G. A. Pocock has called 'the Machiavellian Moment' for the development of European political theory and praxis cannot be underestimated.[65] For this moment, at which secular political self-consciousness was rudely awakened by the fragility of constitutional government, marked the passage of western political thought from the medieval Christian to the modern.

REFORMATION ON THE EVE OF MODERNITY

Whether the Protestant Reformation was medieval or modern in its outlook and consequences has been much debated.[66] It is not obvious, as Hans Rückert observed, that 'the Reformation breaks through to insights in which it anticipates the peculiari-

---

[63] Skinner, in Dunn, *The Unfinished Journey*, p. 68.

[64] Held, *Models of Democracy*, p. 46.

[65] J. G. A. Pocock, *The Machiavellian Moment: Florentine Political Thought and the Atlantic Republican Tradition*, Princeton University Press, 1975.

[66] Hans Rückert, 'The Reformation – Medieval or Modern?' in *Journal for Theology and the Church*, 2, published in *Translating Theology into the Modern Age*, New York: Harper and Row, 1965, pp. 1ff; Ernst Troeltsch, *Protestantism and Progress: the Significance of Protestantism for the Rise of the Modern World*, Philadelphia: Fortress, 1986, pp. 54f.

ties of modern thought'.[67] Even when this is the case, the ethos and theology of the Reformation remain critically distinct from Renaissance humanism, the harbinger of modernity. Yet the Reformation was the bridge across which Christianity passed in its journey from the medieval to the modern world. In doing so, it inevitably became embroiled in the reshaping of the politics of a Christendom fragmenting into strong national monarchies.[68] In seeking the reform of the church, the Reformation triggered new ways of thinking about the state.

The Reformation was a predominantly urban phenomenon. Many of those who became civic leaders in the burgeoning towns and cities of the period were Protestants who played a crucial role in the development of local government.[69] It was in the towns and city councils, rather than at the national level where princes retained power, that modern democratic forms of government and civil society emerged. If the Reformation is taken as a whole and not limited to the contribution of its leaders, then it was, as Steven Ozment suggests, a popular bourgeois movement which, by the standards of the time, brought about 'a democratic revolution'.[70] This is reflected in the view that modern democracy may be regarded a child of the Reformation, but not the offspring of the reformers themselves.[71]

Robert Wuthnow has reminded us that the Reformation was not a unified movement but 'a constellation of reforms, chosen from a larger menu of reforms, rather than a single revision of belief and practice'.[72] Nevertheless, as he goes on to argue, any attempt to understand the impact of the Reformation on society in sixteenth-century Europe and beyond has to take

---

[67] Rückert, 'The Reformation', p. 11.

[68] Lewis W. Spitz, *The Protestant Reformation 1517–1559*, New York: Harper and Row, 1985, p. 36.

[69] A. G. Dickens, *The German Nation and Martin Luther*, London: Edward Arnold, 1974.

[70] Steven E. Ozment, *The Reformation in the Cities: The Appeal of Protestantism to Sixteenth-Century Germany and Switzerland*, New Haven: Yale University Press, 1975, p. 47.

[71] Gooch, *English Democratic Ideas*, p. 7.

[72] Robert Wuthnow, *Communities of Discourse: Ideology and Social Structure in the Reformation, the Enlightenment, and European Socialism*, Cambridge, Mass.: Harvard University Press, 1989, p. 122.

into account the seminal ideas of its major figures, Luther and Calvin, as well as those of their more radical opponents. These provided the ideological basis for the social changes which occurred, but, given their varied backgrounds, experiences, and contexts, it is not surprising that the reformers and their followers developed different approaches to political questions.

The individual and the freedom of conscience

Luther was deeply influenced by the nominalist philosophy of his teachers in Erfurt, and it was nominalism which began, as Heiko Oberman puts it, to push 'open the gates to the modern age', though 'only some gates, and only somewhat modern'.[73] Sitting uneasily on the boundary which separated the medieval from the modern world, the Catholic from the Protestant, the universal Christian from the German national, Luther was both a brake on, and an accelerator of, history.[74] Nowhere is this more evident than in his advocacy of the 'religious sovereignty of the common man' and his political opinion that nothing 'is more ill-mannered than a foolish peasant or a common man when he gets power into his hands':[75] an opinion which led him to encourage the crushing of the Peasants' Revolt in 1524. Let us consider, then, two major constellations of ideas in Luther's theology with this ambiguity in mind.[76]

The first constellation revolved around the importance of the individual. Justification by faith, the corner-stone of all else, stressed the relationship of the individual before God without the mediation of any priest or institution. The priesthood of all believers, a key element in Luther's polemic against Rome, destroyed the division of humankind into clerical and

---

[73] Heiko A. Oberman, *Luther: Man Between God and Devil*, New Haven: Yale University Press, 1989, p. 119.

[74] Dickens, *The German Nation*, p. 13; See Bernhard Lohse, *Martin Luther: An Introduction to His Life and Work*, Philadelphia: Fortress, 1986, pp. 139ff.

[75] Mullett, *Radical Religious Movements*, p. 62.

[76] On Luther's theology see Paul Althaus, *The Theology of Martin Luther*, Philadelphia: Fortress, 1966, and *The Ethics of Martin Luther*, Philadelphia: Fortress, 1972; and on Luther in his context see Heinrich Bornkamm, *Luther in Mid-Career 1521–1530*, Philadelphia: Fortress, 1983.

lay categories, and affirmed the equality of all Christians within the fellowship of the church. The freedom of the Christian person, which was central to Luther's ethics, meant that individual Christians had the right to read Scripture and interpret it for themselves without the tutelage of the teaching magisterium of the church, and to act on the grounds of conscience alone as informed by the Word of God.

Luther's intention, shaped by his own passionate quest for a gracious God, was to reinstate the personal as central to Christian faith. This prepared the way for the discovery of the person as subject, the quest for self-identity and the right to the freedom of conscience, which later became central to the Enlightenment and to liberalism. For Luther, personal faith and freedom did not mean individualism or a denial of social responsibility. The free person was the servant of all. But, in Luther's own lifetime, the individual, rather than the common good, was becoming the focus of Christian witness, and, the more piety became privatized, the less it had to do with public issues. This unintended consequence of Luther's rediscovery of the personal intensified as modernization gained momentum, and became a fundamental element in the secularization of western society and politics.

The privatization of piety was reinforced by the second constellation of ideas in Luther's theology, centred around his teaching on the two kingdoms or realms.[77] By separating the task of the church from the exercising of temporal power, Luther rightly saw the need for the separation of ecclesial and political authority. But this meant that the latter was accountable only to the individual conscience before God, something well typified much later by Otto von Bismarck in Prussia.[78] Lutheran princes were, of course, called by God to rule justly and not out of self-interest.[79] The only role left to the church in the public sphere, however, was preaching the gospel in the hope that rulers might hear and obey. Yet pious princes were

[77] Lohse, *Martin Luther*, pp. 186ff.
[78] Helmut Thielicke, *Theological Ethics: Politics*, Grand Rapids: Eerdmans, 1969, pp. 92f.
[79] Berman, 'Religious Foundations of Law', pp. 16f.

no more exempt from the pursuit of self-interest, despite the bad conscience it might produce, than Machiavellian princes.

Luther's reforming interests were dependent upon, and often coincided with, the self-interests of the princes and the power struggles for German nationhood. Granted, the church was meant to be universal and not nationalist, but social forces determined otherwise. As a result, Protestantism was set on a course which not only reflected the fragmentation of Christendom into nation-states, but also speeded up the process of secularization and gave it theological legitimacy.[80] Christendom was no longer coterminous with the empire under the authority of the pope; but it was alive and well within the new nations of Europe, under the dominion of princes who were often the governors of the church and, in some instances, 'emergency bishops'. In effect, the doctrine of the two kingdoms led the Lutheran church in Germany to an uncritical conservative and sometimes reactionary acceptance of the authority of the state.

A radical separation of church and state

Luther, along with Huldrych Zwingli in Zurich,[81] and John Calvin in Geneva, were what George Williams has designated as 'magisterial reformers'.[82] They pursued their reforming goals within the framework of Christendom, assuming that Christian princes and magistrates were essential to the reformation of the church. This was particularly true at the beginning of the Reformation when the reformers 'reinforced the decision-making power of the regimes that supported it, rather than posing ideas that challenged the state'.[83] By contrast, what Williams calls the radical reformers, often incorrectly labelled collectively as Anabaptists, broke decisively with this relationship to the state. The protest began in Zurich where

---

[80] See the discussion in Dietrich Bonhoeffer, *Ethics*, New York: Macmillan, 1965, pp. 96, 199.
[81] W. P. Stephens, *The Theology of Huldrych Zwingli*, Oxford: Clarendon Press, 1986.
[82] George Williams, *The Radical Reformation*, Philadelphia: Westminster Press, 1962.
[83] Wuthnow, *Communities of Discourse*, p. 154.

Zwingli refused to pursue the Reformation without the support of the city fathers, an example of both the Christendom alliance of church and state, and of the urban context within which much of the Reformation's struggles occurred.[84]

The roots of the Radical Reformation may be traced as much to the lay religious impulse which characterized dissent in the Middle Ages as to the Protestant Reformation.[85] Some of the early leaders were ex-monks and priests, often deeply influenced by the medieval mystical tradition and the more democratic structures of their orders. Apocalyptic in outlook, they were 'the subversives of the sixteenth century', challenging directly both the Christendom ideology of the powerful, the iniquity of a political system based on inequality, and the prevailing social values.[86] The connection between the Peasant Revolts and some radical Christian movements in Germany in the sixteenth century demonstrates the extent to which they embodied and were able to legitimate such egalitarian struggles. They were the religious wing of the dispossessed, at least until the latter either became disillusioned and left Christianity altogether or returned to the bosom of the old faith. These developments later contributed to the alienation of the working class from the church as well as 'the creation of the "democratic-totalitarian" states of the modern world' which became divorced from religious restraints.[87]

The groups of the Radical Reformation varied considerably amongst themselves. Yet collectively they generated ideas and set forces in motion which contributed considerably to the later development of democracy, especially in its more participatory and socialist forms. Some of these antecedents and analogies were their rejection of any clerical status within the church, their understanding of the church as a 'gathered' community comprised of those who freely and willingly joined, their congregational polity in and through which every member was

[84] Leland Harder, ed., *The Sources of Swiss Anabaptism*, Scottdale, Pa.: Herald Press, 1985.
[85] Mullett, *Radical Religious Movements*, p. 65.
[86] Rowland, *Radical Christianity*, p. 101.
[87] Mullett, *Radical Religious Movements*, p. 110.

able to participate in church government, the espousal by some
of pacifism and the rejection by most of nationalism, and a
tolerance towards others which was rare at the time. In a
rudimentary yet real way, they were amongst the first to
advocate human rights.[88] But it was their unequivocal insistence that the church should be free from state support which
fundamentally distinguished them from the magisterial
reformers, and led them to make their most decisive contribution to the birth of the modern secular democratic state.
Civic peace required religious tolerance. For both Catholics
and the Protestant reformers, however, the protest of the
radical reformers was seen as a threat to the stability of
Christendom.

Calvinism and bourgeois democracy

Calvin was a second-generation reformer. His theology
reflected that of Luther, yet his humanist and legal training, as
well as his context, led to a significantly different reforming
ethos which bridged the gap between the medieval and the
modern more decisively than Luther. It was through Calvin
that some of the medieval debates concerning fundamental
law, natural rights, the consent of people, popular sovereignty,
and resistance to tyranny, were reworked in relation
to evangelical teaching and applied in practice within the
political melting-pot of sixteenth- and seventeenth-century
Europe.[89]

Some political historians claim, in fact, that no agent was
more important than Calvin in the history of political thought
in the sixteenth century,[90] and many have noted 'the striking
correlation, both in time and place, between the spread of
Calvinist Protestantism and the rise of democracy'.[91] Repre-

---

[88] Williams, *Radical Reformation*, pp. 862ff.
[89] Herbert D. Foster, 'International Calvinism through Locke and the Revolution of
1688', *American Historical Review* 32, 3, 1927, 487.
[90] J. W. Allen, *A History of Political Thought in the Sixteenth Century*, London: Methuen,
1928, p. 49; Gooch, *English Democratic Ideas*, p. 3.
[91] Robert M. Kingdon and Robert D. Linder, eds., *Calvin and Calvinism: Sources of
Democracy?* Lexington, Mass.: D. C. Heath and Co., 1970, p. vii.

sentative forms of democratic government were initially established and flourished in those countries where the Calvinist or
Reformed tradition was strongest: the Swiss city-states, the
Netherlands, France, England, Scotland, and New England.[92]
Within these contexts, Reformed theologians and jurists, aware
of the power of sin to corrupt those elected to exercise the
power of state, made important contributions to the development of systems of checks and balances which became fundamental to democratic theory and practice.

There is no simple explanation for the development of representative forms of democracy within nations influenced by
Calvinism. Critics argue that the connection is accidental
rather than rational; economic and social rather than theological. Consequently there has been much debate about
whether Calvin and his followers were, in fact, democratic in
any true sense of the word. Marc-Edouard Cheneviére, who
re-opened the debate in 1937, argued that Calvin was essentially aristocratic in outlook, an adversary of modern democracy, believing neither 'in popular sovereignty nor in individual rights'.[93] This opinion has some grounds both in
Calvin's behaviour in Geneva and in his writings.[94] If religious
liberty is a touchstone of modern democracy, then Roland
Bainton's caustic statement that if 'Calvin ever wrote anything
in favour of religious liberty it was a typographical error',[95]
would be a damning indictment. By way of contrast, Jean-
Jacques Rousseau, strange as it may seem coming from him,
praised Calvin and his successors for their contribution to
liberty and the well-being of Geneva.[96]

The young Calvin did not come to Geneva with a ready-

---

[92] Nathaniel Micklem, *The Theology of Politics*, London: Oxford, 1941, p. 48. See also
Troeltsch, *Protestantism and Progress*, p. 65; Foster, 'International Calvinism',
pp. 475ff.

[93] Marc-Edouard Cheneviére, *La pensée politique de Calvin*, Geneva and Paris 1937,
p. 190, quoted in Kingdon and Linder, *Calvin and Calvinism*, p. 15.

[94] John Calvin, *The Institutes of the Christian Religion*, (1559 edition), Philadelphia:
Westminster, 1960, 4.20.8.

[95] Roland Bainton, quoted in Winthrop S. Hudson, 'Democratic Freedom and Religious Faith in the Reformed Tradition', *Church History*, 15, 1946, 179.

[96] Rousseau, 'The Origin of Inequality', *The Social Contract and Discourses*, London: J.
M. Dent & Sons, 1947, p. 152.

made political philosophy or programme.[97] What he
encountered there was an established democratic tradition of
citizen participation in running the affairs of the city.[98] After
all, the citizens themselves had decided to accept the Reformation. Wuthnow suggests that there was no simple relation
between the structure of Genevan politics and Calvin's theology, and that Calvin 'appears to have dealt gingerly and
ambiguously with politics'.[99] Yet Calvin did become deeply
involved in Genevan political affairs, however reluctantly, and
his political thought reflected what was happening there and in
other countries where the Reformation was in progress.[100]
With justification it has been said that Calvin's theology was
framed by politics, at the same time influencing it and being
shaped by it.[101]

Although it is misleading to make the doctrine of the sovereignty of God the key to Calvin's thought, as it was for some of
his later followers, it was none the less a central theme.[102] As a
result, in Calvin's hands key reformation doctrines were far less
prone to the dangers of privatization and subjective individualism, and the prophetic witness to the reign of God in
society was maintained. Much of Calvin's political thought
was derived from the prophetic Deuteronomic code, and
ancient Israel provided him with a model for both church and
state.[103] Even so, Calvin was not a theocrat, insisting, as did
Luther, on a clear distinction between Christ's spiritual
kingdom and civil government. The church was responsible for
preaching the gospel; the state for enabling the church to fulfil

[97] Harro Höpfl, *The Christian Polity of John Calvin*, London: Cambridge University
Press, 1982, pp. 54f.
[98] Ronald S. Wallace, *Calvin, Geneva, and the Reformation*, Edinburgh: Scottish
Academic Press, 1988.
[99] Wuthnow, *Communities of Discourse*, p. 126.
[100] On Calvin's political thought see: André Bieler, *The Social Humanism of Calvin*,
Richmond, Va.: John Knox Press, 1964; William J. Bouwsma, *John Calvin*, New
York: Oxford University Press, 1988. On the way in which Calvinist and Reformed
political thought developed, see Skinner, *Foundations*, vol. 2, pp. 189–348; Troeltsch, *The Social Teaching*, vol. 2, pp. 576–688.
[101] De Gruchy, *Liberating Reformed Theology*, pp. 236ff.   [102] *Ibid.*, pp. 110f.
[103] John T. McNeill 'The Democratic Element in Calvin's Thought', *Church History*,
18, 1949.

its task, and to govern society in such a way that justice, peace, and tranquility flourished. Thus Calvin took a position not essentially different from Luther's two kingdoms, but insisted that the two realms were integrally related under the sovereignty of God, and therefore that the political order was subject to the prophetic witness of the church.[104]

Calvin acknowledged that no particular form of state was ordained by God, but expressed a preference for 'a system compounded by aristocracy and democracy',[105] because it was 'safer and more tolerable for the government to be in the hands of the many', rather than the few.[106] Calvin was an advocate of what we now call 'representative democracy'.[107] This was particularly true with regard to his ecclesiastical polity, though he was not as dogmatic a 'presbyterian' as was his successor Theodore Beza,[108] being willing to accept episcopacy as long as it was shorn of its princely excesses.[109] What was of critical importance for Calvin was not the precise structure of government, but whether both state and church were ruled in a well-ordered way consonant with their respective responsibilities.

The problem of establishing and maintaining political order was the major task of politics in the sixteenth century.[110] But, for Calvin, the responsibility of those in power was not only the maintenance of order, it was also to pursue justice for the poor and needy. Good government vindicated and set the innocent free. In using force to maintain justice, those in authority should act out of a genuine concern for the people.[111] As William Bouwsma comments: 'Calvin and Machiavelli were

[104] *Institutes*, 4.20.1–2.
[105] Following Aristotle, Calvin uses *politia* for popular government. *Institutes* 4.20.8; cf. Aristotle *Politics*, 4.8.
[106] See Hudson, 'Democratic Freedom and Religious Faith', p. 190.
[107] McNeill, 'Democratic Elements in Calvin's Thought'. See also Herbert Darling Foster, 'The Political Theories of Calvinists Before the Puritan Exodus to America', *American Historical Review*, 21, 1916, reprinted in Kingdon and Linder, *Calvin and Calvinism*, pp. 36f.
[108] Basil Hall, 'Calvin against the Calvinists', in *John Calvin*, Appleford, UK: Sutton Courtnay Press, 1966, p. 26.
[109] *Institutes*, 4.4.6,11.   [110] Allen, *History of Political Thought*, p. 512.
[111] *Institutes*, 4.20.8–12.

alike in their realism; but what Machiavelli was prepared to accept for its utility, Calvin hoped to abolish.'[112] The laws which a state adopts and by which it governs were not immutable, but they must be appropriate to each situation. Notwithstanding, the laws of any nation must be in conformity with what Calvin referred to as the 'perpetual rule of love'.[113] As a result, Calvin upheld the principle of equity as 'the goal and rule and limit of all laws'.[114]

A sacred duty to resist tyranny

For Calvin, the obedience and respect of citizens towards duly constituted authority did not cease even if rulers were unjust. Such rulers, Calvin argued, were a judgment from God – a more pious expression of the sentiment that people get the government they deserve. But this did not give them any right to revolt, only to submit and allow God to vindicate his purposes. Despite this, in the celebrated final two paragraphs of his *Institutes*, Calvin argued that the elected representatives of the people not only have a right, but also a duty, to resist and overthrow rulers who claim absolute power and prevent the true worship of God.[115] This possibility of representative magisterial action against tyrants, cautiously left vague in the *Institutes*, prepared the way for later Calvinists to engage in tyrannicide and revolution.

If the struggle against tyranny was central to the development of democracy, then the French Huguenots, the Scottish Presbyterians, and the English Independents, all heirs of the Genevan Reformation, must be accounted key agents in its historical development. The watershed was the massacre of the Huguenots on St Bartholomew's Night in 1572, an event which swept away all restraint from Calvinist political thought.[116]

In 1574, Theodore Beza, Calvin's immediate successor in

---

[112] Bouwsma, *John Calvin*, p. 55.   [113] *Institutes*, 4.20.15.   [114] *Ibid.*, 4.20.16.
[115] *Ibid.*, 4.20.30–1; see also John Calvin, *Commentaries on the Book of the Prophet Daniel*, Grand Rapids: Eerdmans, 1948, vol. 1, p. 38.
[116] Myriam Yardeni, 'French Calvinist Political Thought', in *International Calvinism 1541–1715*, Menna Prestwich, ed., Oxford: Clarendon Press, 1985, p. 320.

Geneva, published a slim but potent volume on the rights of rulers and the duties of subjects in which he declared that 'people were not created for the sake of rulers, but on the contrary, the rulers for the sake of the people'.[117] He went on to insist that 'those who possess authority to elect a king will also have the right to dethrone him'.[118] Beza's theme was taken further by the Huguenot political theorists and activists, and by John Knox and others in Scotland. What began with Calvin as a duty to ensure the freedom of worship, ended with Calvinists engaged in a sacred struggle to ensure the freedom of people from despotism.[119] This was not unique to Calvinists,[120] but their specific contribution was the elaboration of the constitutional means for resistance,[121] and the inclusion of the right to resist within their confessional documents.[122] Insisting that the sovereignty of government was bound by law, and on the right to resist if government transgressed the law, they contributed significantly to what Winthrop Hudson called 'the twin pillars upon which democracy rests'.[123]

A similar contribution to democratic theory was made in the late sixteenth century by Catholic Jesuits who have 'been portrayed as the main founders of modern constitutionalist and even democratic thought'.[124] The leading Jesuit theologian of the day, Francis Suarez, has been regarded by some as 'the first modern democrat', and Cardinal Robert Bellarmine, one of the leading theologians at the Council of Trent, has been praised for revealing 'the true sources of democracy'.[125]

---

[117] Theodore Beza, *Concerning the Rights of Rulers over their Subjects and the Duty of Subjects towards their Rulers*, trans. by H-L Gonin, ed., by A. H. Murray, Cape Town: HAUM, 1956, p. 30.

[118] *Ibid.*, p. 64.

[119] See Robert M. Kingdon, *Myths about the St Bartholomew's Massacres, 1572–1576*, Cambridge, Mass.: Harvard University Press, 1988.

[120] Skinner, *Foundations*, vol. 2, pp. 189f.

[121] Hudson, 'Democratic Freedom and Religious Faith', p. 183.

[122] Scots Confession, article XIV, in *The Book of Confessions*, New York: United Presbyterian Church in the USA, 1970.

[123] Hudson, 'Democratic Freedom and Religious Faith', p. 181.

[124] Skinner, *Foundations*, vol. 2, p. 174, referring to J. H. Fichter, *Man of Spain: Francis Suárez*, New York, 1940.

[125] *Ibid.*

Perhaps it is not surprising that Bellarmine admired Calvin sufficiently to hang his portrait in his study.

The notion of popular sovereignty, the contention that rulers only have legitimacy if they seek to serve the common good, and therefore the right of resistance against tyranny, were common ideas amongst Thomists, and, by drawing on this heritage, Jesuits arrived at a number of radically populist conclusions.[126] The Spaniard Juan de Mariana, for example, argued that the will of the people is expressed by a majority, and that princes who overstepped their authority could be deposed or killed. If princes oppress the state, he wrote, 'their position is such that they can be killed not only justly but with praise and glory'.[127] Indeed, the Jesuit theological legitimation for violent resistance against tyrannical Protestant rulers was much the same as that used by the French Huguenots and John Knox in their support of resistance and tyrannicide.[128] Quite apart from this more radical populist thought, the sixteenth-century Jesuits 'served as the main channel through which the contractarian approach to the discussion of political obligation came to exercise its decisive influence in the course of the following century'.[129] Many of their themes were later picked up and developed by John Locke who likewise argued that they were in accordance with the will of God. Yet Locke was far more an heir of Calvinism, which, through him, made its contribution to the development of democracy in England.[130]

ANGLO-SAXON CHRISTIANITY AND PARLIAMENTARY DEMOCRACY

In response to a mixture of motives ranging from those of Henry VIII to the radical wing of Protestantism, the Church of England separated from Rome.[131] As a result the Church of

---

[126] *Ibid.*, pp. 113ff.
[127] Juan de Mariana, 'Whether it is Right to Destroy a Tyrant? (1599) in Lowell H. Zuck, ed., *Christianity and Revolution: Radical Christian Testimonies 1520–1650*, Philadelphia: Temple University Press, 1975, p. 195.
[128] *Ibid.*, p. 7.   [129] Skinner, *Foundations*, vol. 2, p. 174.
[130] Foster, 'International Calvinism,' pp. 475ff.
[131] A. G. Dickens, *The English Reformation*, London: Fontana, 1967.

England was comprised of factions and parties with divergent interests in which the spiritual and the material were intertwined. Some wished to return to the Roman fold. The Puritans, pushing Calvin's theology to its limits, wanted to purify the church according to Scripture alone. Some accepted episcopacy, some were Presbyterian, and others, the Independents and Baptists, wanted the church to be disestablished and reformed according to congregational polity. And then there were those who sought a *via media* between the Romans and the Puritans. Their chief advocate was Richard Hooker whose *Laws of Ecclesiastical Polity* was one of the most important political and theological texts of the late sixteenth century.[132]

The 'Via Media' in church and state

Written in the 1590s, *Ecclesiastical Polity* was a response to the Puritan *Admonition*, addressed to parliament in 1572, calling for the thorough reformation of the church of England according to the Word of God, and to a second *Admonition* to the same effect, both penned by the distinguished Puritan divine Thomas Cartwright.[133] Cartwright argued that Scripture alone provided the blueprint for church and state. Hooker countered by stating that, while nothing should be done in contradiction of biblical teaching, there are many matters pertaining to civil and church government for which reason must suffice. Hooker was closer to Calvin here than either he or his Puritan opponents recognized.[134]

The title of Hooker's work suggests that his preoccupation was solely church polity, but in his day, and certainly in his mind, there was a thin line separating matters ecclesial and

---

[132] Allen, *History of Political Thought*, p. 185.
[133] Henry McAdoo, 'Richard Hooker', in Geoffrey Rowell, ed., *The Church of England and the Genius of Anglicanism*, London: Ikon, 1992, p. 109.
[134] See Duncan Forrester, 'Richard Hooker,' in Leo Strauss and Joseph Cropsy, eds., *History of Political Philosophy*, New York: Rand McNally and Co., 1963, pp. 314f.; Foster, 'International Calvinism', p. 476.

political.[135] Given his Erastian[136] convictions, there was no way in which Hooker could deal with the polity of the Church of England without also providing a theological rationale for its establishment under the authority of the British monarch. Sovereignty resided both in the monarch and in the people because it resided in a nation, which, according to Hooker, was Christian. The Church of England was the people of England as a whole, and the people were the Church.

In view of this, the validity of church laws became dependent upon the consent of all, and not just bishops and clergy.[137] For Hooker, lay people as represented in parliament, together with the monarch as the supreme layperson representing all the people, comprised the appropriate legislative body for the church. What distinguished the Supreme Governor of the Church of England from Machiavelli's prince, was the fact that she was called to be the servant of the people ruling in terms of the laws of God. The notion that the papacy could interfere in the affairs of either the church or the state was courting treason and was as unacceptable as the idea that the church was a gathered congregation of Puritan 'saints'. Thus it was precisely because Hooker had to find a way to legitimate both monarchy and popular sovereignty in the governance of the Church of England that he developed the philosophical basis for the principle of representation upon which the British parliamentary system was founded.[138] In providing the theological rationale for the *via media*, Hooker unwittingly contributed to the development of political liberalism and the modern sovereign state.[139] His conception of natural law and the social

---

[135] Anthony Quinton, *The Politics of Imperfection: The Religious and Secular Traditions of Conservative Thought in England from Hooker to Oakshott*, London: Faber and Faber, 1978, p. 10.

[136] Thomas Erastus, a Swiss physician in Heidelberg and staunch Zwinglian, argued in his *Explicatio* (London, 1589), that the state had authority over the church in matters of religion.

[137] Paul Avis, *Anglicanism and the Christian Church*, Edinburgh: T & T Clark, 1989, p. 62.

[138] F. J. Shirley, *Richard Hooker and Contemporary Political Ideas*, London: SPCK, 1949, p. 228.

[139] *Ibid.*, p. 201.

contract, 'with their corollaries of "consent" and the "rights of the people", were to form a main stream of political thought, flowing from him to Hobbes, to Locke and America, to Rousseau and France, with world-shaking consequences'.[140] Later English political philosophers did not simply restate what he had taught,[141] however, and, like Hobbes, sometimes arrived at different conclusions from the same premises.[142]

Shaping a Puritan commonwealth

Hooker was not the only nor even the chief Christian contributor to the formation of English liberal democratic traditions. Justifiably A. D. Lindsay attributed this much more to the Anabaptists, Independents, and Quakers. Not only did these groups take the doctrine of the priesthood of all believers more seriously, but they insisted on the self-governing congregation which meant they had practical daily experience of a fellowship in which each and every member had something to contribute. 'Democracy was for them a mystical institution distinct from the practical in which it realized itself.'[143] It meant participation more than representation.

Independents and Presbyterians, with their common Calvinist lineage had much in common, but were separated by their ecclesial polities.[144] Basically the Independents were more 'democratic' in church government, allowing all members to

---

[140] *Ibid.*, p. 225; see also Ellis Sandoz, *A Government of Laws: Political Theory*, Religion, and the American Founding, Baton Rouge: Louisiana State University Press, 1990, pp. 118f.

[141] For a comparison of Hooker's views with those of other political theorists of his period, see Shirley, *Richard Hooker*, pp. 200ff.

[142] *Ibid.*, p. 210.

[143] A. D. Lindsay, *The Churches and Democracy*, London: Epworth, 1934, p. 24. Nathaniel Micklem refers to four streams which contributed to English democracy, viz., Athenian democracy, Renaissance humanism, the theocracy of the Independents, and the individualism of the Anabaptists and Levellers, in *The Idea of Liberal Democracy*, London 1957, pp. 65–8. The word 'democracy' was used in ecclesiastical discussions in England before it became part of English political vocabulary, see Geoffrey Nuttall, *The Holy Spirit in Puritan Faith and Experience*, Oxford, 1947, p. 120.

[144] See the Savoy Declaration, in Williston Walker ed., *The Creeds and Platforms of Congregationalism*, Boston: Pilgrim Press, 1960, pp. 403ff.

participate in the decision-making processes, while for the Presbyterians this task was largely in the hands of elected representatives, the elders. Independency was, in fact, a blending of Calvinism and Anabaptism which occurred amongst the non-conformist exiles in the Netherlands during the reigns of Queens Elizabeth and Mary. Allowing for rhetorical exaggeration, P. T. Forsyth's observation is apposite: Calvin, he remarked, could not have fathered democracy without an 'Anabaptist mother'.[145]

This attempt to hold together Reformed orthodoxy, 'while at the same time evolving a democratic, laicist and localist form of the church with voluntary and effective discipline',[146] was unique amongst the spiritual descendants of Calvin. The most distinctive mark of Independent ecclesiology, however, was not its 'democracy', for it was Christ, the Independents claimed, who really governed the church, but its doctrine of the covenant. Independent congregations were invariably founded on a covenant made by their members one with another and with God.[147] It was a token of commitment, regularly ratified, not unlike the vows affirmed and renewed within monastic and other religious orders. Thus even before Hobbes and Rousseau developed their theories of social contract, covenanting together equipped ordinary people for the responsibilities of civil society by teaching them their duties within the covenant fellowship of believers.[148] If political theorists like Hobbes stressed individualism, Independent divines, like the Quakers, stressed communities in which individuals discovered their equality and expressed their solidarity.

In referring to the role of the Anabaptists in the birth of democracy in England, Lindsay probably had in mind more radically egalitarian groups such as the Levellers and the Diggers. The Levellers comprised two related yet separate groups: those who turned away from Christianity and espoused

---

145 P. T. Forsyth, *Faith, Freedom, and the Future*, London: Independent Press, 1912, p. 297. John Calvin was married to an Anabaptist.
146 Mullett, *Radical Religious Movements*, p. 65.
147 See representative samples in Walker, *Creeds and Platforms*.
148 Albert Peel, *The Christian Basis of Democracy*, London: Independent Press, 1943, pp. 52f.

violent revolution, and those Diggers or True Levellers led by Gerrard Winstanley who rejected violence to achieve their goals. Winstanley more than anyone else symbolized the religious democratic utopian ideal in English history. His work 'beautifully combined political liberty and economic equality, in theological dress'.[149] The unitary principle in Winstanley's thought and programme was 'ownership of the earth'.[150] Lordship over others, he argued, is the source of violence and war, and it will always be so until the earth, which is groaning under such a curse, once again becomes 'a common treasury' and all people are 'of one heart and one mind'.[151]

The Levellers were not as radical in their vision of society as Winstanley and his True Levellers, and they were not particularly religious in their convictions. Often regarded as the first true democrats in English political history, it has been said with good reason that they were the forerunners of Locke and Whig liberalism, rather than of radical democracy.[152] Their main platform, that a person's labour was to be regarded as that person's possession and should therefore be protected from any kind of slavery, was an important step towards recognizing, long before Marx, that labour should not be reduced to a commodity. There was, however, but one step which separated their views of equal right to property from that of Locke's in which people have the right to unlimited property.[153]

The views of the Diggers and Levellers were clearly different from those of the more bourgeois Independents, as the Putney debates demonstrate.[154] Yet it was an Independent, Oliver Cromwell, who welded the parliamentary army together in its revolutionary struggle against the Royalists. For diverse reasons and with different goals in mind, Puritan, Presbyterian and Independent, Digger and Leveller, the middle class and

[149] Zuck, *Christianity and Revolution*, p. 244.   [150] *Ibid.*

[151] Extracts from Gerrard Winstanley, *The True Levellers' Standard Advanced* (1649) published in A. S. P. Woodhouse, ed., *Puritanism and Liberty, Being the Army Debates (1647–9)*, from the Clarke Manuscripts with Supplemental Documents, second edition, London: Dent, 1951, pp. 379ff.

[152] C. B. Macpherson, *The Political Theory of Possessive Individualism: Hobbes to Locke*, Oxford: Clarendon Press, 1962, p. 158.

[153] *Ibid.*, p. 159.   [154] John Dunn, *Western Political Theory*, p. 5, n. 8.

the lower, urban and educated elite and rural proletariat united in an alliance which led to regicide. In embarking on such a course, these aristocratic, bourgeois, and proletarian revolutionaries were not influenced by any political theory emanating from Athens or Renaissance Italy, but by their Christian beliefs. They did not make their appeal on the basis of individualism, but on a conscience informed by their understanding of the Bible, and a new way of regarding social relations.[155] For them, even if they differed in important respects, 'all men were equal not only in the eyes of God but equally qualified to understand the word of God, to participate in church government, and by extension to govern the commonwealth'.[156]

But fundamental social and ideological differences between them made co-operation impossible once the revolution of 1640 was successful. What had united them in the struggle against the monarchy was no longer able to keep them together in designing and consolidating a new order. Some of the political views of the radicals were destructive of any kind of parliamentary government or rule of law, others, like those of Winstanley, demanded a democratic society in which elected officials would change annually as required by the Old Testament. Therefore the choice Winstanley put to Cromwell was 'either to set up the new order and thus remain a true Christian, or merely to continue the old order under a new name, and in so doing to betray the indwelling Christ'.[157]

Cromwell came close to establishing an egalitarian democratic state, but eventually turned against the demands of his radical allies and sought his solution in a republican alternative.[158] In doing so, he consolidated and developed the rudimentary representative parliamentary system of government which already existed, but without the monarchy.[159]

---

[155] Christopher Hill, *Reformation to Industrial Revolution*, Pelican Economic History of Britain, vol. 2, 1530–1780, London: Penguin, 1978, pp. 199, 205.
[156] Dahl, *Democracy and its Critics*, p. 32.
[157] Troeltsch, *Social Teaching*, vol. 2, p. 712.
[158] Zuck, *Christianity and Revolution*, p. 7.
[159] Dahl, *Democracy and its Critics*, p. 27.

Even though Cromwell himself became a benign dictator, and his regime only lasted for two decades in its original form, what the Puritan revolution achieved prepared the groundwork for the 'Glorious Revolution' of 1688 and the parliamentary system which has governed England ever since. Puritanism was a necessary precondition for the emergence of Anglo-Saxon liberalism.[160]

There was a remarkable degree of religious toleration in England after 1640, but, with the restoration of the monarchy, and the attempt to establish religious uniformity through the Act of Uniformity in 1660, a new political climate was created. Bitter conflict forced the question of religious liberty and toleration to the fore. England was now irrevocably a country of Christian pluralism, yet the implications of this were resisted by those who regarded religious uniformity as essential for national unity.[161] Hooker's Erastianism raised the problem of religious toleration 'in a peculiarly awkward form'.[162] But the situation had changed dramatically since his day, and no Act of Uniformity could now achieve its goal. Developing a rationale for toleration was one of John Locke's major contributions to the debate.

Locke, a devout Anglican, went much further in his *Letters on Toleration* (1689) than Hooker, agreeing with the Independents that the church should be a voluntary society. This undermined the essence of a national church.[163] But then Locke was living in a very different historical context almost a century later than Hooker. He had also come under the strong influence of Calvinism and Puritan Nonconformist teaching as a student at Christ Church, Oxford, including that of the leading Independent of his time, John Owen.[164] It is noteworthy that

---

[160] Michael Walzer, 'Puritanism as a Revolutionary Ideology', *History and Theory*, 3, 1963, pp. 165f.

[161] Hill, *Reformation to Industrial Revolution*, p. 191.

[162] Forrester, 'Richard Hooker,' p. 321.

[163] Locke wrote three letters on toleration. In the first he developed the concept of the church as a voluntary society. See I. T. Ramsey, ed., *John Locke, The Reasonableness of Christianity*, London: Adam and Charles Black, 1958, p. 88.

[164] Foster, 'International Calvinism', pp. 480f.; Geoffrey Nuttall *Visible Saints: The Congregational Way, 1640–1660*, Oxford: Basil Blackwood, 1957, pp. 76f.

Owen himself wrote an influential tract, *Of Toleration*, in which he defended the rights of the Nonconformists to dissent and, at least by implication, the rights of others to do likewise,[165] which belies the popular impression that the Puritans epitomized intolerance. This, together with Owen's voluntary understanding of church membership, undoubtedly influenced Locke. Locke also spent some time in the Netherlands with the Remonstrants, a free church which had resulted from the rejection of the hyper-Calvinism of the Synod of Dort in 1612. Locke became, in effect, the carrier of Calvinism, and Nonconformist Calvinism in particular, from the Reformation to the Revolution of 1688. His contribution ensured that, what Foster called the five points of 'political Calvinism' (the rule of law based on the sovereignty of God and the law of nature; the principles of equity and justice; the covenantal or contractual relationship between rulers and people; the sovereignty of the people; and the theory of resistance against tyranny), filtered through to the American Revolution.[166]

THE NEW ENGLAND COVENANT

The development of the doctrine of the covenant within the Reformed tradition, which became the basis of the American federalist tradition, can be traced back behind Locke to the Swiss Reformation, and especially to Heinrich Bullinger, the successor to Zwingli in Zurich.[167] First applied politically by persecuted Reformed communities in seventeenth-century France and Scotland 'to safeguard both the rights of the king and the rights of the people',[168] the covenant had 'awesome

---

165 John Owen, *Works*, vol. 8, Edinburgh: Banner of Truth Trust, 1967, pp. 163ff. This was an appendix to a sermon preached before the House of Commons on 31 January 1648, the day after the decapitation of Charles I.

166 Foster, 'International Calvinism', p. 485; Bernard Bailyn, *The Ideological Origins of the American Revolution*, Cambridge, Mass.: Harvard University Press, 1992, p. 30.

167 Charles S. McCoy and J. Wayne Baker, *Fountainhead of Federalism: Heinrich Bullinger and the Covenantal Tradition*, Louisville, Kentucky: Westminster/John Knox, 1991.

168 James B. Torrance, 'The Covenant Concept in Scottish Theology and Politics and Its Legacy', *Scottish Journal of Theology*, 34, 1981, 323; see also de Gruchy, *Liberating Reformed Theology*, pp. 265ff.

political potency'[169] for it was not simply a human contract, but one which made the will of God its basis. The covenant was a means of limiting the power of the sovereign, as well as activating and channelling the power of the people. It was the theological basis for democratic checks and balances.

The covenant did not necessarily lead to an open, democratic society, however, as was demonstrated in the Puritan New World. New England theocrats might well have been congregational in church polity, but for them the saints who ruled the church were also meant to rule the Commonwealth of Massachusetts. There was a fine line between church meeting and town-house meeting, and their participants and agendas were often identical.[170] The establishment of the Congregational Church as state church in Massachusetts was not conducive to democratization beyond the parameters of the church meeting, and even there it was not readily accepted. In affirming Congregationalism against Presbyterianism John Winthrop nevertheless regarded democracy amongst civil nations as 'the meanest and worst of all forms of government'.[171] For John Cotton it was fit neither for church nor commonwealth.[172] Indeed, throughout the colonial period, the idea of political democracy was regarded in the same way by enlightened thinkers as it had been by Plato and Aristotle.[173] Thus the ideological leaders of New England, the Congregational ministers, were often a stumbling-block to the pursuit of democracy.[174] Puritan New England was authoritarian, patriarchal, and religiously intolerant. The testimony of persecuted Quakers was far more significant in leading the way from state–church authoritarianism to religious tolerance and the acceptance of denominational pluralism.

---

[169] Richard L. Greaves, *Theology and Revolution in the Scottish Reformation: Studies in the Thought of John Calvin*, Grand Rapids: Eerdmans, 1980, p. 124.

[170] Joshua Miller, 'Direct Democracy and the Puritan Theory of Membership', *Journal of Politics*, 53, 1, February 1991, p. 60.

[171] Hudson, 'Democratic Freedom and Religious Faith', p. 177.

[172] Larzier Ziff, ed., *John Cotton on the Churches of New England*, Cambridge, Mass.; Harvard, 1964, p. 27.

[173] Bailyn, *The Ideological Origins of the American Revolution*, pp. 282f.

[174] Perry Miller, *Orthodoxy in Massachusetts*, Cambridge, Mass.: Beacon Press, 1961.

Yet New England Puritanism, for all its faults, did make a decisive contribution to the formation of that major strand within modern American democracy which has led some to speak of 'God's Federal Republic' as its governing symbol.[175] After all, Congregationalists were deeply committed to developing a membership within church and town which was equal and participatory and, once theological and political liberalization began, the transition to a liberal democratic polity was soon made. This was not only because of democratic elements within the tradition, but also because 'the Congregational system was developed by people who were allied with those financial and political leaders whose ends were best served by an extension of the people's liberties'.[176] None the less, it was the doctrine of the covenant, so fundamental to the direct democracy of both Congregational polity and the town meeting, which was the unique contribution which New England Puritanism made to the evolution of democracy, and especially federalism, in the United States.[177]

The idea of the covenant led, as H. Richard Niebuhr argued,[178] to a particular mind-set which challenged the deist view of a mechanical universe in which society 'was largely a self-regulating mechanism' requiring little government intervention. Further, it replaced medieval organic theories of government in which hierarchy and absolute monarchy were an integral part of the cosmic scheme of things. The covenantal idea, in contrast, was based on promises made and kept between rulers and subjects. This, rather than deist or organic views, was the design of the ultimate ruler for the relationship between divinity and humanity; it was therefore the pattern for human government.[179] Such government was neither natural nor contractual. It was not natural because human nature was

175 William Johnson Everett, *God's Federal Republic: Reconstructing our Governing Symbol*, New York: Paulist Press, 1988.
176 Ziff, *John Cotton*, p. 28.
177 Perry Miller, *The New England Mind: The Seventeenth Century*, Boston: Beacon, 1961, pp. 376f.
178 H. Richard Niebuhr, 'The Idea of Covenant and American Democracy', *Church History*, 23, 1954, p. 129.
179 *Ibid.*, p. 132.

fallen; it could not be contractual (how could humanity enter into a contract with God?) because that meant pursuing self-interest rather than common interest, and a limited rather than an unlimited degree of commitment. Covenant, on the other hand, was voluntaristic; it meant freely choosing to make and keep a promise.

It was government of the people, for the people and by the people but always under God, and it was not natural birth into natural society that made one a complete member of the people but always the moral act of taking upon oneself, through promise, the responsibilities of a citizenship that bound itself in the very act of exercising its freedom.[180]

Opinions vary concerning the influence of the Puritan covenant in shaping democracy in the United States.[181] By the time of the Revolution covenantal ideas had already been channelled into the mainstream of political and social thinking and, though very different in ethos, had become part of a new political synthesis.[182] The connection between covenant theology and social-contract theory is self-evident in the American *Declaration of Independence*, especially when compared with the French *Declaration of the Rights of Man and Citizenship*.

The intellectual pioneers of America were deeply influenced by both classical and Christians traditions, the one informing the other. In New England, Athens, and Jerusalem, Aristotle, Calvin, Locke, and Rousseau combined to shape modern American democracy. Calvinism and deism interacted and modified one another. The understanding of the church as a voluntary association, the development of denominationalism as a positive good and, more generally, the growth of religious pluralism, helped cultivate a civil society quite unique from that which prevailed in Europe. This explains Alexis de Tocqueville's astonishment that what was in conflict in the old world, religion and authoritarianism on the one hand, and enlightenment and freedom on the other, were reconciled. 'No

---

[180] *Ibid.*, p. 133.
[181] Robin W. Lovin, 'Equality and Covenant Theology', *Journal of Law and Religion*, 2, 2, 1984, pp. 241ff.
[182] Bailyn, *Ideological Origins*, p. 32.

religious doctrine', he asserted with reference to America, 'displays the slightest hostility to democratic and republican institutions'.[183]

Covenant ideas were not the same as the social contract, nor can the latter simply be regarded as the secularization of the former.[184] Both were attempting to deal with the role played by human choice and action in society, yet they were essentially different. In contract theory everyone was equal by nature, but nature was such that it always sought self-interest; in covenant theory everyone was equal by virtue of sin, but also by virtue of the fact that every vocation was equal in the sight of God. Both these covenantal ideas undermined ancient distinctions of rank and privilege. Contract theory sought ways whereby individual self-interest could be accommodated without destroying social cohesion; covenantal theory sought to transform individual self-interest into a mutual commitment to the common good by the grace, and under the sovereignty, of God.[185]

The original vision of American democracy would have been something quite different if it had not been for this understanding that political society requires responsible citizens freely committed to pursue the will of God, and therefore the interests of all, in society. It is precisely at this point that we may discern the Christian foundations for Civil Rights law in the United States. It is not simply the conviction that all people are born equal, but the conviction that there is a law which is above common law and stands in judgment over it.[186] This means that the political heirs of the covenant idea are not those who seek to protect individual interests, but those whose prime consideration is a moral society of mutual commitment to justice.

---

[183] Alexis de Tocqueville, *Democracy in America*, edited by Phillips Bradley, New York: Vintage Books, 1956, vol. 1, p. 312.

[184] Lovin, 'Covenant Theology', p. 242.

[185] H. Richard Niebuhr, *Radical Monotheism and Western Culture*, New York: Harper, 1970, p. 72.

[186] Robert A. Destro, '"The Religious Foundations of Civil Rights Law" and the Study of Law and Religion in an Interdisciplinary Framework', *The Journal of Law and Religion*, 5, 1, 1987, 39–52; Berman, 'Religious Foundations of Law', p. 32f.

Modern American democracy has in many ways forgotten the covenant dimension to the synthesis which gave it birth. The 'American way of life', especially the right to personal liberty and the pursuit of happiness without any checks, has been legitimated as intended by God and therefore to be protected at all costs. What was intended to be the outcome of an obligation to the command and will of God, has become equated with that will without the obligation – but that development lay in the future. What is clear is that the American Revolution of 1776 was a product of the combined forces of Puritan theology, radical dissent, and Enlightenment thought. This mix provided the rationale for rejecting the British crown, it helped shape the Declaration of Independence and it developed a doctrine of human rights in which individual liberty became the corner-stone of a new political order.[187] How different it was in Europe where the world had come of age by throwing off the tutelage of God.

[187] Sydney E. Ahlstrom, *A Religious History of the American People*, vol. 1, New York: Doubleday, 1975, pp. 49.

CHAPTER 4

The polity of modernity

The European Enlightenment is usually located between the English Revolution of 1640 and that of France in 1789;[1] between John Locke, the Christian believer and Jean-Jacques Rousseau, the Romantic deist. For much of the eighteenth century, there remained a Christian core to European thought which, despite confessional divisions and cultural diversity, retained some semblance of unity.[2] Yet the chasm between an orthodoxy bent on protecting the authority of Bible, creed, and church, and secular thought was becoming unbridgeable, despite liberal Christianity's valiant attempt to redefine the essence of Christianity.

As the consensus at the heart of Christendom began to disintegrate, so the generative seams of democracy in Christianity, whether in the theological reasoning of Locke or on the more sectarian periphery, were increasingly secularized. Hence Berman's observation, quoted at the beginning of the last chapter, that liberal democracy was the first great secular religion in the West, the first ideology which was divorced from Christianity. It was the polity of modernity, and its discourse was that of bourgeois society.

REVOLUTIONS: RADICAL AND BOURGEOIS

Liberalism appealed to reason and conscience rather than to tradition, it advocated resistance to tyranny and affirmed

---

[1] Peter Gay, *The Enlightenment*: An Interpretation, vol. 1, *The Rise of Modern Paganism*, London: Wildwood House, 1973, p. 17.

[2] A. M. C. Waterman, *Revolution, Economics, and Religion: Christian Political Economy 1798–1833*, Cambridge University Press, 1991, p. 4.

individual human rights.[3] Society was no longer conceived of
in organic terms. The individual rather than the collective was
a priori. For liberals, whether Christians or not, rationality,
human autonomy, the doctrine of inevitable progress, and
religious tolerance, were the fundamentals of civilized society.

The first liberals were by no means all democrats, and there
are undoubtedly elements of tension between the two traditions.[4] In fact, liberal suspicions about democracy were partly
responsible for the lack of any major democratic advances in
Britain during the first few decades of the nineteenth century.
At the same time, their views and values resonated well with
the democratic impulses in the political struggles of eighteenth-
and nineteenth-century Britain and France. Liberals themselves were divided, however, between those who wished to
cling to what had already been achieved in the course of
constitutional struggles in England, and those who saw fresh
possibilities in the French Revolution if only its terrors could be
avoided.[5] Liberty required a civil society in which individuals
were able to pursue their personal goals free from the constraints of state control. The means to achieve this was through
insisting that the power of the state was not based on divine
right, but on the sovereign will of the people themselves. This
led inevitably to an espousal of democracy.[6]

Of all the Enlightenment philosophers it was the devout
Locke who contributed most to the early revisioning of democracy within the framework of the liberal tradition. Yet Locke's
seminal *Second Treatise of Government* is remarkably theological
in orientation. His rationale for civil society is based on divinely given natural law which provided him with the basis for
the rights of individuals, notably life, liberty, and property.

---

[3] D. J. Manning, *Liberalism*, London: J. M. Dent, 1976.
[4] Gordon Graham, 'Liberalism and Democracy', *Journal of Applied Philosophy*, 9,2,
1992, 149. For a history of the relationship between European liberalism and
democracy see Guido de Ruggiero, *The History of European Liberalism*, Oxford
University Press, 1927.
[5] R. R. Palmer, *The Age of Democratic Revolution: A Political History of Europe and America,
1760–1800*, Princeton University Press, 1959, pp. 442f.
[6] Georg Sorenson, *Democracy and Democratization*, Boulder, Colorado: Westview Press,
1993, p. 5.

Political society existed to protect such rights, and was therefore based on the consent of those individuals who were its
members. For Locke, citizenship was contingent on the ownership of property, and the state existed primarily to protect such
interests.[7] In appointing a government to act on their behalf,
citizens surrendered much of their own power, but, given the
fact that their representatives were also land and property
owners, the voters knew that those elected would act to protect
their mutual interests. What was at stake was not so much the
protection of the rights of all individuals, irrespective of who
they might be, from the power of the state, but the protection
of these interests.

Locke's liberal individualism was significantly qualified,
giving to the state considerable power, so much so that it has
been argued that he anticipated much of what we find in
Rousseau.[8] None the less, it was Locke's concern for the interests of the individual, for life, liberty, and the pursuit of
happiness, which became the corner-stone of liberal democracy. The state exists, as Jeremy Bentham, James Mill, and the
great exponent of *laissez-faire* economics Adam Smith argued,
to protect individual rights and liberties from a state bureaucracy which controls the political and economic process. It
would be foolish to interfere with the God-given laws of nature
which decreed that every man had the right to the fruits of his
own labour without the intervention of anyone, including the
state. Liberal democracy thus became a way of protecting
individual freedoms, and the separation of civil society from
political society became an essential means to that end. Likewise the symbols and institutions of liberal democracy became
instruments in determining unequal power relations. Instead
of expressing the sovereignty of the people, liberal democracy
legitimated the interests of the dominant class. This was at the
heart of Rousseau's critique, as it has been at the heart of all
socialist understandings of democracy ever since.

Returning to classical Greece and especially Plato, Rousseau

[7] Macpherson, *Possessive Individualism*, pp. 252ff.
[8] G. P. Gooch, *English Democratic Ideas in the Seventeenth Century*, p. 302.

insisted that 'political subjection was essentially ethical and only secondarily a matter of law and power'. He went further. The community, not the individual, 'is itself the chief moralizing agency and therefore represents the highest moral value'.[9] Thus the basis was laid for *The Social Contract* in which Rousseau moved away from the inherent rights of individuals to the 'sacred rights' of a social order in which each person puts himself (the gender is specific) under the supreme direction of the general will.[10] The sovereignty of the people is not surrendered to those elected to represent them – representation, for Rousseau, is a feudal hangover[11] – but neither is sovereignty vested in individuals; it is sovereignty of 'the people'. How the general will was to be ascertained, and how individual rights were to be protected, remained problematic. But clearly the distinction between political and civil society, so fundamental to liberal democracy, was rejected, and the theoretical foundation for the French Revolution, Jacobin egalitarianism, and the terror which followed, was laid.

Rousseau's writings can be interpreted in a variety of ways. This is partly because he was more the romantic dreamer of democratic ideals than the rationalist political philosopher.[12] Attempting to retrieve the direct democracy of Athens, he failed to appreciate the complexity and changed conditions of an industrializing western Europe.[13] None the less, his understanding of the social contract laid the theoretical foundations for the socialist trajectory within the broader democratic tradition. Rousseau's thought also provided the basis for the activities of Robespierre and the Jacobin claim that the Party represented the will of the people. However appropriate Rousseau's critique of the self-interested individualism of liberal democratic theory may have been, he failed to appreciate the dangers attendant upon conflating the state and civil society, and therefore did not anticipate the terror which

[9] Sabine, *Political Theory*, p. 489f.
[10] Rousseau, *The Social Contract*, book I, chapter i.
[11] *Ibid.*, book III, chapter xv.
[12] Elshtain, *Meditations on Modern Political Thought*, pp. 37ff.
[13] Held, *Models of Democracy*, p.79.

engulfed France after the Revolution. His notion of the collective will of the majority provided a mandate for populist dictatorships. Totalitarianism, whether of the fascist right or of the Communist left, was but a hair's-breadth away.

A glance at the names of some of the foremost political philosophers at the height of the Enlightenment – Voltaire, Baron du Montesquieu, and, of course, Rousseau – indicates the extent to which France set the pace and created the pattern for much of what happened in the rest of Europe. Other intellectuals, like the German Gottfried Lessing, 'admired them judiciously and from afar'.[14] The French *philosophes* did not all agree with each other, but they did agree that enlightenment meant freedom from the constraints of traditional Christianity through the rediscovery of the ancient classical world, and that this enabled them to embrace and shape the modern world in the making.

If the earliest *philosophes* were deists, by the time we reach the end of the eighteenth century atheism accompanied by a pronounced anti-clericalism was the intellectuals' creed. The same creed soon became more pervasive amongst the working class. Anti-clericalism identified the church as the antagonist of modern liberties, and therefore as a stumbling-block *en route* to human emancipation.[15] The utopian watchwords were 'liberty, equality and fraternity', not subservience to an authoritarian church and its God. Thus the ideological ground was prepared for the tumultuous events which brought the Enlightenment to its end, though the social forces which fostered revolution were far broader than the ideas which gave it legitimacy.

'Liberté', 'egalité', 'fraternité'

The French Revolution marked the end of the *ancien régime* and the temporal power of the Roman Catholic church in France. The doctrine of the 'divine right of kings' was felled with one

---

[14] Gay, *The Enlightenment*, p. 5.
[15] Owen Chadwick, *The Secularization of the European Mind in the Nineteenth Century*, Cambridge University Press, 1975, p. 115.

blow, and the *Declaration of the Rights of Man* implied, without stating, the sacredness of popular sovereignty. The church was regarded as the custodian of the past, not the harbinger of the future or the saviour of the poor. Thus it was that conservatives 'all over Europe witnessed with astonishment the apocalyptic ending of a civilization, of those values of honour, nobility, respect, paternal authority, and religious faith which had ruled the West since the advent of Christianity'.[16] The Revolution was a massive revolt against Christianity and aristocracy, and the way in which the church responded was to have lasting repercussions. The fluctuations in the fortunes of the Gallican church and its general instability, provided a paradigm for the insecurity which European Christianity began to experience with the dawning of the post-revolutionary industrialized world.[17]

Although the Revolution became blatantly anti-clerical, many Christians and not a few priests were participants in its struggles. The Revolution was not simply a mass uprising of the poor and oppressed, but involved enlightened nobles and other elites as well. Moreover, as in pro-democratic struggles in our own time, the struggle was not confined to the political forums or streets of Paris, but took shape 'in hundreds of town halls, churches, village squares and workshops all over France'.[18] As in the Cromwellian Revolution, at least some aristocrats, nobility, and clergy joined company with 'bourgeoisie' and peasant revolutionaries in order to achieve their goal.[19] Together they thrashed out procedures and policies in the Assembly, and together they proclaimed *egalité* as the first and central principle of the Revolution. It was the Chamber of Clergy which in 1789 insisted on voting by heads rather than estates and so dealt the decisive blow to feudalism.[20]

[16] Biancamaria Fontana, 'Democracy and the French Revolution', in Dunn, *The Unfinished Journey*, p. 107.

[17] Alec R. Vidler, *The Church in an Age of Revolution: 1789 to the Present Day*, London: Penguin, 1965, p. 11; John McManners, *Church and State in France 1870–1914*, London: SPCK, 1972.

[18] Fontana, in Dunn, *The Unfinished Journey*, p. 108.

[19] *Ibid.*, p. 110; Vidler, *The Church in an Age of Revolution*, p. 15.

[20] Franz Horner, 'The Church and Christian Democracy', in Gregory Baum and John Coleman, *The Church and Christian Democracy*, Concilium, Edinburgh: T. and T. Clark, 1987, p. 31.

Unlike the liberal democracy which had taken root in class-divided Britain, the emphasis in revolutionary France was far more on human equality and solidarity (*fraternité*) than personal liberty. *Liberté* did not mean protection of property-owning interests, but freedom from aristocratic and ecclesiastical control. It was also radically qualified by an egalitarianism which insisted that those who had been at the bottom of the social ladder, the majority, should now have access to power in such a way that their interests became determinative for society as a whole. Sovereignty thus rested in the people as a nation, and no person or institution could exercise authority unless it derived from them.[21]

The bloody aftermath of the Revolution in which clergy, especially those in the upper echelons, were one of the main targets of hostility, soon crushed the idealism of those who had espoused its democratic cause as the only true and just form of government. For them the unleashing of state terror proved that social equality and liberty inevitably meant mass violence and the destruction of property. Democracy spelt anarchy and was a luxury which no society could afford. It required an autocratic Napoleon to restore order, and at the same time to ensure the unity and prosperity of the church.[22] No wonder there was increasing revulsion on the part of many who had earlier espoused the cause of the Revolution, and that the scepticism of the churches regarding the possibility of democracy was reinforced.

No wonder, too, that political theorists pondered on why it was that the American Revolution had succeeded in establishing democratic rule, whereas the French had initiated anarchy and despotism. For de Tocqueville, disaster struck because the religious foundations of human equality had been destroyed; for J. S. Mill, it was now necessary to distinguish between the false democracy of majoritarianism, and the true

---

[21] *Declaration of the Rights of Man and Citizens*, 27 August 1789, in John Hall Steward, ed., *A Documentary History of the French Revolution*, New York: Macmillan, 1951.

[22] Vidler, *The Church in an Age of Revolution*, p. 19.

democracy of representative government.[23] Throughout
Europe, church leaders regarded the French Revolution as
anti-Christian, and they were not slow to connect the chaos
and terror which resulted with unbelief and moral licence. In
Britain and Germany especially, the 'anti-clerical and anti-
ecclesial attitude of leading revolutionaries in France and the
bloody terror of the revolutionary epoch left many Protestants
disenchanted with the democratic ideal'.[24]

According to the historian William Lecky, the Methodist
Revival saved England from 'the contagion' of the French
Revolution and prevented it from sharing the same fate as
France.[25] The Revival, in fact, turned working-class discontent
into evangelical piety and fervour, and brought about sufficient social change to prevent revolution. Yet its leader, John
Wesley, was an 'unbending high Tory',[26] and, while a strong
critic of the slave-trade, he was by no means a democrat either
in politics or in the organization of his societies. A Methodist
leader, Jabez Bunting, declared in 1827: 'Methodism was as
much opposed to democracy as to sin.'[27] Certainly the theology
of the Anglican establishment firmly rejected any thought of
Christian support for liberal ideas, let alone revolution.[28] And
'old Dissent', the Congregationalists and Baptists (Methodism
being 'new Dissent'), were well and truly part of the middle
class, concerned more about their own status with regard to the
established Church of England than they were about the poor.

Federalism, suffrage, and the market

The American Revolution in 1776 predated the French, but
the theorists of the new Constitution were deeply influenced by

[23] John Stuart Mill, *Considerations on Representative Government*, London: Everyman
edition, 1910, p. 256. Quoted in Charles S. Maier, 'Democracy since the French
Revolution', in Dunn, *The Unfinished Journey*, p. 131.

[24] Huber, 'Christianity and Democracy', in John Witte, ed., *Christianity and Democracy
in Global Context*, Boulder: Wedgewood Press, 1993, p. 44.

[25] William E. H. Lecky, *History of England in the Eighteenth Century*, London: Longmans
Green, vol. 3, 1902, p. 146.

[26] Hill, *Reformation to Industrial Revolution*, p. 276.

[27] Robert Currie, *Methodism Divided: a Study in the Sociology of Ecumenism*, London:
Faber, 1968, p. 165.

[28] Waterman, *Revolution, Economics, and Religion*, p. 5.

ideas emanating from France and Britain. Central to the debate, as reflected in the Federalist Papers (1787–8),[29] was the question of the feasibility of direct, participatory democracy as advocated by Rousseau. Paper No. 10, written by James Madison and generally regarded as the most important, was primarily concerned with the problem of governing a large and diverse population of conflicting interests without resorting to that kind of force which denies human liberty.[30] Faction, Madison argued, derives from human nature, and finds expression in a variety of forms, but most commonly in the unequal distribution of property. Government cannot get rid of the causes of such faction, but good government is able to control its effects. This cannot be done through the direct participation of every citizen in government, for such a 'pure democracy' can only function in small-scale communities where diversity is minimal, and even then it was problematic. The only workable model, Madison argued, would be a republic large enough to provide a good selection of electoral candidates as well as the necessary checks and balances to allow diversity and protect liberty. A balance was required between electors who are acquainted with local circumstances and interests, and those able 'to comprehend and pursue great and national objects'.[31]

If the Federalists rejected Rousseau's 'pure democracy' because it could not deal with the conflicting interests of a pluralist state, Mary Wollstonecraft, the earliest feminist exponent of democracy, faulted Rousseau for denying women an independent role in political life.[32] Inspired by the French Revolution and the role which women played in it, Wollstonecraft was also aware of the way in which both the Enlightenment liberal ideologists and revolutionary legislation ignored women.[33] *The Rights of Man* were essentially that. Until there

---

[29] *The Federalist Papers*, New York: New American Library, 1961; Morton J. Frisch and Richard G. Stevens, *The Political Thought of American Statesmen*, Itasca, Illinois: F. E. Peacock Publishers, 1973, pp. 39ff.

[30] *The Federalist Papers*, No. 10, pp. 77ff.   [31] *Ibid.*, p. 83.

[32] Elshtain, *Meditations on Modern Political Thought*, pp. 47f.; Held, *Models of Democracy*, pp. 79f.

[33] Richard J. Evans, *The Feminists*, London: Croom Helm, 1979, p. 16.

was a fundamental change in the private sphere, there could be little meaningful change in the public. Not only must the 'divine right of kings' be abolished, but also the 'divine right of husbands'.[34] What was at issue, Wollstonecraft argued in her tract *A Vindication of the Rights of Woman*, published shortly after the French Revolution, was not whether women had the rational ability to participate in politics, but the fact that they were denied the necessary education to do so. Wollstonecraft was unable to present an alternative to the prevailing models of democracy which could take this into account,[35] but she anticipated contemporary feminist reactions to liberal democracy.

Scottish academics and divines who had imbibed the values of the Enlightenment also contributed to their political propagation in critical response to the French Revolution. It was in Scotland that Adam Smith, and a generation later, T. R. Malthus, worked out their economic theories and provided the basis for what has been called Christian Political Economy.[36] This theology of economics, adopted by the distinguished Church of Scotland churchman, Thomas Chalmers, was in essence a blessing of market forces, free trade, economic individualism, and moral paternalism in the name of Christianity. In effect, however, it led to the secularization of political economy, placing it beyond the constraints of Christian ethics.[37] Chalmers was as opposed to mercantilism as he was to anything else which had a 'tendency to disturb the existing order of things, or to confound the ranks and distinctions' which obtained in society.[38] The Protestant work ethic required a free-market economy, but not a democratic society.

Scottish influence was remarkably strong in the United States throughout the nineteenth century, and many of the intellectual, religious and economic ideas of the Scottish Enlightenment found a ready audience across the Atlantic; but

[34] Held, *Models of Democracy*, p. 81.   [35] *Ibid.*, p. 84.
[36] Waterman, *Revolution, Economics, and Religion*, p. 5.
[37] *Ibid.*, p. 11.
[38] Thomas Chalmers, address at the laying of the foundation-stone of New College, Edinburgh in 1846. *New College Edinburgh: A Centenary History*, compiled by H. Watt, Edinburgh: Oliver and Boyd, 1946, p. 3.

liberal democratic ideas were not part of this legacy. In the United States democratic ideas were not propagated so much by Presbyterians and Congregationalists as by revivalist Methodists and Baptists. Set on fire by the Second Great Awakening in the nineteenth century, they pioneered Protestant expansion along the western frontier, rejecting the religious and political establishment of the eastern colonies as they took possession of the land.[39] Thus, while democracy became secularized in Europe, it became wedded to a popular revivalist Christianity in North America, with a stress on the moral regeneration of the individual validated by a productive life.

Democratic rhetoric in the United States was not matched in practice, however, beyond the homogeneous confines of the white Anglo-Saxon Protestant community. That 'all men were equal' was accepted doctrine, but this excluded slaves and women. In the South, theological legitimation was provided in support of the ownership of slaves by Christians.[40] The debate about slavery, and the civil war which followed, was to tear American Protestantism apart and seriously compromise its witness to human equality and social justice.

The Second Great Awakening helped energize the struggle for women's rights in the United States.[41] Patriarchy was deeply entrenched in the churches, but, as a result of the Awakening, Christian women began to play leading roles in those social movements, including the anti-slavery movement, which emerged. This led to the Women's Rights Convention at Seneca Falls, New York State, in 1848, which passed a resolution declaring 'that all men *and women* are created equal', and providing a detailed account of the way in which the rights of women were denied in both church and society.[42] This marked the beginning of the modern feminist movement, but it also

---

[39] Nathan O. Hatch, *The Democratization of American Christianity*, New Haven: Yale University Press, 1989.

[40] Ahlstrom, *Religious History of the American People*, vol. 2, pp. 91ff.; Albert J. Raboteau, *Slave Religion: The 'Invisible Institution' in the Antebellum South*, New York: Oxford University Press, 1978.

[41] Evans, *The Feminists*, pp. 44f.

[42] Martin E. Marty, *Pilgrims in their Own Land: 500 Years of Religion in America*, London: Penguin, 1985, pp. 205f.

revealed a tension between the struggle for women's suffrage and racial equality which would long remain problematic in the struggle for democratic rights.[43]

Liberal democracy and its failed revolution

Liberal democratic theory reached its best expression in the writings of the nineteenth-century English philosopher J. S. Mill who, to some extent at least, was supportive of the rights of women. Like the Federalists, Mill insisted that the best option for ensuring liberty was representative government in which all educated people (that is, those able to read, write, and do arithmetic), including women, were able to participate actively in the political process.[44] Unless they did so, democratic rights would be forfeited by default. What was needed was individual resourcefulness and initiative which prevented people from being dependent upon others, on the one hand, and allowed them to realize their full potential, on the other.[45] Without liberty of conscience, pursuit of personal interest, and organization, no matter what kind of government is in place, society itself could not be free. 'The only freedom', Mill wrote, 'which deserves the name, is that of pursuing our own good in our own way, as long as we do not attempt to deprive others of theirs, or impede their efforts to obtain it'.[46]

In contrast to others within the liberal democratic tradition, Mill was all for strengthening democracy so that it could not be subverted by class interests. With Britain's strongly classist society in mind, he maintained that, without the necessary checks upon class domination, constitutional government was 'but solemn trifling'.[47] Unless the domination of a particular class could be restrained, democracy was not the best form of government. The challenge was 'to find the means of preventing this abuse, without sacrificing the characteristic advan-

---

[43] Susan Thistlethwaite, *Sex, Race and God: Christian Feminism in Black and White*, New York: Crossroad, 1989, p. 41.
[44] J. S. Mill, *Utilitarianism, Liberty, and Representative Government*, pp. 114f., 276f.
[45] *Ibid.*, p. 208.
[46] *Ibid.*, p. 75.   [47] *Ibid.*, p. 277.

tages of popular government'.[48] Mill's liberal democracy had a social conscience.

In 1848, at the mid-point of Mill's career, revolution erupted again in Paris and then, in a series of chain reactions, spread across Europe, having a particularly significant impact on Germany.[49] Although its precise character varied from country to country,[50] overall it was a bourgeois revolution against authoritarian regimes, and liberals, fearful that the same fate would overtake this Revolution as had happened in 1789, were determined to control its outcome. For the first time, political parties were formed in Germany and some other countries, and liberal politics began to exert an influence. But liberalism was unable to deal with the rising tide of nationalism, or with the 'social question', as the plight of the poor and the 'class struggle' was then called.

Across Europe, liberalism and constitutionalism were severely defeated, leading in Prussia to the consolidation of traditional conservative forces ('throne and altar') and the triumph of Bismarck's authoritarian regime.[51] For good reason, then, 1848 has been labelled the year of the 'failed bourgeois revolutions'.[52] This was the context within which Marx and Engels founded the Communist League and published the *Communist Manifesto*. A bourgeois revolution was not what Marx had in mind, with the result that he despondently left Germany, never to return. But if 1789 meant the overthrow of aristocracy, and 1848 the failure of the middle class, the turn of the proletariat was next.[53]

CHRISTIAN POLITICAL LIBERALISM AND SOCIALISM

In response to the European revolutions, conservative European intellectuals and Christians, from Edmund Burke to

[48] *Ibid.*
[49] William Carr, *A History of Germany: 1815–1945*, London: Edward Arnold, 1969, pp. 41f.
[50] Krishan Kumar, 'The Revolutions of 1989: Socialism, Capitalism, and Democracy', *Theory and Society*, 21,3, pp. 325f.
[51] Carr, *A History of Germany*, p. 94
[52] Kumar, 'The Revolutions of 1989', p. 327.
[53] Wuthnow, *Communities of Discourse*, p. 361.

Joseph de Maistre and F. J. Stahl, called for the restoration of Christendom, a rediscovery of those common values which bound society together in the past. All of them shared the conviction that the Enlightenment had been a disaster, an apostasy, which had led inexorably to revolution and now threatened to destroy the social fabric of Europe. Nowhere was this better expressed than in Holland, where the neo-Calvinist Groen van Prinsterer attacked all forms of liberalism as the basis of unbelief and revolution.[54]

An avalanche of de-Christianization

The failure of German Protestantism to identify with the people in 1848 and after, led to the further alienation of the working class from the church, driving it eventually to embrace Marxism and other secular forms of socialism.[55] The churches failed abysmally to appreciate both the appalling working conditions and the democratic aspirations of the people.

While the luminaries of German liberal Protestantism, from Friedrich Schleiermacher to Adolf von Harnack, were generally positive in their response to the Enlightenment, like their fellow intellectuals – jointly and aptly named the 'German mandarins' – they were resolute in their resistance to liberal democracy and their attachment to the Prussian monarchy.[56] Numbered amongst them were right-wing Hegelians who developed strong theological connections between Christianity and German nationalism. This German Protestant antipathy to democracy was fuelled by the rise of the Social Democratic Party which waged a particularly venomous campaign against Christianity and the churches during the last third of the nineteenth century.

[54] Guillaume Groen van Prinsterer, *Unbelief and Revolution*, translated and edited by Harry van Dyke with Donald Morton, Amsterdam, 1975. First published in 1847.
[55] Robert M. Bigler, *The Politics of German Protestantism: The Rise of the Protestant Church Elite in Prussia, 1815–1848*, Berkeley: University of California Press, 1972.
[56] George Rupp, *Culture Protestantism: German Liberal Theology at the Turn of the Twentieth Century*, Missoula, Montana: Scholars Press, 1977; Fritz K. Ringer, *The Decline of the German Mandarins: the German Academic Community, 1890–1933*, Cambridge, Mass.: Harvard University Press, 1969.

Conservative Christian reactions to the Enlightenment and revolutionary change failed to meet the moral attack which Voltaire had launched against Christianity, namely, that it stood for injustice and bondage rather than human equality and liberty. The churches were, as Kaspar indicates, 'blind to the Christian roots of autonomy, and blinder still to the Christian potentialities of the modern era'.[57] The doctrines of human rights, social equality, and freedom of thought, were linked in their minds not only with the Enlightenment's undermining of Christian faith, but also with political instability. So whereas previously atheism had been something espoused by liberal intellectuals, it was now channelled into the working class and a massive de-Christianization process took place in much of Europe.[58] As Jacques Maritain later put it: 'The working classes sought their salvation in the denial of Christianity; the conservative Christian circles sought theirs in the denial of the temporal exigencies of justice and love.'[59]

There were exceptions to prove the rule. In France, Félicité de Lammenais developed a Catholic form of democracy (*Démocratie chrétienne*) after the Napoleonic wars,[60] in order that liberal Catholics could counter the secularization of politics without putting a brake on liberalization.[61] But the movement was soon undermined by the Vatican.[62] Any attempt to reconcile Catholicism with liberalism was condemned by Rome in the 1830s,[63] and in 1864 Pius IX promulgated his *Syllabus of Errors* in which he categorically rejected progress, liberalism, and democratic organization. Every call for social justice was equated with godless revolution.

---

[57] Walter Kaspar, *Theology and Church*, London: SCM, 1989, p. 55.
[58] William O. Shanahan, *German Protestants Face the Social Question*, vol. 1, *The Conservative Phase 1815–1871*, University of Notre Dame Press, 1954, pp. 345f.
[59] Jacques Maritain, *Christianity and Democracy*, San Francisco: Ignatius Press, 1986, p. 21. First published as *Christianisme et démocratie*, New York, 1943.
[60] McManners, *Church and State in France*, pp. 81ff.; John C. Cort, *Christian Socialism*, Maryknoll, N.Y.; Orbis, 1988, pp. 88ff.
[61] Horner, 'The Church and Christian Democracy', in Baum and Coleman, *The Church and Christian Democracy*, pp. 28f.
[62] Michael P. Fogarty, *Christian Democracy in Western Europe, 1820–1953*, London: Routledge and Kegan Paul, 1957.
[63] Maier, in Dunn, *The Unfinished Journey*, p. 143.

There were also French Protestants who were convinced of the need for democracy. Notable amongst them was Edmond de Pressensé, a French Reformed scholar, who ministered in Paris during the 1848 Revolution and became much involved in the democratic movement of the time.[64] In England, a remarkable group of Anglicans, John Ludlow, Charles Kingsley, and F. D. Maurice, established the Christian Socialist Movement in 1848, and sought to influence the Chartists in the rejection of *laissez-faire* capitalism. They were not radical in their socialism,[65] but they were deeply aware of the fact that Christianity would lose the working class if it did not identify with the political struggles of the victims of the Industrial Revolution.

Radical religious dissent had long been the home of democratic and egalitarian ideas, especially within popular culture, but the capitulation of the churches in Europe to authoritarian regimes and bourgeois values led to the virtual extinction of such forms of Christianity.[66] As Protestantism, notably in Germany, became more pietist and aligned itself with territorial authoritarian rule, and as Catholicism, despite the success of the counter-reformation in the re-Catholicization of rural Europe, became more clericalized and closely connected to the *anciens régimes*, so the influence of Christian social radicalism lost its popular support.[67] Christianity was now widely viewed as a middle-class religion controlled by aristocratic elites. The common people either piously followed their lead, especially in the feudal rural areas, or they became part of that 'avalanche of de-Christianization' which followed industrialization.[68] Between the First Communist International in 1864 and the First World War in 1914, Marxist socialism became the creed of the working classes throughout most of Europe.

[64] Donald W. Norwood, *The Case for Democracy in Church Government*, unpublished Ph.D. thesis: University of London, 1983, p. 79.

[65] John Atherton, *Christianity and the Market: Christian Social Thought for Our Times*, London: SPCK, 1992, p. 135.

[66] Mullett, *Radical Religious Movements*, pp. 110f.   [67] *Ibid.*, pp. 107f.

[68] *Ibid.*, p. 109.

Voluntaryism and the Nonconformist conscience

The situation was somewhat different in England, where parliamentary democracy was well established by the nineteenth century, and where Free Church Nonconformity played an increasingly significant political role on the side of liberal democratic politics. As descendants of the seventeenth-century separatist Puritans, and considerably strengthened as a result of the eighteenth-century Evangelical Revival, 'old Dissent' (Congregationalists and Baptists) produced many of the political radicals of the late eighteenth century.[69] By the beginning of the nineteenth century Nonconformity was a political force with which British politicians had to reckon in a way that had not been true since the Cromwellian period.[70] Traditionally aligned since 1688 with the *laissez-faire* liberalism that became the charter of Whig politicians, it 'was almost inconceivable that anyone brought up in traditional Dissent could be a Tory'.[71] To gauge their significance, active Nonconformists outnumbered active Anglicans at the turn of the twentieth century, even though, relative to the population, Nonconformity was already in decline.[72]

Nonconformists and liberal Whigs shared the same concern for civil and religious liberty.[73] Disestablishment and religious voluntaryism was the cry. Moreover, in the same measure that they both attacked religious establishment, they opposed the remnants of feudal society. They were 'free-traders', supporters of the Anti-Corn Law League, against war and for social reform. There was Nonconformist agreement with liberalism that 'the laws of political economy were the foundation of social harmony', which meant that hard work alone would result in prosperity and benefit the community.[74] But, despite their liberalism, not all Whigs were members of the Liberal

---

[69] Hill, *Reformation to Industrial Revolution*, p. 277.
[70] D. W. Bebbington, *The Nonconformist Conscience: Chapel and Politics, 1870–1914*, London: George Allen and Unwin, 1982, p. 1.
[71] David M. Thompson, *Nonconformity in the Nineteenth Century*, London: Routledge and Kegan Paul, 1972, p. 10.
[72] Bebbington, *The Nonconformist Conscience*, p. 2.   [73] *Ibid.*, p. 8.
[74] *Ibid.*, p. 10.

Party, nor were all Nonconformists convinced democrats.[75]
Some Congregationalist leaders, supportive of democracy,
were careful not to equate it with their ecclesial polity.[76]

None the less, Nonconformity was more committed to liberal
democracy than was the Anglican establishment.[77] So the
struggle for a more democratic society, in which the morality of
political leaders and the welfare and interests of the people
were paramount, was regarded by Nonconformist leadership
as a particular responsibility of their churches. Modelling their
programmes on the anti-slavery crusades of the 1830s,
throughout the nineteenth-century campaigns against other
social ills became the order of the day.[78] This was reflected in
what was probably 'Nonconformity's most enduring memorial'
within the history of English religion,[79] the 'Nonconformist
conscience'.

The Nonconformist conscience had three features: 'a conviction that there is no strict boundary between religion and
politics; an insistence that politicians should be men (sic) of the
highest character, and a belief that the state should promote
the moral welfare of its citizens'. All of these, comments D. W.
Bebbington, 'were new in the late Victorian period'.[80] Politics
was not something to avoid as worldly, but something to
engage in actively for the sake of social reform. Nonconformist
leaders thus supported the emerging trade union movement,
even though they also supported *laissez-faire* economics.[81] But
their support amongst the poor, as distinct from the 'respect-
able' working class, was minimal.[82] By the end of the century,
with the exception of the Primitive Methodists, 'Nonconformity was probably more homogeneously middle class than it

---

[75] See Vivien Hart, *Distrust and Democracy*, Cambridge University Press, 1978.
[76] For example, R. W. Dale, and P.T. Forsyth. See Norwood, *Case for Democracy*.
[77] There were some notable Anglicans who were strongly committed to the Liberal
    Party. See Philip Hesketh, *'The Wail of Jeremiah': the Early Life of C. F. G. Masterman,
    1873–1927*, unpublished Ph.D. thesis, University of London, 1993.
[78] Bebbington, *The Nonconformist Conscience*, p. 15.
[79] Munson, *The Nonconformists*, p. 306.
[80] Bebbington, *The Nonconformist Conscience*, p. 11.
[81] Thompson, *Nonconformity*, pp. 12f.
[82] *Ibid.*, pp. 13f.; Bebbington, *The Nonconformist Conscience*, pp. 5f.

had been at the beginning',[83] and it was becoming rapidly out of touch with the labour movement whose representatives would soon replace the Liberal Party as the dominant opposition to the Conservatives within parliament.[84] At the same time, it was within Nonconformity that many future labour leaders first learnt their moral and democratic values as well as their rhetorical and organizational skills – even if they subsequently left the fold.

Nonconformity made at least four major contributions to the development of English liberal democracy.[85] Firstly, it fought and won the battle against the conservative establishment for the freedom of religion and of thought, without which political liberty would not have been able to flourish. Secondly, it provided a good education for people from the middle and working classes, excluded by the establishment from the public schools and universities, and thus enabled some to become liberal and labour leaders. Thirdly, in contrast to what happened in much of the rest of Europe, Nonconformity countered anti-clericalism, and indicated that Christianity was not in principle against democratic social change. Finally, Nonconformity injected a sense of commitment, idealism, and social activism into British public life which had been largely absent before. But English Nonconformity seldom espoused a more socialist democratic agenda, as was the case amongst some Anglicans and Roman Catholics.

Anglican socialists and Catholic democrats

If Nonconformists were generally liberal in their politics, Anglicans were part of the Tory establishment. There were, however, significant exceptions to this latter alignment, none more so than Stewart Headlam and those Anglo-Catholic socialists who established the Guild of St Matthew in 1877. In retrospect this was a remarkable event, for between 1854 and

---

[83] Thompson, *Nonconformity*, pp. 14f.
[84] Stephen Mayor, *The Churches and the Labour Movement*, London: Independent Press, 1967.
[85] Thompson, *Nonconformity*, pp. 16f.

1877 there was virtually no socialist activity in Britain, even though Karl Marx was in residence there.[86] Later, in 1889, Charles Gore and Henry Scott Holland formed the Christian Social Union.[87] The Union was liberal and reformist in approach, unlike the Church Socialist League, founded in 1906 by two priests, Conrad Noel and W. E. Moll, who preferred Headlam's radicalism and regarded the Union as irrelevant to the real issues. Noel, for whom the worst social hindrances were bishops, brewers, and brothels, and the deadliest foes the Press, the Liberal Government and the Party system, was also a founder of the British Socialist Party.[88]

The Anglo-Catholic socialists, whether reformist or revolutionary, were deeply rooted in a sacramental approach to Christian faith and practice. This made them highly critical of the kind of individualism which they associated with evangelical piety and liberal democracy. In this, as in other respects, they were in continuity with that organic understanding of church and society which we have already noted in medieval Thomism. Whether these Anglican socialists really had much influence in generating political action on behalf of the poor may be doubted, but they were deeply concerned about poverty. Unlike the more radical socialists among their fellow priests, they also believed that the class issue could best be resolved through the democratization of the political process. The charter of the Union, *Lux Mundi*, published in 1889, attributed both democracy and socialism to the work of the Spirit.[89] In the eucharist, as in society, the Spirit was at work to transform the material into that corporate 'body of Christ' of human equality and solidarity.

The way was thus prepared for later developments in the early decades of the twentieth century, when William Temple (later Archbishop of Canterbury), and the distinguished social

[86] Cort, *Christian Socialism*, p. 153.
[87] Stanley G. Evans, *The Social Hope of the Christian Church*, London: Hodder & Stoughton, 1965, pp. 154ff.; Cort, *Christian Socialism*, pp. 154ff.
[88] Cort, *Christian Socialism*, p. 159.
[89] Michael Ramsey, *From Gore to Temple*, London: Longmans, 1960, p. 14. Charles Gore, ed., *Lux Mundi: a Series of Studies in the Religion of the Incarnation*, Oxford, 1904.

historian R. H. Tawney, who profoundly influenced Temple,[90] gave their support to Labour and broke the long historical connection between the established church and Tory politics. Together they contributed significantly to the liberalization and democratization of British politics and the establishment of the Welfare State.[91] From the 1880s until Temple's death in 1944, Christian socialism dominated the mainstream of Anglican thought.[92] What is of particular note is Temple's conviction that respect for individual personality is the root of democracy, and the herd-instinct its greatest danger:[93] an important reminder that the rejection of possessive individualism is not incompatible with respect for individual persons. If respect for the individual goes, organic societies degenerate into totalitarian Fascism.

In the final decades of the nineteenth century, significant changes became apparent in the social teaching of the Roman Catholic church. A new era dawned with the publication of Pope Leo XIII's now celebrated encyclical *Rerum Novarum* in May 1891.[94] Cautiously balanced, the ties with feudalism and monarchy were broken and both *laissez-faire* liberal capitalism and socialism were condemned, though the former more than the latter.[95] This was an enormous step for the Catholic church, far 'ahead of contemporaneous Christian praxis by comparison with the *average* level of consciousness in the church community at the end of the nineteenth century'.[96] The papacy was beginning to respond positively to the cries of the workers and the poor. Anticipating the change was the support which Cardinal Manning of Westminster gave to the Dockers'

---

[90] John Kent, *William Temple: Church, State and Society in Britain, 1880–1950*, Cambridge University Press, 1992, pp. 16f.

[91] *Ibid.*, pp. 53f.

[92] Kenneth Leech, 'The Radical Anglo-Catholic Social Vision', *Discussion Paper 2*, Centre for Theology and Public Issues, New College, Edinburgh, 1989, p. 3.

[93] William Temple, *Essays in Christian Politics*, London: Longman, Green and Co., 1927, pp. 73f.

[94] John A. Coleman, SJ, ed., *One Hundred Years of Catholic Social Thought: Celebration and Challenge*, Maryknoll, N.Y.: Orbis, 1991.

[95] McManners, *Church and State in France*, pp. 86f.

[96] Enrique Dussel, *A History of the Church in Latin America*, Grand Rapids: Eerdmans, 1981, p. 216.

Strike in England in 1889, much to the dismay of the government.

It was within this milieu that new attempts were made to develop organizations and structures through which the vision of *Rerum Novarum* could be put into effect. This led, *inter alia*, to the rebirth of *la démocratie chrétienne* which soon made a significant impact on French politics, laying the foundation for similar developments in other parts of Europe where Catholic political parties were founded.[97] As previously, the Catholic 'Christian democrats' were concerned about both the laicization of the church and the democratization of society. What was new amongst some was a socialist commitment, a response to what was happening amongst the working class. Hence some 'Christian democrats' were militantly opposed to bourgeois economic values.[98] Although *Rerum Novarum* marked an about-face in Catholic social teaching,[99] it was cautious and ambiguous, making it possible for Catholics to claim support for both a socialist and a more liberal capitalist position. Hence the ideological dichotomy within Catholic political organizations and parties in Europe, and the later tendency, particularly in Germany, for Christian Democratic Parties to be aligned with the right rather than the left.

If the French Revolution signalled the beginning of the end of Christendom, then the outbreak of the First World War, when the 'Christian nations' of Europe and North America engaged in such devastating conflict, signalled the end of the beginning. During 1914 to 1918, a period which encompassed the Russian Revolution, the old order died and the twentieth century was violently born. These traumatic events shattered the liberal myth of inevitable progress and raised fundamental questions about the cosy relationship between liberal Protestantism and nationalism. In prophetic response, Karl Barth

---

[97] McManners, *Church and State in France*, pp. 94f.
[98] Paul Misner, *Social Catholicism in Europe: From the Onset of Industrialization to the First World War*, London: Darton, Longman and Todd, 1991, p. 320.
[99] John J. Mitchell, Jr., 'Embracing a Socialist Vision: The Evolution of Catholic Social Thought, Leo XIII to John Paul II', in James E. Wood, Jr., ed., *Readings on Church and State*, Waco, Texas: Baylor University, 1989.

and other 'dialectical' theologians turned again to biblical eschatology in order to find a prophetic alternative to liberal Protestantism, and a way to relate Christian faith to the irrational and tragic dimensions of human history.[100] For Barth and others like him, this required a radical break with Christendom and liberal politics, and a Christian decision for socialism.[101]

THE CHURCHES, WEIMAR, AND NAZISM

The political history of Germany since the Reformation militated against democratic government. Key terms within western liberal democracy such as individuality, freedom, community, or nation, had a very different connotation in German tradition.[102] As Bismark perceived, the chief means for maintaining German unity was by appealing to national sentiment and the conservative elements in the legacy of Luther. Humiliation at Versailles in 1918 intensified rather than doused the flames of German nationalist aspiration and fervour. None the less the Weimar Republic established in August 1919 had a constitution which was remarkably democratic, giving women suffrage for the first time in German history. Some argued then, and others have done so since, that Weimar failed precisely because its constitution was too democratic to deal with the realities which faced Germany at the time. But the problem in German history, as Karl Dieter Bracher has observed, has never been 'too much but too little democracy'.[103]

[100] James M. Robinson ed., *The Beginnings of Dialectic Theology*, vol. 1, Richmond, Va.: John Knox, 1968.

[101] Mark Kline Taylor, ed., *Paul Tillich: Theologian of the Boundaries*, Philadelphia: Fortress, 1991, pp. 18f., 67ff. In making this decision, Barth found particular inspiration in the life and work of German and Swiss Christian Democratic Socialists, notably Christoph Blumhardt. See Barth, 'Friedrich Naumann and Christoph Blumhardt', in Robinson ed., *The Beginnings of Dialectic Theology*, pp. 35ff.

[102] Klaus Scholder, 'Modern German History and Protestant Theology', (1963) in Klaus Scholder, *A Requiem for Hitler and Other Perspectives on the German Church Struggle*, London: SCM, 1989, p. 48.

[103] Karl Dieter Bracher, *The German Dictatorship: the Origins, Structure and Consequences of National Socialism*, London: Penguin, 1973, p. 616.

In defence of 'throne and altar'

From its beginnings, the Weimar Republic was torn apart by left-wing strikes and right-wing *putsches* in an increasingly volatile context which was exacerbated by the collapse of the German economy in 1923. Democracy was widely regarded as being incapable of solving the nation's severe social and economic problems. Decisive and timely action by the *Reichstag* was stymied as politicians found themselves trapped between trade unions and powerful industrial and military elites. Compromises failed to solve the crises which ensued. Neither the Communists nor right-wing elites, supported by the military, trusted the Social and Liberal Democrats, believing that only a strong, centralized, and authoritarian government could resolve the crisis. By October 1929, when Wall Street crashed, the situation had deteriorated to chronic levels, with unemployment at an alarmingly high level. Rule by presidential decree became inevitable as democratic procedures were rejected by old enemies amongst the elites, and by the mass mobilization of the disaffected middle class under Hitler's leadership. Industrialists and President Hindenburg regarded Hitler as personally despicable, but an indispensable ally in destroying parliamentary rule.

Those groups committed to democracy still had considerable support even in 1930, but the *Reichstag* could do little to prevent the rot amongst a panic-stricken population, or stop Hitler without the help of the president. Such help was not forthcoming. The Communists did not want a democratic resolution of the problem and, while they engaged in bitter battle with the Nazis, they equally rejected the Social Democrats as 'social fascists'.[104] Many Communists held firm against Nazism and became the first victims of concentration camps. Yet many workers who had marched under the red flag switched their allegiance to Hitler when it became evident that their interests would be better served.

In July 1932, the Nazis increased their parliamentary seats

---

[104] *Ibid.*, p. 463.

from a mere twelve to a massive two hundred and thirty. Hitler unashamedly made it plain that he intended to use his newly won parliamentary power to bring an end to democracy. In fact, the Nazis were in disarray at the time, and, had there been the political will amongst those with power, Hitler could have been stopped in his tracks. But the traditional pillars of the government, the president and his advisers, as well as the churches and the intellectual elite,[105] had already rejected a parliamentary solution to Germany's problems. They thus found themselves virtually without any other option but to open the door and welcome in Hitler.[106]

Christian attitudes towards Weimar varied, but on the whole they were wary and lukewarm.[107] The Catholic Centre Party was one of the major players in the Republic, and the Catholic hierarchy and laity generally gave their support to the task of building a more democratic society in line with revisionist Vatican social teaching. Between 1919 and 1933, five of the Chancellors were devout Catholics and the situation was more favourable to the Catholic church than it was to the Protestants. The firm leadership of the papacy was in strong contrast to both a weak *Reich* and a fragmented Protestantism.[108] At the same time, the constitutional policy of the Weimar Republic with regard to Catholic schools was of major concern to the hierarchy, hence the plans to establish a concordat between the Vatican and Germany.[109] With the memory of Bismark's *Kulturkampf* still fresh in their minds, the hierarchy was particularly concerned about protecting Catholic interests rather than wider social issues.

There was some early Catholic opposition to Hitler and Nazi ideology, notably by Cardinal Michael von Faulhaber and Count Conrad von Preysing, bishop of Berlin, who was later

[105] Alice Gallin, *Midwives to Nazism: University Professors in Weimar Germany, 1925–1933*, Macon, Georgia: Mercer University Press, 1986.
[106] Bracher, *German Dictatorship*, pp. 221f; Mary Fulbrook, *A Concise History of Germany*, Cambridge University Press, 1993, p. 178.
[107] See Klaus Scholder, *The Churches and the Third Reich*, vol. 1, 1918–34, London: SCM, 1977, pp. 3ff.
[108] Scholder, 'Eugenio Pacelli and Karl Barth', (1980) in *Requiem for Hitler*, pp. 64f.
[109] Scholder, *Churches and the Third Reich*, vol. 1, pp. 146ff.

connected with some leading individuals in the resistance movement.[110] But, in reaction to Nazi attacks upon the priesthood and Catholic internationalism, protest was mixed with 'strong affirmations of patriotism and national loyalty'.[111] It was a leader of the Centre Party and a canon lawyer, Ludwig Kaas, who advocated co-operation with the Nazis, and then in July 1933 concluded the negotiations for the concordat. But now, with Hitler in power, the context was totally different. The concordat effectively silenced official Catholic opposition and gave international respectability to the regime.[112] Moreover, as the country became ungovernable, and fears about a Communist take over increased, the right wing of the Centre Party became more influential. In 1933 the Centre Party was ditched by the hierarchy and dissolved, which meant that the one possible political power base which could have opposed Hitler was surrendered without a shot being fired. Following the example of the hierarchy, Catholics generally gave their support to Hitler, and Franz von Papen, previously leader of the Centre Party, helped engineer Hitler's seizure of power.[113]

The various autonomous Protestant *Landeskirche* (Lutheran, Reformed, or Church of the Union in which Lutheran and Reformed were united) had little time for Weimar. For them it was a symbol of a decadent culture. With its hopes pinned on the restoration of the monarchy, Protestantism was the bastion of reaction, and nationalism part of its theological creed.[114] Some support was given when Hindenburg became president in 1925, but that was because he was anti-democratic and monarchist in his sympathies. German Protestants were by tradition not only anti-Communist, but also anti-democratic

[110] Klemens von Klemperer, *German Resistance against Hitler: the Search for Allies Abroad*, London: Oxford University Press, 1992, p. 46.

[111] Gordon C. Zahn, 'Catholic Opposition to Hitler: The Perils of Ambiguity', in James E. Wood, Jr., ed., *Readings on Church and State*, Waco, p. 297.

[112] Klemperer, *German Resistance against Hitler*, p. 38; Scholder, *The Churches and the Third Reich*, vol. 1, pp. 64f.; Scholder, 'Political Resistance or Self-Assertion as Problem for Church Governments', (1985) in *Requiem for Hitler*, p. 131.

[113] Klemperer, *German Resistance against Hitler*, 1992, p. 38.

[114] Scholder, *Requiem for Hitler*, p. 49.

and anti-Semitic, so that whatever qualms they might have had regarding Hitler or Nazi propaganda, they felt an affinity with the 'national revolution'. Hence their strong antipathy to the League of Nations and the emerging ecumenical movement – regarded by many pastors as a betrayal of the Reformation and Germany – and their commitment to the *Volk*.[115] This was true even of some church leaders who later became ardent opponents of the regime, such as Martin Niemöller.

In a curious disregard for their own traditional understanding of the political realm, Protestant theologians did not esteem the Weimar government as ordained by God, but as a usurper of the divinely established order of 'throne and altar', and therefore unworthy of loyalty and obedience.[116] They might not have liked Hitler, but they accepted him as a leader who could rescue the nation from disaster. '"Yes to the state, no to democracy" was the slogan of many Protestants who accepted voluntarily the transition to the dictatorship of Adolf Hitler.'[117] Some leading Lutheran theologians even provided Nazism with theological legitimation.[118] But, even amongst the more critical, there was an inability to discern the inseparable linkage between the gospel and human rights.[119]

The 'Kirchenkampf' and the resistance

Dietrich Bonhoeffer was one of very few German theologians who perceived the real nature of the Nazi menace from the beginning, just as he was virtually the only theologian involved in the German resistance.[120] On the day on which Hitler was installed as Chancellor, Bonhoeffer attacked the *Führerprinzip* in a sermon preached on state radio. True leadership, he

---

[115] James A. Zabel, *Nazism and the Pastors*, Missoula, Montana: Scholars' Press, 1976, pp. 77f.

[116] Klemperer, *German Resistance against Hitler*, p. 38.

[117] Huber, in Witte, *Christianity and Democracy*, p. 45.

[118] Robert P. Erikson, *Theologians under Hitler*, New Haven, Conn.: Yale University Press, 1985.

[119] Franz Hildebrandt, *Gospel and Humanitarianism*, unpublished D.Phil., Cambridge University, 1941.

[120] Eberhard Bethge, *Dietrich Bonhoeffer: Theologian, Christian, Contemporary*, London: Collins, 1970, pp. 626ff.

declared, could never be equated with dictatorship and blind obedience to it.[121] Not surprisingly the sermon was cut off in midstream.[122]

Many Protestant pastors tried to remain neutral, and some joined the Nazi aligned *Deutsche Christen*, but a significant number became members of the Confessing Synod of the *Evangelische Kirche*, and joined in the *Kirchenkampf* ('church struggle') against the Nazi attempt to control the church. Constituted on the basis of the Barmen Declaration adopted at its first synod in October 1934,[123] the Confessing church[124] regarded its task primarily as a struggle for the gospel and the freedom of the church from Nazi ideology. British and North American Christians wrongly perceived it as a struggle for religious liberty and democracy.[125]

With their memories of Weimar still vividly alive, the delegates at Barmen did not want 'the state to become locked into the form of the liberal, constitutional state'.[126] Many were prepared to work within the Third Reich as given by God. The Lutheran doctrine of the 'two kingdoms' was deeply rooted. At the same time, the Barmen Declaration was one of the few representative documents of the period which rejected totalitarian rule.[127] In stressing the common responsibility of rulers and ruled, the Declaration implicitly pronounced 'in favour of democratic structures'.[128] As the conflict intensified, so class,

---

[121] Dietrich Bonhoeffer, '*Der Führer und der einzelne in der jungen Generation*', in *Gesammelte Schriften*, vol. 2, Munich: Chr. Kaiser Verlag, 1956, pp. 22ff.

[122] Bethge, *Dietrich Bonhoeffer*, pp. 193f.

[123] See especially Scholder, *The Church and the Third Reich*; John Conway, *The Nazi Persecution of the Churches*, New York: Basic Books, 1968; Guenter Lewy, *The Catholic Church and Nazi Germany*, New York: McGraw-Hill, 1964.

[124] There was no Catholic equivalent of the Confessing church, but Catholic Action, the Catholic Youth League, and Catholic trade unionists, were courageous in their resistance to Nazism.

[125] Karl Barth, 'Karl Barth Answers a Question', *The British Weekly*, 22 April 1937.

[126] Eberhard Jüngel, *Christ, Justice and Peace: Toward a Theology of the State*, Edinburgh: T. and T. Clark, 1992, p. 52.

[127] Barth, the main drafter of the Declaration was a social democrat, and opponents were not slow to condemn Barmen as being tainted by his Calvinist democratic convictions. See Jüngel, *ibid.*, p. 42.

[128] See Article Five of the Barmen Declaration. Huber, in Witte, *Christianity and Democracy*, p. 45; Huber, 'The Barmen Declaration and the Kairos Document: On

age, and gender differences between the members of the Confessing church became less significant than was traditionally
the case within German Protestantism.

At the same time, many Confessing church pastors failed to
recognize the danger of aligning Christianity with German
nationalism, and some were even members of the National
Socialist Party.[129] The dividing line within the Confessing
church was drawn by the question of the legitimacy of the Nazi
regime. Was it right to work within the system in order to
change it, or was it necessary to resist and overthrow it?[130]
Bonhoeffer chose the latter path. In doing so he opened up new
possibilities for the future of Christianity in Germany,
especially in post-war East Germany. But the Confessing
church as a whole, despite the courage and suffering of many of
its members, was too compromised and concerned about its
own survival to fulfil its early promise. Most tragically, it
remained silent on the persecution of the Jews.[131]

Whatever the faults of the Confessing church, Hitler and the
Nazi leadership regarded it as a political threat. Any organization which sought to retain its own autonomy, especially one
which had such a large and widespread membership, was an
enemy. The mere existence of a church which asserted its
freedom was an affirmation of a civil society which defied
totalitarian rule. In a situation where all other opposition was
being systematically crushed, it was self-evident to the Nazis
that this expression of freedom held out the promise of resistance, and resistance on one issue implied resistance to the
whole system. Even if the churches were only an 'involuntary
resistance movement'[132] they were a threat to Nazi domination. The church was a symbol of values which transcended
and judged those espoused by the regime.

This was made dramatically explicit by the belated papal

the Relationship between Confession and Politics', *Journal of Theology for Southern
Africa*, 75; Jüngel, *Christ, Justice and Peace*, p. 15.
[129] Zabel, *Nazism and the Pastors*, p. 226.   [130] Bracher, *German Dictatorship*, p. 476.
[131] Eberhard Bethge, 'Dietrich Bonhoeffer and the Jews', in John D. Godsey and
Geffrey B. Kelly, eds., *Ethical Responsibility: Bonhoeffer's Legacy to the Churches*, New
York and Toronto: Edwin Mellen, 1981.
[132] Bracher, *German Dictatorship*, p. 474.

attack on National Socialism in the encyclical *Mit brennender Sorge* read from all Catholic pulpits on 21 March 1937.[133] A year earlier the Confessing church had issued a memorandum to all its pastors and congregations condemning the illegal character of the concentration camps and the actions of the Gestapo, as well as challenging the assumption that Hitler's will was 'the norm not only of political decisions but also of the morality and rights of our people'.[134] But by now, especially as he prepared for war, Hitler had given up on winning over the church to his aims, and had resolved to leave the church question until the larger struggle had been fought and won.[135]

In sum, the role of the churches, as distinct from the courageous witness of many individual Christians, in resisting National Socialism, was limited in scope and much of it came too late. Significantly, no German bishops, either Catholic or Protestant, were arrested by the Gestapo for political reasons during the war. Resistance came 'from pastors, communities and individual Christians' who 'had to bear the full burden of the persecution', quite often without any support from their respective church authorities.[136] Protestants and Catholics became involved in the Kreisau Circle which plotted the attempted assassination of Hitler, and, like Bonhoeffer, died as a result of its failure. Such resistance arose out of a troubled Christian conscience combined with a deep sense of loyalty to the Fatherland; it was elitist, patriotic, and national in ethos, as can be detected even in Bonhoeffer's own writings.[137] There was a growing sense of revulsion with regard to what Hitler and his cohorts were actually doing to the life of the nation, rather than a commitment to any democratic alternative.

Bonhoeffer himself, as a German Lutheran, was not a con-

---

[133] Nathaniel Micklem, *National Socialism and the Roman Catholic Church*, London: Oxford University Press, 1939, pp. 170f.

[134] Bracher, *German Dictatorship*, p. 477.

[135] Scholder, 'Politics and Church Politics in the Third Reich', (1983) in *Requiem for Hitler*, p. 155; Bracher, *German Dictatorship*, p. 483.

[136] Scholder, 'Political Resistance or Self Assertion', in *Requiem for Hitler*, p. 138.

[137] Keith Clements, *A Patriotism for Today: Dialogue with Dietrich Bonhoeffer*, London: Collins, 1986.

vinced democrat, at least, not of the liberal variety. He was also sceptical about the chances of democracy solving Europe's problems in the post-war era, and deeply fearful of what he called 'bolshevism'.[138] He was only too mindful of the failure of Weimar and its consequences. Yet Bonhoeffer's theology, his understanding of human freedom, sociality, and justice, as well as his participation in the resistance, all had far-reaching democratic implications. Moreover, for Bonhoeffer, the deep schism between the witness of the church and the values of modernity had been breached by those Christians and their secular compatriots who were involved in the struggle against tyranny and the struggle for a new and just political order. Reflecting on this, Bonhoeffer remarked:

Reason, culture, humanity, tolerance and self-determination, all these concepts which until very recently had served as battle slogans against the Church, against Christianity, against Jesus Christ himself, had now, suddenly and surprisingly, come very near indeed to the Christian standpoint.[139]

This perceptive insight is of particular significance for our project. It indicates how in the struggle against tyranny and for democracy in our century – the case studies in the next three chapters will further substantiate this – secular humanists and Christians have found each other, and discovered the extent to which the emancipatory values of truth, freedom, and justice are as, if not more, deeply rooted in biblical prophetic faith than the Enlightenment. This points us forward to our final chapter where we will discuss the theological basis for a genuinely just democratic global order, and where we will suggest how democracy as the polity of modernity may overcome the latter's contradictions. But it also brings us more immediately to a brief consideration of the way in which ecumenical Christianity has retrieved democracy as an essential element in Christian political witness in the course of the twentieth century.

[138] Bonhoeffer, 'The Church and the new order in Europe', in *Gesammelte Schriften*, vol. 1, Munich: Chr. Kaiser Verlag, 1965, pp. 362ff.
[139] Bonhoeffer, *Ethics*, p. 55.

AN ECUMENICAL RETRIEVAL OF DEMOCRACY

The churches of those countries ranged against Nazism and Fascism, together with their political leaders, regarded the Second World War as a struggle for democracy. As a result there was a strong tendency to equate democracy with the will of God. With this in mind, shortly before the outbreak of the Second World War, T. S. Eliot rejected the prevailing notion that it was self-evident that 'democracy is the only regime compatible with Christianity'.[140] None the less, there were other Christian theologians and leaders, such as Barth in Switzerland, Bishop Temple and A. D. Lindsay in England, Reinhold Niebuhr in the United States, and the French Catholic philosopher Jacques Maritain in exile in New York, who, at a more profound level than the popular, recognized that the struggle against totalitarianism and the struggle for democracy were intrinsically related to the Christian gospel. Careful not to equate democracy with liberal individualism or capitalism, they added a new depth to the Christian understanding of democracy, and to the debate about a new just post-war world order. In doing so, they were also influential in shaping the social thought of the World Council of Churches which came into existence in 1948.

Throughout the war the ecumenical movement provided support for Christians and churches engaged in the struggle against totalitarianism. To begin with, such solidarity was understandably tentative, given the fledgling character of the movement and the need to define goals and strategies, but the onslaught of Fascism and Nazism swiftly sharpened the ecumenical mind. This led, in turn, to the beginnings of what has since become a worthy history of Christian solidarity with those engaged in the struggle against the enemies of equality, freedom, and justice in their respective countries. Thus the rise and fall of the Third Reich was the catalyst which re-opened the Christian debate about democracy, and helped churches to retrieve it as part of their own Christian inheritance in the struggles for democracy after the war.

[140] T. S. Eliot *The Idea of a Christian Society*, London: Faber and Faber, 1939, p. 15.

Democracy as a theme in itself, however, has not been a subject of much discussion within the World Council of Churches during the twentieth century.[141] This lack should not be misconstrued. Part of the reason was the virtual identification of democracy with western interests which meant, especially during the cold war era, that Christian support for democracy was equated with political allegiance to the West – a major problem for an ecumenical council seeking to serve member churches across the ideological divide of East and West. The fact that much right-wing Christianity today equates its cause with the defence of western interests under the ideological rubric of liberal democratic capitalism, remains a problem. None the less, a perusal of the literature indicates a long and intense concern about the need for a just democratic world order, as was already evident at the celebrated Oxford Conference on Life and Work in 1937, and at the founding Assembly of the WCC at Amsterdam in 1948.[142] Throughout the century, in response to Fascism, nationalism, Communism and liberal capitalism, the desirable human society has been described in ways which 'espouse forms of democratic organization, people's participation and human rights and responsibilities' – the key phrases being a responsible society; a just, participatory, and sustainable society, and now justice, peace, and the integrity of creation.[143]

Nothing demonstrates more dramatically the shift in Christian social thought with regard to democracy than that which has taken place within Roman Catholic social teaching during the past century since the publication of the seminal encyclical, *Rerum Novarum*, in 1891.[144] Inspired by John XXIII and

---

[141] Neither democracy nor liberal democracy feature as specific entries in the *Dictionary of the Ecumenical Movement* (edited by Nicholas Lossky, José Míguez Bonino, John S. Pobee, Tom F. Stransky, Geoffrey Wainwright, and Pauline Webb, Geneva: WCC, 1991) though socialism does. The same is true of Paul Albrecht's essay on 'The Development of Ecumenical Social Thought and Action', in Harold E. Fey, ed., *The Ecumenical Advance: A History of the Ecumenical Movement*, vol. 2, 1948–68, pp. 233ff.

[142] Ruth Rouse and Stephen Charles Neill, eds., *A History of the Ecumenical Movement, 1517–1948*, London: SPCK, 1967, pp. 597ff., 719f.

[143] José Míguez Bonino, in *Dictionary of the Ecumenical Movement*, p. 417.

[144] Coleman, *One Hundred Years of Catholic Social Teaching*, pp. 13ff.

directed by Vatican II, Catholic social teaching has sought to affirm democracy as the best way to promote the common good, while critically distancing itself from both the individualism and capitalism of liberal democracy and the collectivism and state economies of socialism. At the same time it has affirmed the liberal values of freedom and tolerance, while giving its support to what is broadly speaking a social democratic welfare approach to economics and labour questions. Catholic social teaching has yet to 'propose workable alternative institutions and ideals to the regnant liberal and socialist institutions',[145] but it is positively engaged in the current debate.

There can be little doubt, then, that the long history of Christian antipathy towards democracy, which began with the Enlightenment and the birth of modernity, is largely at an end. There can also be no doubt that the ecumenical church today regards the democratic *vision* as consonant with, even if not identical to, that of the prophets of ancient Israel and its own vision of a just world order, or that the democratic *system* provides the best available way of embodying that vision within political structures and amidst historical realities.

[145] *Ibid.*, p. 39.

Churches and the struggle for democracy

CHAPTER 5

Civil rights and liberation in the Americas

In this and the next two chapters we shall consider several case studies in order to illustrate and analyze the role which churches have played in the struggle for democracy since the end of the Second World War. In doing so we will pay close attention to the understanding of democracy and related theological insights which emerged in the process.

We have chosen five very different contexts for these studies: the United States of America, Nicaragua, sub-Saharan Africa, the former German Democratic Republic, and South Africa. These broadly represent the global context, the varieties of Christian denomination, and the different ways in which churches have participated in the democratic process. They are also paradigmatic in illustrating the issues which are fundamental to the relationship between Christianity and democracy at the end of our century, and cumulative in their impact and significance, even though the specifics of each is quite different from the others.

THE CIVIL RIGHTS MOVEMENT IN THE UNITED STATES

The theme song of the Civil Rights movement in the United States in the 1960s, 'We Shall Overcome', has been sung around the world by those engaged in the struggle for freedom and justice. From San Salvador to Soweto, from Berlin to Beijing, it has symbolized the best of America's offerings to a humanity in search of a better world.[1] For the oppressed of the

---

[1] Vincent Harding, *Hope and History: Why We Must Share the Story of the Movement*, Maryknoll, N.Y.: Orbis, 1990, p. 28.

world, it is not the democratic ideology of America as superpower which is admired and desired, but the democracy which
was expressed in the black struggle for civil rights and the
democratic vision of Martin Luther King, Jr. Few political
struggles have demonstrated so clearly both the shortcomings
of liberal democracy and yet its potential as the basis for
moving towards a more just order.[2] Equally few have shown
how civil religion can have such conflicting results – American
expansionism, on the one hand, and a genuine concern for
global human rights, on the other – and be justified by Christians in terms of their divergent reading of the gospel.[3]

The roots of the Civil Rights struggle may be traced back to
the beginning of the colonial period and the way in which
African slaves were treated, largely by Christian colonists, even
though slave-owning was condemned by many churches long
before the Civil War.[4] As the Civil War approached, and as the
tensions which separated South and North grew in intensity, so
some of the major churches, notably the Baptists, Methodists,
and Presbyterians, divided over the issue of slavery.[5] Yet for as
long as a century after the Civil War, legitimated by the North
as a fight for the freedom of slaves, African Americans
remained second-class citizens in 'a *Herrenvolk* democracy'[6]
ravaged by racism. In the South, the discrimination was crass
and often brutal; in the North, it was more subtle. Yet, as Anna
Hedgeman, one of the few women in a leadership position
within the Civil Rights movement points out, this difference
was not one of basic philosophy: 'In the South the weapon was

[2] On the Civil Rights movement and especially the role of Martin Luther King Jr., see
David J. Garrow, *Bearing the Cross: Martin Luther King, Jr., and the Southern Christian
Leadership Conference*, New York: Vintage Books, Random House, 1988.

[3] Andrew Michael Manis, *Southern Civil Religions in Conflict: Black and White Baptists and
Civil Rights, 1947–1957*, Athens, Ga.: University of Georgia Press, 1987, pp. 108f.

[4] Robert D. Linder, 'A Christian Approach to the Contemporary Civil Rights
Movement', in Robert G. Clouse, Robert D. Linder, and Richard V. Pierard, *Protest
and Politics: Christianity and Contemporary Affairs*, Greenwood, S.C.: Attic Press, 1968,
p. 125.

[5] H. Richard Niebuhr, *The Social Sources of Denominationalism*, New York: Meridian
Books, 1957, pp. 236ff.

[6] James Melvin Washington ed., Introduction, *A Testament of Hope: The Essential
Writings of Martin Luther King, Jr.*, p. xvi.

a meat axe; in the North, a stiletto. Both are lethal weapons. It was a long time before I knew that they are as lethal to the wielders as to the victims.'[7]

From Reconstruction until the Second World War the struggle for black civil rights was muted and without much effect. The major agency for securing such rights was the National Association for the Advancement of Colored People (NAACP) whose approach was to work through the system to achieve its goals. The NAACP scored a major victory with the 1954 Supreme Court decision which declared that the 'separate but equal' education policy, in place since 1896, was inherently unequal. But the strategy of the NAACP was as slow in changing social reality as it was deliberate in its intent. The Civil Rights movement was born, by way of contrast, out of a growing impatience with the daily reality of racism.

Baptists: black and white

Women were in the forefront of the struggle from the beginning, though few ever made it into the ranks of the Civil Rights movement's leadership.[8] The rights of women were not regarded by males as part of the agenda, and their cause was often opposed in the supposed interests of the broader struggle. None the less, the movement began with a courageous act of civil disobedience when middle-aged Rosa Parks refused to give up her bus seat to a white passenger. This led to the Montgomery Bus Boycott and 382 days of protest action by the local black community. Soon the protest gathered wider support within the black community in the South. In the process, a young Baptist pastor in Montgomery, Martin Luther King, Jr., became the acknowledged spokesperson, the founder of the Southern Christian Leadership Conference (SCLC) in 1957 and the national leader of the growing movement.[9]

[7] Anna Arnold Hedgeman, *The Trumpet Sounds: A Memoir of Negro Leadership*, New York: Holt, Rinehart, and Winston, 1964, p. 39.
[8] Paula Giddings, *When and Where I Enter: The Impact of Black Women on Race and Sex in America*, New York: Bantam Books, 1984, pp. 261ff.
[9] Garrow, *Bearing the Cross*, chapters 1–2.

King's training, skills, and charisma made him the obvious choice for this role, but his rise to leadership would not have been possible without the support of a growing number of other black Baptist pastors in the structures of the SCLC staff. As James Washington reminds us: 'no part of the middle-class black leadership felt the need and pressure to overthrow segregation more than did black ministers. They counseled the victims of this infamous system. They buried the victims of white mob violence. They laboured to relieve the psychic and economic depression largely caused by racist injustice. And they were among the first to openly denounce and actively oppose racist oppression.'[10] The meetings of SCLC resembled Baptist Sunday services; its statements were clothed in, and its actions justified by, reference to prophetic passages of Scripture.[11]

Not all within the black church supported King or the SCLC. Some preferred to avoid political issues; others preferred the more cautious approach of the NAACP; yet others opted for the more radical approach of the Black Power movement, or the leadership of Black Muslim Malcolm X.[12] But many students rallied to King's cause through the formation of SNCC (Student Non-Violent Co-ordinating Committee), and, as the Civil Rights movement gathered momentum, so the black church increasingly threw its weight behind King's leadership. Without this the Civil Rights movement would have been an impossibility. During 1964 alone thirty-eight black churches in Mississippi were fire-bombed, sufficient and compelling evidence of the role of the black church,[13] and an indication of the nature and extent of white opposition.

The origins of the black or Afro-American church can be traced to the religion of the slaves and their decision, as Cornel

---

[10] Washington, *A Testament of Hope*, p. xvii.

[11] Adam Fairclough, *To Redeem the Soul of America: the Southern Christian Leadership Conference and Martin Luther King, Jr.*, Athens, Georgia: The University of Georgia Press, 1987, p. 1.

[12] For a comparison of King and Malcolm X see James H. Cone, *Martin and Malcolm and America: A Dream or Nightmare*, New York: Orbis, 1991.

[13] Linder, in Clouse, et al., *Protest and Politics*, p. 122.

West puts it, to 'choose to follow Jesus'.[14] Unwelcome in the dominant white Baptist and Methodist churches, they created, sustained, and controlled the only black institution which became 'the most visible and salient cultural product of black people in the United States'.[15] From the outset it was a dissenting tradition which 'provided many black slaves with a sense of somebodiness, a personal and egalitarian God who gave them an identity and dignity not found in American society', just as it was Baptist congregational polity which gave them control over their own churches.[16] The resultant piety – a blend of African spirituality and evangelical faith – was a mechanism for coping with harsh reality, but also a resource for defiance.[17]

From the end of the Civil War to the beginning of the Civil Rights movement, the black church as an instrument of solidarity and liberation 'collapsed under the weight of a ghettoized version of American fundamentalism'.[18] Protest was limited and there was widespread demoralization.[19] Blacks had become vulnerable to the propaganda that decreed their inferiority. In spite of its dissenting origins, the black church had become authoritarian, patriarchal, dominated by populist preachers, and stifling of creativity and democratic participation.[20]

A similar denial of their dissenting heritage occurred within the Southern Baptist Convention[21] which had also become hierarchical and patriarchal in ethos, and which increasingly

[14] Cornel West, *Prophetic Fragments*, Grand Rapids: Eerdmans, 1988, p. 4.
[15] *Ibid.*
[16] *Ibid.*, p. 43.
[17] Vincent Harding, 'Religion and Resistance Among Antebellum Negroes, 1800–1860', in John M. Mulder and John F. Wilson, eds., *Religion in American History: Interpretative Essays*, Englewood Cliffs, N.J.: Prentice-Hall, 1978, p. 271; see also E. Franklin Frazier, *The Negro Church in America*, New York: Schocken Books, 1964; Raboteau *Slave Religion*.
[18] Gayraud S. Wilmore and James H. Cone, *Black Theology: A Documentary History, 1966–1979*, Maryknoll, N.Y.: Orbis, 1979, p. 245.
[19] Peter J. Paris, *The Social Teaching of the Black Churches*, Philadelphia: Fortress, 1985, p. 71.
[20] Frazier, *The Negro Church in America*, p. 86.
[21] At least 25 per cent of the white South, and even more of the black, was Baptist by affiliation in the 1950s, though separated in two major denominations (the white Southern Baptist Convention and the black National Baptist Convention). Manis, *Southern Civil Religions in Conflict*, p. 6.

used its congregational polity to protect local white community interests. When these were threatened by the Civil Rights movement, Baptist fundamentalism blended with white racism and a distorted patriotism to provide the basis for much of the opposition. Their vision was of 'a traditional, homogeneous and evangelically Christian' country in which American democracy, which meant the 'southern way of life', was protected against the inroads of international Communism – of which the Civil Rights movement was the vanguard. This reveals the shadow-side of American 'civil religion' which restricted the American dream to whites and remained ever fearful of the demands which others might make or enact.[22] Blacks perceived that 'America was only a potentially Christian nation' and that external threats were 'insignificant compared to the internal threat of hypocrisy with respect to the nation's deepest values'.[23]

Racial bigotry was a fundamental threat to America's democratic and moral tradition. But racism, as King argued, was also a blatant denial of Christian unity, which made the conquest of segregation 'an inescapable *must* confronting the church'.[24] There were several specific things which King believed the church could do: deal with the fears, suspicions, and misunderstandings which lead to racism; communicate the real intentions and desires of blacks; make Christian non-racial community a reality; and get rid of segregation in its own ranks. The church, King noted, has a schism in its own soul that it must close.[25]

Some white ministers and congregations in the South sought ways to defy the racist norms of their culture, and most of the major denominations, from Roman Catholic to Methodist, and smaller churches such as the Mennonite and Quaker, issued statements in support of the Civil Rights movement. But this

[22] Cornel West, *The American Evasion of Philosophy: A Genealogy of Pragmatism*, Madison, Wisconsin: University of Madison Press, 1989, p. 5.
[23] Manis, *Southern Civil Religions in Conflict*, p. 106.
[24] King, *Stride Towards Freedom: The Montgomery Story*, New York: Harper & Row, 1958, p. 205.
[25] *Ibid.*, pp. 207f.

was not true of the majority of white Christians.[26] Most white
church leaders in the South stood critically aloof, and many of
those in the North, who initially supported King, retreated
once the movement impinged on their interests. Support for
King only became more popular amongst whites after the
emergence of Black Power made his non-violence the better of
two evils.[27]

The tragedy in all this was that a cause so clearly Christian,
and so obviously in line with the Bill of Rights, met such
opposition.[28] Nothing better illustrates what Gunnar Myrdal
called the 'American dilemma': how to remain committed to
the equality enshrined in the Constitution and teachings of
Christianity, yet maintain white superiority and control.[29] Few
white Americans realized the extent to which democracy in the
United States was compromised by the disenfranchizement of
blacks in the South,[30] and the extent to which the future of
democracy was dependent upon the success of the Civil Rights
struggle.

King: a prophetic democrat

Although the Civil Rights movement was much bigger than
King, he was its prophet and his philosophy was firmly
stamped upon its policies and programmes.[31] There was, in
Vincent Harding's words, a 'dialectical movement between an
inspired and inspiring people and an inspired and inspiring
pro-democratic leader'.[32] But King did more than provide

---

[26] John C. Bennett, *The Radical Imperative*, Philadelphia: Westminster Press, 1975. See
Wilmore and Cone, *Black Theology: A Documentary*, p. 176.

[27] James H. Cone, *Black Theology and Black Power*, New York: Seabury, 1969, p. 79.

[28] Linder, in Clouse, et al., *Protest and Politics*, p. 122.

[29] Samuel Eliot Morison, Henry Steele Commager, and William E. Leuchtenburg,
The Growth of the American Republic, vol. 2, seventh edition, New York: Oxford
University Press, 1980, pp. 685ff. Myrdal's hypothesis is the point of departure for
one of the seminal books on the 'black church', C. Eric Lincoln, *Race, Religion, and
the Continuing American Dilemma*, New York: Hill and Wang, 1984.

[30] King, 'Civil Right No. 1: The Right to Vote', *New York Times*, 14 March 1965, in
Washington, *A Testament of Hope*, p. 182.

[31] On the development of King's thought, see John J. Ansbro, *Martin Luther King, Jr.:
The Making of a Mind*, New York: Orbis, 1984.

[32] Harding, *Hope and History*, p. 35.

leadership, he also began to change perceptions within the white churches as well as the broader community.[33] He was able to bridge the protest piety of the black church in the South and the progressive intellectual culture of the North, and thus build a political alliance vital for the success of the movement.[34]

The ideological basis King developed was a creative blend of the black slave protest tradition, the 'Social Gospel', Gandhi's non-violent philosophy of resistance derived in part from Jesus' Sermon on the Mount, and what West calls the prophetic American civil religion which 'fuses secular and sacred history and combines Christian themes of deliverance and salvation with political ideals of democracy, freedom and equality'.[35] Drawing on Hegel's insight that history moves towards its goal through struggle, King regarded prophetic Christianity as the source of empowerment for that struggle, and his eschatological vision of 'the Beloved Community' as its norm and goal.[36] Understood in this way, Christianity and a just democracy were inseparable.[37] This blend of prophetic Christianity and the vision of democracy embodied in the American Constitution and its Bill of Rights, was one of the most significant models of the interconnectedness between the two traditions in the history of Christianity. In continuity with those who moulded together Christian and secular elements in founding the Republic, King sought to make that legacy racially inclusive. A just democracy was impossible within the homogeneous society envisaged by whites for whom personal liberty meant segregation; it was only possible in a pluralistic society where desegregation would be the norm.

King's espousal of American democracy and its universal mission was not a sanctification of its political expansionism, but a concern that the civil rights for which he was fighting in the United States would help human rights everywhere.[38] In

---

[33] Bennett, *The Radical Imperative*, p. 176.
[34] Fairclough, *To Redeem the Soul of America*, p. 5.
[35] West, *Prophetic Fragments*, p. 4.   [36] Ansbro, *Martin Luther King*, pp. 187f.
[37] See for example King's Speech at the Golden Anniversary of the National Urban League, 1960, in Washington, *A Testament of Hope*, p. 151.
[38] King, 'Facing the Challenge of a New Age', an address, December 1956, in Washington, *A Testament of Hope*, p. 136.

1961 King had already declared that history 'has thrust upon the present administration an indescribably important destiny – to complete a process of democratization which our nation has taken far too long to develop, but which is our most powerful weapon for earning world respect and emulation'.[39] For this reason he eventually came out against the Vietnam War, distancing himself from the political establishment and its chauvinist understanding of democracy and anti-Communism. King was committed to internationalizing the American ideals of democracy, freedom, and equality as the measure of both domestic and foreign policies.[40] At the same time he appealed to the growing victory against colonialism in Africa and elsewhere in support of his own internal crusade. 'The Negro freedom movement', King declared, 'reflects this world upheaval within the United States. It is a component of a world era of change, and that is the source of its strength and durability.'[41]

There can be little doubt that the Civil Rights movement was one of the inspirations behind the Church and Society Conference sponsored by the World Council of Churches in Geneva in 1966,[42] and subsequently the Programme to Combat Racism launched after the Fourth Assembly of the WCC held at Uppsala in July 1968. King had been scheduled to speak at the Assembly, but was assassinated earlier in the year. King's influence, and the example of the Civil Rights movement, have had a lasting impact on Christians engaged in democratic struggles in our time, notably in South Africa, but also elsewhere in Africa. As recently as September 1993, the Catholic bishops in Nigeria quoted King in their communiqué to President Babangida: 'It is time to stand erect as free citizens of a free nation.'[43]

[39] King, 'Equality Now: The President has the Power', first annual report on the Civil Rights movement, *Nation*, 192, 4 February 1961, in Washington, *A Testament of Hope*, p. 159.

[40] West, *Prophetic Fragments*, p. 12.

[41] King, 'Hammer on Civil Rights', fourth annual report on Civil Rights movement, *Nation*, 198, 9 March 1964, in Washington, *A Testament of Hope*, p. 169 ; see West, *Prophetic Fragments*, p. 11.

[42] *The World Conference on Church and Society: Official Report*, Geneva: WCC, 1967.

[43] *Communique of Plenary Meeting of the Catholic Bishops' Conference of Nigeria* 7–11 September 1993, 6,c.

Ballot or bullet?

In the early days of the Civil Rights campaign, King was convinced that the struggle for world-wide justice was irreversible. But there was an urgent need to 'speed up the coming of the inevitable'.[44] The way to do this was through non-violent action, legislation, and education, rather than violent revolution: the ballot rather than the bullet. King argued that voting was 'the foundation stone for political action'.[45] However the struggle for suffrage and for voter registration could not be separated from non-violent direct action, for such social protest was 'the hammer of social revolution'.[46] White society and even its 'democratic' institutions would not change without continual creative action which would prick the nation's conscience and force the recalcitrant to accept the need for change.[47] But the means adopted for the struggle were crucial to the nature of its outcome.

We must seek democracy and not the substitution of one tyranny for another. Our aim must never be to defeat or humiliate the white man. We must not become victimized with a philosophy of black supremacy. God is not interested merely in the freedom of black men, and brown men, and yellow men; God is interested in the freedom of the whole human race.[48]

King's non-violent strategy was essentially the way of democratic struggle, a critical building-block for the retrieval of democracy. If the primary reason for uprooting racism was the fact that it was morally wrong, then means could not be used to combat it which were themselves immoral.[49] Resistance, King argued, must always be dignified and disciplined, and never be allowed to 'degenerate to the crippling level of violence'.[50]

Yet King also acknowledged that, unless non-violent action

[44] King, 'Challenge of a New Age', in Washington, *A Testament of Hope*, p. 141.
[45] King, 'Civil Right No. 1', in *ibid.*, p. 183.
[46] King, 'Hammer on Civil Rights', in *ibid.*, p. 169.
[47] King, 'Civil Right No. 1', in *ibid.*, p. 188.
[48] King, *Stride Towards Freedom*, p. 220.
[49] King, 'The Rising Tide of Racial Consciousness', *YWCA Magazine*, December 1960, in Washington, *A Testament of Hope*, pp. 147f.
[50] *Ibid.*, p. 148.

led to meaningful change, it would be discredited and this would force others to resort to violent strategies to achieve their goals.[51] King was deeply concerned about the rise of the Black Power movement, led by Stokely Carmichael, opposing it from the outset as counter-productive to the cause of civil rights. After 1965, however, especially after the violent riots in Watts, and with the worsening of the Vietnam War, many activists, who had previously supported King's philosophy of non-violence and his dream of a truly democratic America, despaired both of such tactics and such hopes. Even King himself began to wonder whether his dream could be realized in the way in which he had hitherto pinned his hopes, though he remained committed to non-violent and non-racial strategies to the end of his life. Perhaps the only way forward was in critical tandem with those who chose other strategies of political engagement.

One of the serious lacunae in the Civil Rights movement was its failure to grapple in any depth with economic issues, or to draw the connection between racism and class stratification.[52] King had read Marx, and, though he firmly rejected Communism as un-Christian and even evil, he recognized in Marx's protest the voice of a Hebrew prophet concerned about the poor.[53] King wanted a world 'in which men will no longer take necessities from the masses to give luxuries to the classes; a world in which all men will respect the dignity and worth of all human personality'.[54] Hence he continuously sought ways to keep the movement in touch with the mass of the people. Towards the end of his life he also began to endorse a more socialist democratic vision which, on the basis of the rule of law and the protection of individual liberties, promoted 'a "person-centred rather than a property-centred and profit-centred"

[51] King, 'Negroes are Not Moving too Fast', *Saturday Evening Post*, 237, 7 November 1964, in *ibid.*, p. 180.
[52] James H. Cone, *For My People: Black Theology and the Black Church*, New York: Orbis, 1984, pp. 176f.
[53] Ansbro, *Martin Luther King*, pp. 183f.
[54] King, 'Facing the Challenge of a New Age', in Washington, *A Testament of Hope*, p. 144.

economy'.[55] But there was no clear economic policy which guided the thinking of the movement as such. Moreover, the economic gap between whites and blacks in the United States widened rather than closed in the decade that followed the signing of the Civil Rights Act. That is one reason why, despite the successes which the movement achieved, 'liberation did not follow; Black Power did'.[56]

The possibility that King's dream might turn into a nightmare was given its most powerful articulation by Malcolm X. In several speeches in 1964 Malcolm X spoke with dramatic effect of the need for using both the ballot and the bullet in order to achieve the goals of the black nationalist cause. What separated Americans, he argued, was not whether they were Baptists, Methodists, or Muslims, but the fact that they were black or white. The cards were stacked against blacks ever being able to be truly American. Speaking in a Methodist church in Cleveland, Ohio, Malcolm X spoke of American democracy as 'disguised hypocrisy', of which blacks were the victims. 'I don't see any American dream', he declared, 'I see an American nightmare.'[57] Blacks and whites could not overcome together for the 'black man (sic) was on his own'.

Malcolm X's reference to the 'bullet', as James Cone comments, was in continuity with his previous understanding of black strategy. His recognition of the ballot, however, opened up the way for some meaningful contact and co-operation with King.[58] Kept apart by different backgrounds and perspectives, the one coming from the ghettos of the urban North and a convert to the militant Black Muslims, the other from the rural South and a product of Baptist piety and American liberalism, Malcolm X and King represented two distinct paths trod by Afro-Americans. Just as political events were beginning to shatter King's earlier dreams and confidence in the American democratic system, so Malcolm X's exposure to other parts of

[55] West, *Prophetic Fragments*, p. 9.
[56] Herbert O. Edwards, 'Black Theology and Liberation Theology', in Sergio Torres and John Eagleson, eds., *Theology in the America*, Maryknoll, NY.: Orbis, 1976, p. 188.
[57] Quoted in Cone, *Martin and Malcolm and America*, p. 1.   [58] *Ibid.*, pp. 198f.

the world was pushing him towards a more co-operative and universal perspective within the struggle for black empowerment.[59] Thus, as Cone concludes, both King and Malcolm X provided a profound critique of American Christianity, and especially white Christianity, the one speaking as a prophet from within, the other as a critic from without. For both the target was racism, but it was also anything else which oppresses and dehumanizes people whether black or white; for both the vision was of a just world in which 'the beloved community of humankind' would be realized.[60]

Women's rights and prophetic pragmatism

Writing in the 1830s, de Tocqueville expressed his conviction that American democracy was providential for the world. Others earlier this century, before the rise of totalitarianism, surmised that there was a natural, irreversible, social trend whereby such democracy would spread throughout the globe.[61] And the events of 1989 have revitalized that debate, with some political scientists optimistically asserting that the United States can promote global democracy.[62] What they have in mind is at best classical liberal democracy with its free and fair elections, fundamental liberties and individual freedoms, multi-party systems, non-partisan security forces, and an independent judiciary. At worst, they have in mind North American military and economic hegemony.

Yet, as King, and more recently Cornel West and feminist theologians such as Rosemary Radford Ruether and Rebecca Chopp have recognized, there are other vital dimensions to the founding vision of American democracy that have to be part of the global retrieval of democracy, in critical tension or even confrontation with liberal democratic capitalism. These dimensions can also be traced to the vision of the 'founding fathers'

---

[59] *Ibid.*, p. 211.   [60] *Ibid.*, p. 318.

[61] See Samuel Huntington, 'Will More Countries Become Democratic?' *Political Science Quarterly*, 99, 2, Summer 1984, 196.

[62] Graham T. Allison, Jr., and Robert P. Beschel, Jr., 'Can the United States Promote Democracy?' *Political Science Quarterly*, 107, 1, Spring 1992.

and some of their successors, even though they themselves were trapped within their own racial and gender particularities despite the universal claims of their rhetoric.

The extent of the challenge facing women in the struggle for civil rights in the United States can be ascertained from the fact that the Equal Rights Amendment, which would have given constitutional force to the elimination of gender discrimination, was first proposed in 1923. Opposed by powerful political and church groups now as well as then, it was rejected.[63] Likewise since the passing of the Civil Rights Act in 1964, which explicitly prohibited discrimination in employment on the basis of race, sex, ethnicity, or national origin, 'and thirty years of affirmative action programs, men and women remain markedly unequal in the work place'.[64] The more recent attempt to get the Equal Rights Amendment passed through Congress indicates yet again the uphill nature of the task.

The struggle for women's rights in the United States can be traced back well into the nineteenth century. A significant segment of its leadership was Christian, or at least motivated by Christian notions of human equality, freedom, and justice.[65] The contemporary struggle for women's liberation and equal rights grew out of the radicalization of American politics during the Civil Rights struggles and the resistance to the Vietnam War in the 1960s. This in turn led to the development of feminist and womanist theologies, and to the emergence of the women's movement within the churches.

In her autobiographical account of the development of her theology, Ruether recounts how her experience as a white, middle-class Catholic student of the Civil Rights struggle in Mississippi was the catalyst which awoke her political consciousness and made her existentially aware of the reality of

---

[63] Patricia Altenbernd Johnson and Janet Kalven, *With Both Eyes Open: Seeing Beyond Gender*, New York: Pilgrim Press, 1988, p. 4.

[64] M. E. Hawkesworth, *Beyond Oppression: Feminist Theory and Political Strategy*, New York: Continuum, 1990, p. 55.

[65] Anne E. Carr, *Transforming Grace: Christian Tradition and Women's Experience*, San Francisco: Harper & Row, 1988, pp. 5ff.

racism and oppression.[66] Only later, in reaction to Catholic teaching on sexuality and especially contraception, did she become engaged in feminist liberation theology,[67] recognizing her own oppression as a woman within the church and society. Reflecting much later on feminism and democracy, Ruether asked whether there was a way to integrate the liberal, social, and radical feminist visions of society. Each of these traditions, she argued 'shows its limitations precisely at the point where it tries to become final and to encapsulate itself within its own system'. But each 'remains insightful and authentic to the extent that it also remains open-ended'. Her vision was of an integrative society which affirms the values of democratic participation, dismantles sexist and class hierarchies, restores ownership and management of work to the workers; an organic society in which women and men share together in all aspects of life and 'an ecological society in which human and nonhuman ecological systems have been integrated into harmonious and mutually supportive, rather than antagonistic, relations'.[68]

Ruether recognized the utopian character of her vision, and the immense obstacles to its realization, but suggested communitarian experiments as one strategy for its realization, as well as projects which would work at different elements in the vision separately. Rebecca Chopp has taken the discussion further and related it to the current debate about multi-culturalism and particularity. Feminist theology, she claims, cannot be properly understood unless placed in the locus between Christianity and democracy. But, when this happens, it can become a significant resource for developing a new relationship between Christianity and democracy, contributing to its multicultural and non-patriarchal transformation.[69] Feminist theology 'as a form of cultural politics', Chopp writes, 'envisions

---

[66] Rosemary Radford Ruether, *Disputed Questions: On Being a Christian*, New York: Maryknoll, N.Y.: Orbis, 1989, p. 76

[67] *Ibid.*, pp. 119f.

[68] Rosemary Radford Ruether, *Sexism and God-Talk: Toward a Feminist Theology*, Boston: Beacon Press, 1983, pp. 232f.

[69] Rebecca S. Chopp, 'A Feminist Perspective: Christianity, Democracy, and Feminist Theology', in Witte, *Christianity and Democracy*, p. 111.

new forms of flourishing for both common and personal good'.[70]

Fundamental to this discussion is Cornel West's notion of 'prophetic pragmatism' as a reclaiming of that pragmatic tradition in the American heritage of which the basic impulse is 'a plebian radicalism that fuels an antipatrician rebelliousness for the moral aim of enriching individuals and expanding democracy'.[71] The tradition is essentially heterogeneous, critical of hierarchy and authoritarian structures, socially transformative, and open-ended. From this perspective 'the nature, narratives and practices of democracy' have to be continually reinterpreted. This rebellious dimension to the American dream recognizes that the globalization of democracy should not be confused with the extension of western or capitalist domination. It should promote freedom with justice in ways which respect human particularities and the values of multi-cultural contexts. This has been very much in mind amongst those Christians and churches in the United States who have been involved in, and concerned about, Latin American issues. We turn, then, to our next case study, that of Nicaragua, a country of particular significance in the current process of democratization, but one at the mercy of North American interests camouflaged in the rhetoric of global democracy.[72]

DEMOCRACY AND THE STRUGGLE FOR LIBERATION IN NICARAGUA

From the beginning of the colonial era the indigenous peoples of Central America have been oppressed and steadily reduced to poverty. The revolutionary struggles of the nineteenth century were liberal bourgeois uprisings of Creole landowners against Spanish control which led to the establishment of elitist oligarchies.[73] Nicaragua became independent from Spain in

---

[70] *Ibid.*, p. 125.   [71] West, *American Evasion*, p. 5.

[72] William I. Robinson, *A Faustian Bargain: U.S. Intervention in the Nicaraguan Elections and American Foreign Policy in the Post-Cold War Era*, Oxford: Westview Press, 1992, pp. 1ff.

[73] Enrique Dussel, *A History of the Church in Latin America: Colonialism to Liberation*, Grand Rapids: Eerdmans, 1981, pp. 75ff.

1821. With the discovery of gold in California in 1848, the country took on strategic importance as a link between the Atlantic and the Pacific. Control of Nicaragua became a matter of international economic importance, especially for Britain and the United States. The latter eventually became the dominant power and has helped make or break most Nicaraguan governments ever since.[74]

During the nineteenth century, Conservative and Liberal political parties emerged in most Latin American countries and Nicaragua was no exception.[75] The Conservative Party represented the older Hispanic feudal aristocracy and closely identified with the interests of the Catholic church. The Liberal Party represented the growing bourgeoisie and was anti-clerical in attitude and policy, though supported by Protestant missions. It pursued a '*laissez-faire* capitalism which was materialist in character and exploitative in its social effects'.[76]

As in Europe, during the early decades of the twentieth century Christian Democratic parties were formed which embodied the new direction being taken in Catholic social teaching. Influenced by Jacques Maritain, who lectured in Latin America in the 1930s,[77] the new Christian Democrats 'provided a mass basis for social reform and democracy'. Located as a 'third position' (*tercerismo*) between liberal individualism and collectivist socialism, they represented 'a populist welfare-state liberalism' which, while Catholic by commitment, was similar to reformist democratic parties, whether liberal or socialist, in Europe, the United States, and the British Commonwealth.[78]

The Cuban Revolution in 1959 was a watershed in Latin American politics. This brought the Cold War directly into the

[74] Joseph E. Mulligan SJ, *The Nicaraguan Church and the Revolution*, Kansas City, Mo.: Sheed and Ward, 1991, pp. 21ff.

[75] James DeFronzo, *Revolutions and Revolutionary Movements*, Oxford, Boulder: Westview Press, 1991, p. 190.

[76] Sigmund, 'Christian Democracy, Liberation Theology', in Witte, *Christianity and Democracy*, p. 189.

[77] See Gustavo Gutiérrez, *A Theology of Liberation: History, Politics, and Salvation*, Maryknoll, N.Y.: Orbis, revised edition, 1988, pp. 35f., 191, n. 8.

[78] Sigmund, in Witte, *Christianity and Democracy*, p. 191.

region, and led to the radicalization of many student activists, including Christians. The success of the revolution held out the promise of liberation for all those who were oppressed, but it also led to the development of a strong anti-Communist reaction aided and abetted by the United States. In pursuing its goal of controlling the hemisphere, the United States helped develop strong militia indoctrinated with the ideology of 'national security'. The eventual result was widespread rule by military dictatorships supported by big business and expanding multi-national corporations. From 1936 until 1979 Nicaragua was ruled by the corrupt and brutal Somoza dynasty[79] with the support of successive United States governments, and by means of a National Guard trained and equipped by the United States.[80]

Sandinistas, Catholics, and Contras

From the early seventies progressive Catholics joined others in the anti-Somoza revolutionary struggle led by the Sandinista Liberation Front (FSLN)[81] which had been formed in 1961.[82] After the Somoza family misappropriated aid sent to help victims of the Managua earthquake in 1972, such popular support for the Sandinistas escalated, and by 1977 it embraced a wide range of Nicaraguan society, including members of the Conservative Party. The Somoza regime was eventually overthrown in 1979, an event hastened by the withdrawal of the support of the United States by President Jimmy Carter in terms of his human rights policy.[83]

---

[79] Anastasio Somoza became president in 1936. After his assassination in 1956 he was succeeded by his son Luis who died in 1967, and then by another son, Anastasio Jr., who remained in power until the revolution in 1979 forced him to flee to the United States. He was assassinated in Paraguay in 1980.

[80] DeFronzo, *Revolutions*, pp. 194f.

[81] Augusto César Sandino had been a general who refused to be party to a sell-out of Nicaraguan sovereignty to the Americans in the 1920s. A fervent nationalist, Sandino then led a guerrilla war seeking the liberation of Nicaragua from US military occupation and political control. In 1934 he was murdered by National Guard soldiers with the backing of the US ambassador. See Mulligan, *The Nicaraguan Church*, p. 35f.

[82] DeFronzo, *Revolutions*, pp. 197f.   [83] *Ibid.*, p. 101.

When the FSLN came to power it had the support of a large and ideologically diffuse following, ranging from hard-line Marxist–Leninist revolutionaries to middle-class Catholics and members of the Conservative Party, notably Violeta Chamorro. Even prior to this there were three major ideological factions within the FSLN. The largest, the *Terceristas* (Third Force), was more socialist than Marxist, and included many Catholic and Protestant social activists committed to both the gospel and socialism. Led by Daniel Ortega, who later became president of Nicaragua, the *Terceristas* group eventually proved to be the most effective in overthrowing the Somoza regime. Ideologically more moderate than the other FSLN factions, it determined the policies and character of the post-revolutionary government, welding together a pluralist alliance and transforming itself into a democratic political party.[84] This reflected a new realism throughout Latin America that acknowledged that revolutionary aspirations had to be channelled into democratic policies in order to achieve economic viability and stop the cycle of violence which led from one military dictatorship to the next.

The problems of national reconstruction were immense. The legacy of the Somoza regime and the civil war was appalling. The country was in economic ruin, adding to the already massive poverty which had characterized the position of the majority for generations. Compounding this was the relentless hostility of the United States government towards the FSLN after the 1980 elections brought Ronald Reagan to the White House. Reagan made it publicly clear that the Sandinistas had to be removed from power at any price.[85] For his administration, the left was an illegitimate actor in the political arena.[86] Not only did Reagan prevent Nicaragua from receiving funding from the International Monetary Fund,[87] but he gave massive support to the Contras ('counter-revolutionaries') led

[84] *Ibid.*, p. 199. [85] *Comment: Nicaragua*, London: CIIR, 1987, p. 24.
[86] Alejandro Bendaña, 'The Future of Democracy in Central America: Lessons from Nicaragua', *Working Papers* CEI, No. 1, May 1991, p. 18.
[87] Jenny Pearce, 'A Short History of Latin America', in George Gelber ed., *Poverty and Power: Latin America after 500 Years*, London: Cafod, 1992, p. 59.

by former members of the National Guard, business leaders, and disenchanted Atlantic Coast farmers who wanted to overthrow the FSLN government.[88] From Reagan's perspective, the Sandinista government was a totalitarian Communist regime which was a threat to the region and the interests of the multinationals. The problem was not that Sandinista Nicaragua lacked democracy, 'but that it was *too* democratic'. It provided 'a dangerously attractive model' for the surrounding countries under United States dominance.[89] 'The United States', William Robinson writes, 'was not out to help democratize Nicaragua; it was out to destabilize and destroy the democratic experiment itself'.[90]

Indicative of the extent of the United States' interference was the judgment of the International Supreme Court of Justice at The Hague in 1986 which insisted that the United States end its assault on Nicaragua and pay reparations for war damage.[91] As César Jerez, a leading Jesuit in Nicaragua, noted in 1984, what was at stake in Nicaragua was 'national sovereignty, regained by the poor through revolution'.[92] The Esquipulas Accords,[93] initiated by Nicaragua in October 1986, indicated the Sandinista government's commitment to establishing a 'Zone of Peace, Democracy and Co-operation' in Central America, without the interference of the United States or other major powers.[94]

The counter-revolutionary war ended formally with elections held in February 1990 as part of the changing international new order. The FSLN lost the elections to the UNO, a coalition party backed by the United States, a triumph for the low-intensity warfare that had been waged.[95] The elections

---

[88] Robinson, *A Faustian Bargain*, p. 111.

[89] *Ibid.*, p. 152; DeFronzo, *Revolutions*, p. 222.

[90] Robinson, *A Faustian Bargain*, p. 153.   [91] DeFronzo, *Revolutions*, p. 214.

[92] César Jerez SJ, *The Church and the Nicaraguan Revolution*, CIIR Justice Papers, London, no. 5, 1984, p. 20.

[93] The summit meetings of Central American presidents was formally instituted in Esquipulas, Guatemala, in May 1986.

[94] Mauricio Herdocia, 'The Esquipulas Accords and the Declaration of Central America as a Zone of Peace, Democracy and Cooperation', *Working Papers of the Center for International Studies*, no. 1, May 1991, pp. 27f.

[95] Robinson, *A Faustian Bargain*, p. 147.

were pronounced and accepted as 'free and fair', but the United States had helped to create conditions which made it almost impossible for the Sandinistas to win.[96]

Yet the electoral failure of the Sandinistas cannot be wholly laid at the door of United States interference. The FSLN did make serious mistakes.[97] The ham-handed treatment of farmers in the Atlantic Coast region, the military draft, and anti-religious rhetoric were major errors. The torture of the Miskito Indians during 1981–2 constituted a serious violation of human rights.[98] Like most parties in power the FSLN abused its position and lost the ability to be self-critical. Critics from the left within the Party complained that a 'people's democracy' had been replaced by a technical bureaucracy.[99] When it came to the elections, the FSLN was far too confident of its popular base, and miscalculated the extent of its support.[100] None the less an evaluation of its human rights record concluded that it was not bent on totalitarian rule, that few abuses could be attributed to its security apparatus, and that there was an 'increasing willingness to put on trial and punish members of the armed forces accused of abuses of power'.[101]

Despite losing the election the FSLN remained the single largest and most popular party without whose support the UNO coalition could not rule. In awarding an honorary doctorate to Daniel Ortega after his defeat at the polls, the president of the Central American University, César Jerez, highlighted the major contribution which the revolution had made to democracy:

Those who had struggled for years to gain power, suffering imprisonment and death, did not cling to that government but, in the face of an unexpected defeat, had the strength to accept the will of the people. For the first time in Nicaraguan history, a peaceful transition was possible.[102]

---

[96] DeFronzo, *Revolutions*, p. 224.
[97] 'Nicaragua after the 1990 Elections', *Update*, CIIR, November 1990, p. 2.
[98] DeFronzo, *Revolutions*, p. 209.   [99] Mulligan, *The Nicaraguan Church*, p. 145.
[100] Robinson, *A Faustian Bargain*, p. 153.
[101] *Right to Survive: Human Rights in Nicaragua*, London: CIIR, 1987, pp. 123f.
[102] Jerez, *Church and the Nicaraguan Revolution*, pp. 12f.

If this was the first time in history that triumphant revolutionaries forgave their enemies,[103] South Africa might well claim to
be the second. In both cases, the influence of the Christian
gospel is striking.

Hierarchy versus 'popular church'

We need to distinguish between the role of the church, both
Catholic and Protestant, within the revolutionary liberation
struggle and its subsequent role in the process of democratic
reconstruction from 1979 to 1990.[104] Three major groupings
within the Catholic church need to be kept in mind.[105] The
first was the sizeable anti-Communist, anti-Sandinista and
reactionary group, which also provided a home for extreme
right-wing elements. The second group, in the tradition of
Christian Democracy, comprised those who took a 'third way'
between the anti-Communist reactionaries and the Sandinista
revolutionaries. They advocated justice, freedom, brother-
hood, and democracy, but rejected revolution.[106]

The third group identified with the FSLN and the revolution out of Christian commitment. Reacting to the repressive
character of the regime, informed by an evangelical commitment to the poor and a Marxian social analysis as expressed in
liberation theology, this segment of the church was identified
as the 'popular church' as distinct from the 'official church'
controlled by the hierarchy.[107] The popular church had strong
support from many expatriate priests and nuns, especially
Jesuits, as well as the support of Catholic and Protestant
churches in the United States who consistently opposed anti-
Sandinista policy and support for the Contras.[108]

---

[103] *Ibid.*, p. 13.
[104] For a historic overview, see P. Berryman, *The Religious Roots of Rebellion*, New York:
Orbis, 1984.
[105] Mulligan, *The Nicaraguan Church*, p. 300.   [106] *Ibid.*, p. 22.
[107] Luis Serra, 'Ideology, Religion and Class Struggle in the Nicaraguan Revolution',
in Richard L. Harris and Carlos M. Vilas, ed., *Nicaragua: A Revolution under Siege*,
London: Zed Books, 1985, p. 153.
[108] *Comment*, 1987, p. 26. It has been estimated that about 54 per cent of the 240
Catholic priests in Nicaragua opposed the Sandinista revolution in 1983. Significantly, 61 per cent of all priests were expatriates. See *Envio*, December 1983.

From the mid-sixties, liberation theology provided the theological foundation for those Christians who became involved in the revolutionary struggle against oppressive regimes throughout Latin America.[109] Its genesis was a growing awareness that the church needed to shift its allegiance from support for the ruling classes, and take 'a preferential option for the poor' as mandated by the Latin American Bishops' Conference (CELAM) in Medellín in 1968 and again at Puebla in 1979,[110] attended by John Paul II. For liberation theologians, but not for the majority of Catholic leaders, who adopted the 'third way' position, this meant a radical and risky realignment with the forces of socialist revolution.[111]

Out of a long experience of the failures of liberal democracy in the history of Latin America, liberation theologians had little faith in its reformist ability to bring about the basic structural changes needed in society. Appreciative of some aspects of Christian Democracy, they were conscious that it gave rise, as Gustavo Gutiérrez expressed it in his critique of Maritain, 'to fundamentally moderate political attitudes', which were a long way from 'radically new social forms'.[112] For liberation theologians, the historical point of departure for witness was not the Enlightenment and the liberal agenda it created, but the irruption into history of the oppressed and believing poor.

Central to the liberation theological project were the *comunidades eclesiales de base* or 'ecclesial base communities' (EBC). These began to emerge, after Vatican II, in various parts of Latin America, expressing a new evangelical concern for marginalized urban and rural communities. By 1979 there were probably more than 300 EBCs in Nicaragua alone[113] and they were at the heart of the popular church.[114] Comparatively

---

109 Alfred T. Hennelly, ed., *Liberation Theology: A Documentary History*, Maryknoll, N.Y.: Orbis, 1990.
110 *Ibid.*, pp. 89ff., 225ff.
111 Giulio Girardi, *Faith and Revolution in Nicaragua*, Maryknoll, N.Y.: Orbis, 1989.
112 Gutiérrez, *A Theology of Liberation*, p. 36.
113 Serra, in Harris and Vilas, *A Revolution under Siege*, p. 152.
114 Leonardo Boff, *Ecclesiogenesis: The Base Communities Reinvent the Church*, London: Collins, 1986.

small in total numbers, the EBCs played a vital role in the revolutionary struggle. Comprised of small groups of Catholics who met regularly for Bible study and prayer, usually led by laypeople, they became centres of *concientización* for the empowerment of local communities in their struggles for justice.[115] Although more might have been expected of the EBCs in the democratization process which followed liberation,[116] they were none the less remarkable experiments in participatory democracy within the church and local communities, analyzing issues and mobilizing the grass-roots with regard to political issues and action. They were 'microcosms of that equality, popular participation and mutual support which characterize "a more fraternal and humanized world"'.[117]

Much of the conflict within the Catholic church in Nicaragua centred on the role of the archbishop of Managua, Miguel Cardinal Obando y Bravo, leader of a hierarchy described as 'one of the most conservative politically and theologically in Latin America'.[118] Enthroned as archbishop in 1970, and made the first cardinal in Central America in 1985, Obando has been described as a progressive,[119] a moderate, and a reactionary.[120] But perhaps he is best understood as a Nicaraguan version of conservative Christian Democracy, espousing the third way between capitalism and socialism, though increasingly on its more reactionary wing.[121]

In 1974 Obando and his fellow bishops were publicly critical of the Somoza regime, and in 1977 they denounced the 'state of terror' which existed,[122] but they refused to give any support to the FSLN, regarding the armed struggle as un-Christian and unjustified. When it became clear in 1978–9 that the Somoza

---

[115] *Church and Politics: Internal Upheaval and State Confrontation in Nicaragua*, Centro Antonio Valdivieso, Central American Institute, 5, 1, January 1986.

[116] W. E. Hewitt, 'Religion and the Consolidation of Democracy in Brazil: the Role of the Communidades Eclesiais de Base (CEBs)', *Sociological Analysis*, 51, 2, 1990, pp. 139ff.

[117] Rowland, *Radical Christianity*, p. 140.

[118] Mulligan, *The Nicaraguan Church*, p. 225.

[119] Paul E. Sigmund, *Liberation Theology at the Crossroads: Democracy or Revolution?* New York: Oxford University Press, 1990, p. 123.

[120] Mulligan, *The Nicaraguan Church*, p. 116.   [121] *Ibid.*, p. 208.

[122] Sigmund, *Liberation Theology*, p. 123.

regime was beginning to collapse, Obando and the hierarchy became more supportive of those engaged in the armed struggle, notably in the Joint Pastoral Letter of the Nicaraguan Bishops published in November 1979. In it the bishops affirmed the 'revolutionary process', but equally clearly articulated their 'third way' stance by expressing the hope that a new Nicaraguan society would not be 'capitalist, nor dependent, nor totalitarian'.[123] For those Catholics supportive of the FSLN, such support was welcome but it was always equivocal: 'too little, too infrequent, too inaudible, and in some cases too late'.[124] The Catholic community was radically divided.

Soon after it came to power, the FSLN issued an historic statement on religious freedom. It was 'the first declaration of a Marxist-inspired political movement *in power*' which stated that religion is 'a right of conscience for every citizen of the state'. It also acknowledged 'that in recent Nicaraguan history Christian faith has shown itself to be an active force for justice even at the level of the institutional churches'.[125] But for the bishops, the Sandinista regime was totalitarian and atheist, manipulating people for its own political ends, creating division within the church, encouraging class hatred and militarism, and placing the country within the orbit of Soviet and Cuban power and influence.[126] For the hierarchy, revolution, and anti-clericalism had curtailed the political, religious, ideological, and social space previously occupied solely by the church as the only source of morality or social programmes.[127] It meant 'popular democracy', which Obando regarded as an enemy of democratic freedom, just as he regarded the *comunidades eclesiales de base* as a threat to the hierarchical order and control of the church.

Although they supported the popular uprising against the Somoza regime in 1979, the bishops could not 'justify the rising

---

[123] Translated as 'Christian Commitment for a New Nicaragua', Joint Pastoral Letter of the Nicaraguan Bishops, 17 November 1979, published by CIIR and Cafod London.
[124] Mulligan, *The Nicaraguan Church*, p. 123.
[125] Jerez, *Church and the Nicaraguan Revolution*, pp. 15f.
[126] Serra, in Harris and Vilas, *A Revolution under Siege*, p. 160.
[127] Mulligan, *The Nicaraguan Church*, p. 221.

up of the poor masses to gain more and more political and economic power in Nicaraguan society'.[128] This coincided with growing opposition amongst bourgeois groups who had likewise supported the FSLN in the final overthrow of the Somoza regime.[129] The visit of John Paul II to Nicaragua in 1983, when he was heckled by the large crowd in Managua for not condemning the Contras, led to a worsening in the relationship between the hierarchy and the FSLN and those Catholics which supported the movement. In concert with the Reagan administration, Obando did everything possible to curtail the ability of the FSLN to govern, and to prevent priests from participating in government structures.

The growing gap between the hierarchy and the Sandinistas with the popular church, can be seen in the reaction to the 'Call to Dialogue' issued by the bishops in 1984.[130] Although calling for reconciliation, the bishops expressed no criticism of the Contras, but seemed to be taking their side. In fact, after becoming a cardinal in 1985, Obando openly associated with the Contras, convinced that the Sandinistas could and must be overthrown.[131] Despite all this the Sandinistas nominated Obando as president of the committee for National Reconciliation in 1987 which attempted to bring the counter-revolutionary war to an end.

The ideological war against liberation theology was one of the main elements in the counter-revolutionary struggle. Published in 1980, the *Sante Fe Papers* provided the basis for Reagan's policy towards Nicaragua, and similar situations in the Third World, locating the struggle against the Sandinistas within the context of the 'cold war'. Behind the rhetoric of human rights was a concern to keep Central America within the United States' sphere of influence, and especially to ensure the interests of the multinationals. It did not mean giving democratic rights to the people, but a free capital market. All

---

[128] *Ibid.*, p. 171.   [129] *Ibid.*, p. 213.

[130] 'Call to Dialogue', Bishops of Nicaragua, 22 April 1984, in Hennelly ed., *Liberation Theology*, pp. 375ff.; Patricia Hynds, 'Bishops' Letter Deepens Church–State Estrangement', 24 May 1984, Hennelly, *Ibid.*, pp. 381ff.

[131] Jerez, *Church and the Nicaraguan Revolution*, p. 11.

those who opposed such policies, including the liberation theologians, were labelled 'anti-democratic' and had to be discredited and overthrown. Throughout this period the CIA and
'Christian Democratic' groups in Germany and other Catholic
countries engaged in a vitriolic attack on liberation theology
and its exponents in many Third World countries. Right-wing
Christianity became an instrument of the counter-revolution,
with Christian leaders professing a commitment to democracy,
but not wanting 'people to exercise power effectively'.[132]

Our focus has been upon the dominant Catholic church, but
many Protestants supported the struggle against Somoza and
were subsequently supportive of the Sandinista government.[133]
Protestantism had always been predominantly middle class,
and identified with the growth of political liberalism earlier in
the century. This democratizing alliance had broken the back
of Catholic hegemony and allowed Protestant missions into the
country. Protestantism, it has been argued, was 'the most
organized element of civil society in Nicaragua'.[134] But Protestantism has also been divided between older 'mainline'
denominations (Baptists, Methodists, and Presbyterians),
which have been more supportive of the FSLN, and newer,
more fundamentalist and right-wing groups whose proclamation has included a strong anti-Communist, anti-Sandinista
note.[135]

Pentecostalism in particular grew exponentially during the
decades of the revolutionary struggle and after,[136] especially
amongst the poor,[137] and often at the expense of the 'base
communities'. The number of Protestant and Pentecostal

---

[132] *The Road to Damascus: Kairos and Conversions*, A Document signed by Third World
Christians from seven nations: South Africa, Namibia, South Korea, Philippines,
El Salvador, Nicaragua, and Guatemala, Johannesburg: Skotaville, 1989, para-
graph 78, p. 17.

[133] 'Nicaragua', *Comment*, CIIR, 1987.

[134] Roberti Zub, 'The Growth of Protestantism – From Religion to Politics', *Envio*, 11,
137, December 1992, 19.

[135] Duncan Green, *Faces of Latin America*, London: Latin American Bureau, 1991,
p. 183.

[136] In Latin America Protestant membership (including Pentecostalism) grew from 5
to 40 million between 1970 and 1990. See Green, *Faces of Latin America*, p. 170.

[137] Zub, 'The Growth of Protestantism', p. 21.

pastors in Nicaragua far exceeded that of Catholic priests, and many of them were more evidently at work amongst peasant communities in search of converts.[138] As has been aptly said, 'it was not the revolution but pentecostalism that offered personal experience and shelter to many' in a very threatening environment.[139] Pentecostalism correlated well with the biblical ethos of the 'base communities', but promised miraculous redemption and a way of escape from harsh reality, rather than stressing political struggle as the way to achieve future hopes.

President Daniel Ortega, a Catholic, had always had a good relationship with Protestants, but there was a significant swing towards the UNO in the 1990 election.[140] One reason was that in the early eighties some Sandinista leaders tried to discredit evangelical pastors and confiscate church property.[141] Since then, evangelical churches have engaged more directly in politics. In February 1992, they formed the National Justice Party (NJP) to contest the next elections, with a good chance of winning a large number of seats in the parliament. According to Roberti Zub, 'Protestants – the majority of them pentecostal, poor and neglected – are leading the formation of new political parties.'[142] The programme of the new NJP centres does not address right-wing concerns, but those of human rights, service of the poor, and women's issues, which are brought together under the rubric of 'building a state according to the Bible'.[143]

In certain respects the NJP seems to have taken over the agenda of the 'base communities'. Thus, many Protestants have shifted decisively from an 'a-political' stance to a thoroughly political one, and it has been surmised that 'traditional parties tied to specific societies or labour unions and broad-based parties such as the FSLN could be replaced by religious parties'.[144] This direct involvement of more evangelical

---

[138] Green, *Faces of Latin America*, p. 180.
[139] Zub, 'The Growth of Protestantism', p. 29.
[140] *Ibid.*, pp. 22f.   [141] *Ibid.*, p. 25.   [142] *Ibid.*, p. 29.
[143] Newsbrief in *Envio*, 11, 137, December 1992, p. 28.
[144] Zub, 'The Growth of Protestantism', p. 28.

and fundamentalist Protestant churches in the political process is a widespread phenomenon throughout Latin America, Africa, and in some parts of Asia. Its implications for global democratization have yet to be assessed.

Liberation theology and democracy

In the light of the failure of the FSLN to retain power through the ballot-box, the Sandinista aligned Antonio Valdivieso Ecumenical Center in Managua issued a self-critical evaluation of the role of the popular church and liberation theology within the democratic revolution.[145] This document has particular significance for our assessment of the role of the popular church and its supporting liberation theology in the democratic struggle and transition in Nicaragua and elsewhere, and is therefore helpful in providing a way of focussing more critically on the issues.

First of all, the authors acknowledge that the victory of the UNO coalition, the collapse of Communism in eastern Europe, and the emergence of the United States as the only superpower (i.e. the 'new world order'), created a crisis for Nicaragua and civilization as a whole. The utopianism that had guided the revolution had failed to materialize and the electoral defeat had apparently put an end to any socialist hopes.[146] Liberal democracy had become the dominant popular ideology. Serviced by the churches it was linked to the 'bourgeois project of "national reconciliation"' as the way of national salvation.[147] This raised fundamental questions about the way in which 'revolutionary Christians' had interpreted 'the option for the poor', and undercut the coherence which they had perceived 'between the perspectives of the Realm of God and of the Sandinista historical project'. Thus it had to be asked whether 'revolutionary Christians' had been mistaken in their analysis

---

[145] *Nicaraguan Revolutionary Christians Face the Crisis of Civilization*, Managua, Nicaragua: Antonio Valdivieso Ecumenical Center, 1991. Published in English by Circus Publications, New York, April 1991.
[146] *Ibid.*, p. 6.   [147] *Ibid.*, pp. 11f.

and commitment, and should now 'return to the fold of the "true church"'.[148]

Secondly, in response, the authors of the document recast their theology of liberation in terms of a *theologia crucis*.[149] Christians are not called to be on the side of the poor and oppressed because they will eventually triumph, they argued, but precisely because they 'are the conquered of today'.[150] Christians are always in conflict with the dominant culture, and it is through identification with the weak that all political programmes, projects, and systems have to be evaluated. The 'triumph of capitalism' is an experience of crucifixion for it means death not life for the majority of people.[151]

Thirdly, the authors rejoiced in the fact that many militant Christians who had opted out of the Christian community had now returned to 'find a source of fidelity and revolutionary creativity in the dynamism of faith'. They had returned to their former communities and discovered in them 'spaces for nurturing, reflection, prayer, friendship and common searching'.[152] Rather than causing a loss of faith, there was a renewed awareness of responsibility and the need to reaffirm basic convictions and commitments. This imposed 'on revolutionary Christians and the popular church the need to take a strong position in opposition to the bourgeois technocratic government', and become a source of creativity in the next phase of the struggle for justice.[153]

Fourthly, this new commitment enabled the people to become the subjects of their own history and thus to determine the kind of society they wanted without the interference of the United States. The sovereignty of the people was at stake. The

[148] Uriel Molina Oliù OFM, a leading liberation theologian in Nicaragua had equated the reign of God and the Sandinista historical project. See L. Boff and V. Elizondo, eds., *La Iglesia Popular; Between Fear and Hope*, *Concilium*, 176, December 1984.

[149] By *theologia crucis*, as distinct from what Luther referred to as the 'theologia gloriae' of papal triumphalism, is meant a theology which finds its strength in 'weakness' (cf. I Corinthians 1:25) rather than in identification with the centres of ecclesiastical or political power.

[150] *Nicaraguan Revolutionary Christians*, p. 15.   [151] *Ibid.*, p. 9.

[152] *Ibid.*, p. 13.

[153] *Ibid.*, p. 14.

society envisaged was 'not in effect anywhere', nor could it be 'scientifically shown to be possible'.[154] What was proposed was a search for new ways of being a revolutionary movement, and new models of society independent of the dead legacy of European Communism.[155] This meant the abandonment of the armed struggle, and an acceptance of the loss of political and military power; conversely it meant the espousal of non-violence as 'the historical force of truth, right, justice and love'.[156] Christians could help the revolutionary movement recover its original non-violent inspiration and make Nicaragua a laboratory in which the revolutionary and the non-violent traditions of struggle could create a new cultural synthesis, thus contributing to 'humanity's search in the crisis of civilization'.[157]

Fifthly, the document expressed the need for the popular church to be more autonomous and critical in its relationship to the FSLN. This meant being more attentive to 'appropriate tasks as believers, and more faithful also to the people in the continuing critical and self-critical effort'.[158] It also meant strengthening the autonomy of the popular church in relation to the institutional church through the development of lay leadership and appropriate forms of spirituality. Only in this way could the task of reconciliation not become captive to the 'bourgeois ideology of reconciliation'. Reflecting on the role of the popular church the authors also stressed the need for Christians to be engaged in the task of educating people for liberation and democracy.[159] Electoral defeat had demonstrated 'that the popular classes are not revolutionaries spontaneously' and that the need for education would have to be unceasing.

What is of particular significance in this chastened response of liberation theology to democratization in Nicaragua is the

[154] *Ibid.*, p. 17.
[155] Peadar Kirby, 'A "New Left" Emerges in Latin America', *Conjuncture*, 5, 8, August 1992.
[156] *Nicaraguan Revolutionary Christians*, p. 19.   [157] *Ibid.*, p. 26.
[158] *Ibid.*, p. 25.
[159] *Ibid.*, pp. 22ff.

way in which the revolutionary struggle has been reaffirmed, but placed within 'the constitutional democratic framework' in which the struggle evolved.[160] The basic commitment to the poor, and therefore to a socialist future, remains, but it has to be worked out in the sphere of democratic and practical politics. Utopian vision alone is inadequate if not dangerous. As Frei Betto put it: 'Liberating utopia needs to translate itself into feasible "topias", realizable in the world of the poor as a condition for new roads to social transformation'.[161]

Although Martin Luther King Jr., started at a different ideological and theological point to these Nicaraguan liberation theologians, and although their contexts were very different, there is a remarkable convergence in their understanding of democracy and its relation to Christian witness. There is an acceptance of the importance of the democratic system as the 'site of struggle' for democratic transformation; a rejection of the equation of democracy with capitalism; a commitment to non-violence as the only appropriate strategy consonant with democratic change; an affirmation of an integral link between the struggle for democratic transformation and Christian witness; and a recognition of the need for a spirituality necessary for that task.

There is, however, a further link which has to do with King's understanding of the responsibility of the United States in global democratization to which we earlier referred. Nicaragua is a prime example of what Robinson calls 'low-intensity democracy' whereby the United States in particular, and the North in general, seek to control the democratic process in the South in such a way that they retain their privileges.[162] Powerful countries can and do undermine the capacity of nations, especially at the economic level, to determine democratically their own future.[163] An imposed process of democratization

[160] *Ibid.*, p. 25.
[161] Frei Betto, 'Did Liberation Theology Collapse with the Berlin Wall?' *Religion, State, and Society*, 21, 1, 1993, p. 37.
[162] Robinson, *The Faustian Bargain*, p. 159.
[163] Interview with Ed de la Torre, Catholic activist from the Philippines, in *The New Nation*, Johannesburg, 19–25 June 1992, p. 11.

might bring about a new sense of freedom to some, but it might also accentuate recession and deepen 'the effects of economic crisis as the economy opens further to the competitive winds of the world and global capital'.[164] Thus an emphasis on national sovereignty by a small and weaker country may be an appropriate means of defending democratic rights and freedoms against dominant powers, even though the doctrine of national sovereignty has serious drawbacks in other respects for world peace and global democratization.

The Nicaraguan experience clearly demonstrates the importance of NGOs and the role of the church in building civil society. Democracy requires educating people to participate in the political process, the need to develop a culture of human rights and tolerance, and an ability to break out of dogmatic ideological positions in seeking solutions to the problems which divide a country. Votes are not won through 'years of indoctrination', but through dealing with the economic, social, and political realities,[165] not just in the urban areas where political parties are usually based, but in rural areas which are often neglected and forgotten by those in power.[166]

Most Latin American democracies will probably remain provisional and unconsolidated for some time. The establishment of a just and lasting democratic social order takes time and effort. Whether the end-product will be some form of liberal or social democracy is debatable, though the odds seem to point beyond both to new forms appropriate to the region and its human and social resources.[167] For the time being, fragile liberal pluralist democracies have been established in some countries, and these, along with market economies, have been accepted, however reluctantly, by many on the left.[168]

---

[164] See Joel Rocamora and Barry Gills, 'Low Intensity Democracy', *Third World Quarterly*, 13, 3, 1992, pp. 501f.

[165] Zub, 'The Growth of Protestantism', p. 29.

[166] Marvin Ortega, 'The State, the Peasantry and the Sandinista Revolution', *The Journal of Development Studies*, 26, 4, July 1990, pp. 122f.

[167] Laurence Whitehead, 'The Alternatives to "Liberal Democracy": a Latin American Perspective', *Political Studies*, 40, 1992, 146ff. See also Jamie Osorio, 'Liberalism, Democracy and Socialism', *Social Justice*, 19, 4.

[168] Pearce, in Gelber, *Poverty and Power*, p. 63.

Liberation theologians have likewise expressed 'a new appreciation of the virtues of representative government, however
flawed' as well as 'a certain pessimism about the possibility of
revolutionary transformation'.[169] In fact, Paul Sigmund sees
the emergence of a consensus in which the left promotes 'communitarian grass-roots democracy, the center participation
and human rights, and the right free market economies and
civilian consensus government'.[170] Such a consensus neither
will nor need resolve all the tensions, but it might provide a
crucible in which just and contextually appropriate democratic models could develop for the region and more widely in
the southern hemisphere.

[169] Sigmund, in Witte, *Christianity and Democracy*, pp. 202f.   [170] *Ibid.*, p. 205.

CHAPTER 6

The post-colonial struggle for democracy in sub-Saharan Africa

The Second World War was a watershed in African political development. Drafted by their colonial rulers into fighting for world democracy and freedom, Africans were fired with determination to achieve that same goal for themselves.[1] The ensuing struggle against colonialism eventually led to the independence of most sub-Saharan African countries in the 1960s beginning with Ghana in 1957. Throwing off the yoke of British, French, Belgian, and eventually Portuguese imperial rule, they became members of the United Nations in their own right.

The newly independent countries were launched on the basis of British or French parliamentary systems, imposed from above with the agreement of the new political elites. These either failed to deal satisfactorily with the problems of ethnic division and economic development or were simply rejected for ulterior motives. One-party states (for example, Zaire, Kenya, Zambia) and socialist experiments (for example, Congo, Tanzania) emerged to take their place. However justified, the costs were exceedingly high. In many countries the ruling power bloc was identified with a dominant ethnic group, so that the attempt to build new national identities heightened rather than eliminated ethnic divisions or tensions. Conflict, civil war, and military coups became endemic, and have remained a constant threat to democratic rule in many countries. With the notable exception of the churches, civil society virtually

---

[1] Basil Davidson, *The Black Man's Burden: Africa and the Curse of the Nation-State*, London: James Currey, 1992, p. 164; Kwame Anthony Appiah, *In My Father's House: What Does it Mean to be an African Today?* London: Methuen, 1992, pp. 6f.

disappeared and the power of the state became all-encompass-
ing.[2] The euphoria of liberation celebrated at independence
dissipated in repetitive failure and growing alienation.[3]

The inability of the newly independent governments to deal
with the enormous economic problems facing their countries
was a major destablizing factor. Many countries had reasonable economies at independence, but these were not built on
solid economic foundations. Development required massive
injections of aid from either the West or the Soviet bloc, much
of it fostering militarization fed by 'cold war' ideology. Within
a short time, economic conditions became chronic, exacerbated by cyclical drought conditions and governmental corruption. By the early seventies many countries were on the
verge of economic collapse, faced with increasing poverty and
the need to repay huge debts to western nations and the
International Monetary Fund. Development programmes had
failed, and the quality of life for most people had fallen significantly.

Independence did not affect traditional gender relations.
The new governments were patriarchal and women remained
oppressed. As Ruth Meena observes, with specific reference to
southern African countries, governments 'hijacked the
women's movements by creating women's political wings of the
ruling party as the only legitimate political forum for women'.[4]
As a result, women's organizations simply reflected the
undemocratic nature of the ruling parties, and became instruments of political mobilization for them, rather than an
independent voice which represented their own demands.

The failure of multi-party democracy and development aid
to achieve its goals led many in the West to assume that the
region was a lost cause for democracy and development. That
assumption remains widely held. But it is superficial, unfair,

---

[2] Adrian Hastings, *A History of African Christianity, 1950–1975*, Cambridge University
Press, 1979, p. 187.
[3] Davidson, *Black Man's Burden*, p. 10.
[4] Ruth Meena, 'Gender Research/Studies in Southern Africa: An Overview', Ruth
Meena ed., *Gender in Southern Africa: Conceptual and Theoretical Issues*, Harare: SAPES
Books, 1992, p. 18.

and short-sighted. Multi-party democracy, after all, has not worked in some parts of Europe, and it has worked reasonably well in some African countries where conditions have been conducive.[5] Sub-Saharan Africa, in fact, compares favourably with eastern Europe.[6]

Colonialism cannot be blamed for everything which went wrong after independence, but it was responsible for many of the problems faced by the new governments. Imperial strategies of 'divide-and-rule' in the frantically indecent scramble for Africa,[7] the 'invention of ethnicity',[8] and the creation of new nation-states in which ethnic groups became fragmented 'tribes', must be held accountable for many of the traumas of post-colonial Africa. Modern tribalism, unlike that which existed in pre-colonial Africa, is a creation of colonialism 'utterly destructive of civil society'.[9] Colonialism undermined indigenous political institutions and their natural development. It put vast obstacles in the way of 'every reasonable avenue of African progress out of preliterate or prescientific societies into the "modern world"'.[10] Not only was colonial rule undemocratic, but its bureaucratic administration undermined traditional systems of rule in which 'mutually balancing segments' had been held together.[11] Independence did not mean the creation of genuinely African democracies, but the

---

[5] Prior to 1990 there were well-established multi-party democracies in The Gambia (1965), Botswana (1966), Zimbabwe (1980), Senegal (1977), and Namibia (1989).

[6] Davidson, *Black Man's Burden*, pp. 266ff.

[7] Thomas Packenham, *The Scramble for Africa*, Johannesburg: Jonathan Ball, 1991.

[8] Ethnicity is the product of social forces within different historical contexts. 'Tribalism' is the attempt to give ethnic groups a primordial status in order to provide legitimation for a group's self-interest. See Terence Ranger, 'The Invention of Tradition in Colonial Africa', in Eric Hobsbawn and Terence Ranger eds., *The Invention of Tradition*, Cambridge University Press, 1983, pp. 211ff; and Ranger, 'The Invention of Tradition Revisited', in Terence Ranger and Olufemi Vaughan eds., *Legitimacy and the State in Twentieth Century Africa: Essays in Honour of A. H. M. Kirk-Greene*, London: Macmillan, 1993; Gerhard Maré, *Ethnicity and Politics in South Africa*, London: Zed., 1992.

[9] Davidson, *Black Man's Burden*, p. 11.   [10] *Ibid.*, p. 42.

[11] M. Fortes and E. E. Evans-Pritchard, *African Political Systems*, London: Oxford University Press, 1963, p. 16.

Africanization of colonial institutions and economic structures,[12] and often the transference of political ineptitude and incompetence. Little was done to prepare the new nations for independence or multi-party politics.

There are many religious traditions in sub-Saharan Africa, but three are dominant: African traditional religion, Islam, and Christianity. Traditional religion remains a pervasive force permeating even those cultures which have been transformed by Islam or Christianity. Islam has predominated in north Africa since the seventh century, forming an inverted crescent from west Africa across the north and down the east coast. In more recent times it has become a growing contender for dominance in other parts of the continent.[13] This has far-reaching implications for the political future of the continent and the role of the churches.

Christianity was established in north Africa and Ethiopia from early on, but its expansion throughout the rest of the continent was coterminous with European colonization in the nineteenth century. Christianity has subsequently become the dominant religion in much of the sub-Saharan Africa, and its rapid growth since the Second World War suggests that Africa will have one of the largest concentrations of Christians on any continent by the beginning of the twenty-first century.[14] Part of this growth must be attributed to the way in which African Christianity has managed to overcome its foreign image and become indigenous. This can be seen particularly in the phenomenal growth of the African Independent church move-

---

[12] Kabiru Kinyanjui, 'The Challenge of African Churches and Countries', in Masamba ma Mpolo, Reginald Stober, and Evelyn V. Appiah, eds., *An African Call for Life*, Geneva: WCC, 1983, p. 81.

[13] See Ali A. Mazrui, 'Religion and Political Culture in Africa', *Journal of the American Academy of Religion*, 53,3, December 1985, 817ff.

[14] David B. Barrett ed., *World Christian Encyclopedia: A Comparative Study of Churches and Religions in the Modern World, AD 1900–2000*, Nairobi: Oxford University Press, 1982, global table 2, p. 4.

ment in which African culture and Christianity have blended together.[15] The expansion of Christianity in Africa has there-fore been not only numerical, but also an 'expansion into a new scale of complexity'.[16]

While the colonial powers hindered rather than helped prepare the way for democratic rule after independence, such preparation did take place within Christian missionary institu-tions. These were not democratic in themselves, but they inculcated western parliamentary democracy as the ideal form of political organization. Perhaps more so than anywhere else, a liberal democratic ideology was built into the foundations of the churches in Africa.[17] In much of sub-Saharan Africa, 'the principles of unity, democracy and self-government were developed in the church long before they were even dreamed of in the state'.[18] Thus, whatever the faults of the missionaries, the 'African revolution' was 'a harvest of Christian missions'[19] and 'a triumph of Christian ideals'.[20] Not surprisingly, Christians were often the leaders in the struggle for independence, and missionaries the first foreigners to sense the rising tide of nationalism, to stress its importance in their home countries, and to help shape its course, fearful that it might otherwise become Marxist.[21]

As a result, at independence there was a significant group of

[15] The classic discussion on the subject is Bengt G. M. Sundkler, *Bantu Prophets in South Africa*, London: Lutterworth, 1948.
[16] Hastings, *A History of African Christianity*, p. 262.
[17] Adrian Hastings, 'The Churches and Democracy: Reviewing a Relationship', pp. 10f. Paper presented at the Conference on 'The Christian Churches and Africa's Democratization' held at the University of Leeds, September 1993, spon-sored jointly by School of African Studies (SOAS) at the University of London, and the Department of Theology and Religious Studies, at the University of Leeds. Forthcoming in Paul Gifford, ed., *The Christian Churches and Africa's Democratisation*, Leiden: Netherlands: E. J. Brill, 1995.
[18] Eridadi Mulira, quoted in Tom Tuma and Phares Mutibwa, eds., *A Century of Christianity in Uganda: 1877–1977*, Nairobi: Church of Uganda, 1978, p. 131.
[19] A. Adegbola, 'A Christian Interpretation of the African Revolution', *All Africa Conference of Churches Bulletin*, 3,3, June 1965, p. 111.
[20] *Ibid.*, p. 114.
[21] A. T. Tom Tuma and Phares Mutibwa, *A Century of Christianity in Uganda, 1877–1977*, pp. 133f.; Ian Linden, *The Catholic Church and the Struggle for Zimbabwe*, London: Longman, 1980, pp. 48f.

missionary-educated leaders in many countries who had espoused, or at any rate been introduced to, western democratic values, and trained in democratic procedures. Moreover, close personal relationships were forged between many future church and political leaders who shared common values and a vision for the future of their countries. At the same time, however, the churches and missionary institutions failed to help create a more broadly based democratic culture within the wider society. Relatively small ruling elites of political, church, and business leaders, often belonging to one dominant ethnic group, formed informal coalitions which sought 'to exercise hegemonic control over the society',[22] preferring to perpetuate their own privileged status after independence rather than to share power with other groups.[23] This often led to the co-option of the churches as uncritical servants of the state, giving legitimacy to policies which were morally suspect, socially disastrous, and counter-productive to Christian witness. When governments were later discredited, so were those churches and their leaders which had given them uncritical allegiance. This has sometimes curtailed their ability to participate critically and constructively in what has become known as the second liberation struggle.

The link between government and church elites was made more serious because of the ethnic character of many denominational divisions. This was a product of the comity arrangements entered into by Protestant missions whereby regions were apportioned to different missionary societies. However rational an arrangement, it stimulated ethnic consciousness and identity along religious lines. In some instances this seriously compromised churches when their particular ethnic community came to power. A notable example was the close tie between the Presbyterians and the powerful Kikuyu in Kenya

[22] Jean-Francois Bayart, *L'Etat en Afrique: La politique du ventre*, Paris: Fayard, 1989, quoted in Timothy Paul Longman, 'Socio-Political Change and the Christian Churches in Rwanda', to appear in Paul Gifford, *The Christian Churches and Africa's Democratisation*.
[23] Maxwell Owusu, 'Democracy and Africa – a View from the Village', *The Journal of Modern African Studies*, 30,3, 1992, 375.

which, under the leadership of Jomo Kenyatta, led the struggle for independence. This made it difficult for the Presbyterian church in post-independent Kenya to address the nation's conscience on issues closely linked with Kikuyu hegemony.[24]

The Roman Catholic church was less affected by connections with ethnic groups than the Protestant churches because it had not been party to comity agreements. After Vatican II, which occurred during the early days of independence, the Roman Catholic church became more ecumenically involved and often provided the leadership in responding to political matters. As bishops' conferences were established throughout Africa, their regular pastoral letters became important instruments in the political witness of the Catholic church, and more broadly within the ecumenical community. As far back as 1953, before the birth of Tanzania, the bishops of Tanganyika had issued a watershed pastoral letter on *Africans and the Christian Way of Life* in which they dealt with the political, economic, and educational development of the country.[25] Likewise the bishops of future Zimbabwe unequivocally denounced social injustice in what was then Rhodesia in their pastoral letter, *Peace through Justice*, published in 1961.

The political significance of the African Independent or indigenous churches in the struggle for independence has generally been regarded as ambiguous, but the popular image of them being a-political is misleading.[26] The question is not whether they were political, but the nature of their political activity.[27] There can be little doubt, for example, that the Kimbanguist church was of considerable importance in the struggle against Belgian colonial rule in Zaire, even though its intentions were not explicitly political.[28] Likewise in Kenya, with the exception of the Presbyterians, it was not on the whole

---

[24] Hastings, *A History of African Christianity*, p. 190. [25] *Ibid.*, p. 100.

[26] Michel Legrain, 'Indigenous African Churches and the Quest for Democracy', in James Provost and Knut Walf, eds., *The Tabu of Democracy within the Church*, Concilium, vol. 5, London: SCM, 1992.

[27] Terence O. Ranger, 'Religious Movements and Politics in Sub-Saharan Africa', *African Studies Review*, 29,2, June 1986, 1ff.

[28] Marie-Louise Martin, *Prophetic Christianity in the Congo: the Church of Christ on Earth through the Prophet Simon Kimbangu*, Johannesburg: Christian Institute, n.d.

the mainline churches, but the indigenous churches who 'embraced the nationalists and supported the struggle for independence'.[29] In Zimbabwe, where the mainline churches were strongly divided in their political loyalties, usually along racial and ethnic lines, some indigenous churches played a critical role in the liberation war.[30]

In so far as the mainline churches were identified with those who came to political power, the African indigenous churches provided autonomous space and resources for the empowerment of those who were on the periphery of politics. As such they challenged an all-inclusive state in a way which was sometimes impossible for churches compromised by their uncritical loyalty to the state. Like the Pentecostals in Latin America, the indigenous churches had greater appeal for the rural poor than either the Roman Catholic church or mainline Protestantism, not least because of their emphasis upon healing, and their ability to help rural migrants to adapt to urban environments.

The co-option of the churches by the state was not always related to ethnic connections, but sometimes, as in Zaire and Liberia, to a more general system of patronage of the churches by political leaders. President Mobutu Sese Seko's 'authenticity' campaign in Zaire, and his strategy to control the churches through creating one united church organization, were particularly effective in co-opting Protestants, though the Catholic hierarchy also eventually succumbed.[31] Likewise, the patronage of the churches by President William Tolbert, a Baptist leader of world prominence, gave the churches of Liberia considerable standing within the nation, but prevented them from fulfilling any critical role. After Tolbert's murder the churches were so compromised that they could not mediate in

---

[29] Agnes Abuom, 'The Role of Kenyan Churches', unpublished Leeds Conference paper, pp. 7f.

[30] Matthinus Daneel, *Fambizano*, Gwero: Mambo Press, 1989.

[31] The Catholic bishops produced two Declarations in 1975, *Notre foi en Jésus-Christ and Déclaration de l'épiscopat face á la situation présente*, in which they opposed Mobutu's campaign. By 1988 Mobutu had won many of the bishops to his side. See Paul Gifford, 'Church Timidly Toes Line in Zaire', *National Catholic Reporter*, 29 September 1988, p. 14.

the wars which erupted in the decade of President Samuel Doe's rule.[32] With the exception of one or two leaders, the churches automatically justified True Whig Party dominance, and with a flourish of biblical rhetoric gave legitimacy to Doe's oppressive regime.[33]

Even though many of the leaders of the liberation movements were educated in missionary institutions, the churches, and especially foreign missions, were widely regarded as appendages of colonialism and therefore as unreliable allies in nation-building in the post-independence period. At independence many of the churches were themselves still controlled by foreign mission boards and missionaries. This meant that they were themselves largely unprepared for the role which was thrust upon them as they became self-governing. In some instances it took considerable time for them to break free from the negative image of being the instruments of colonialism, and to become churches in their own right. Symbolic of this endeavour was the moratorium on missionaries proposed by the All African Conference of Churches (AACC) in 1974.[34]

Whether churches were supportive of the struggle for independence or not, it often did not make much difference once independence was achieved. After comparing the role of the churches in the struggle for independence in three different countries, Rwanda, Uganda, and Ghana, Adrian Hastings concluded that 'neither the support nor the opposition seemed to matter very much once power was attained'. At the same time, the churches became increasingly cautious about intervening in the political arena.[35] There were exceptions to Hasting's observations, but there can be little doubt that on the whole the post-independent governments either wanted the full allegiance of the churches, or else they wanted them

---

[32] See Paul Gifford, *Christianity and Politics in Doe's Liberia*, Cambridge University Press, 1993; Paul Gifford, 'The Role of Liberian Christianity during the Civil War', to appear in Gifford, *The Christian Churches and Africa's Democratisation*.

[33] *Ibid.*

[34] Decision of the AACC Third Assembly, held in Lusaka, Zambia, in May 1974. See the discussion of the decision by the General Secretary of the AACC, Canon Burgess Carr, in his report to the General Committee of the AACC, October, 1974.

[35] Hastings, *A History of African Christianity*, p. 155.

sidelined in purely 'spiritual' activities. As most of the churches were pietistic in orientation, eschewing prophetic social witness, they generally concurred. Preferring church–state peace and patronage to conflict, they were often only too willing to be co-opted and, as a result, they were unable to oppose the rise of dictatorships, clientelism and corruption in the post-independent years. Such critical and prophetic witness as there was, was usually ecumenical in character, rather than denominational.

A CRITICAL ECUMENICAL WITNESS

The first representative African ecumenical conference, held on the eve of independence in Ibadan, Nigeria, in 1958, had expressed the need for the indigenization of Christianity in relation to the continent-wide quest for African political and cultural selfhood and identity. The conference also raised issues concerning economic justice, human rights, and the place of women and youth in society, which were otherwise overlooked both in the churches and the political sphere.[36] In this way, from the beginning, the ecumenical movement in Africa encouraged the churches to participate in nation-building, but to do so critically. With independence there was an upsurge in ecumenical activity, symbolized by the formation of the AACC in 1964, which kept this prophetic vision alive.[37]

The ecumenical movement was unable to penetrate deeply into the structures of the various denominations, and its vision of an increasingly united Christian witness engaged in nation-building and social justice often failed to overcome the tena-

---

[36] The AACC and the WCC jointly sponsored a Human Rights Consultation in Khartoum, Sudan, in February 1975, at which the nature and causes of human rights violations in Africa were identified, called on the churches to become active in promoting such rights, and to promote the role of women. AACC Press Statement, 21 February 1975. See also 'The Confession of Alexandria' adopted by the AACC in February 1976, published in Mpolo, Stober, and Appiah, eds., *An African Call for Life*, pp. 136ff.

[37] Harold Fey, ed., *The Ecumenical Advance: A History of the Ecumenical Movement*, vol. 2, 1948–68, London: SPCK, 1970, pp. 73f.

cious grass-roots allegiance to denominational and ethnic identities. At the same time, in some conflict arenas, notably in Nigeria and the Sudan in the late sixties and early seventies,[38] the AACC fulfilled an important mediating role. It was largely responsible for bringing the seventeen-year-old civil war in Sudan to an end,[39] though the conflict tragically resumed later. Likewise, ecumenical effort on behalf of human rights did make an important difference in some countries, especially as the AACC and its member churches were able to muster international support. The Roman Catholics had the additional clout of Vatican diplomacy. Even so, the churches, like the Organization of African Unity, were powerless to prevent ruthless regimes from pursuing their policies, as in Idi Amin's Uganda where Anglican Archbishop Janani Luwum was murdered by soldiers six days after he and his fellow bishops had attacked the abuse of human rights by the regime.[40]

The great leaders of African independence, such as Kwame Nkrumah, Julius Nyerere, and Kenneth Kaunda, were often admired and supported by the churches and the AACC, but they were not regarded by all as beyond criticism.[41] That they may have been agents of divine providence in history did not mean that they were not prone to corruption.[42] Indeed, the close relationship between some churches and the new governments began to sour in some countries soon after independence. Already during Ghana's First Republic (1957–66), there were church leaders who expressed criticism of the government for political and other excesses.[43] In Congo, where the church rather than the state had provided education, hospitals, and other essential services, the harmonious relation-

---

[38] *Engagement*, The Report of the Second AACC Assembly, Abidjan, 1969, pp. 96f.

[39] 'Sudan: Church Diplomacy Pays Off', *AACC Bulletin*, 5,11, July/August 1972, pp. 5f.

[40] Tuma and Mutibwa, *A Century of Christianity in Uganda*, pp. 171f.

[41] Gabriel Setiloane, 'The Ecumenical Movement in Africa: From Mission to Moratorium', in Charles Villa-Vicencio and John W. de Gruchy, eds., *Resistance and Hope: South African Essays in honour of Beyers Naudé*, Cape Town: David Philip, 1985, p. 143.

[42] Adegbola, 'A Christian Interpretation of the African Revolution', pp. 119f.

[43] Kwesi Dickson, 'The Church and the Quest for Democracy in Ghana', to appear in Gifford, *The Christian Churches and Africa's Democratisation*.

ship ended in the revolution of 1963. This introduced 'scientific socialism', and in its wake unleashed a reign of terror, including the persecution of the church and clergy and their exclusion from the social and political life of the country.[44] In Tanzania, both the Lutheran and Catholic churches became increasingly uneasy about the concentration of power in the hands of a few political elite who were trained in eastern Europe, and who sought to control the masses through centralized power and statism.[45] By 1972 the policy of *Ujamaa* was suspected as being anti-religious.[46] The Catholic bishops' pastoral letter published that year, *Peace and Mutual Understanding*, rejected the policy as unacceptable, indicating that the Catholic church would become involved in development along different lines.[47]

In Zambia between 1976 and 1982 there was also considerable church resistance to the introduction of 'scientific socialism' into the school curriculum. After discussions with President Kaunda in 1982, the churches indicated that, while they rejected Marxist humanism, they were prepared to accept Kaunda's understanding of 'Zambian humanism' and the socialism which was based on it because they were consonant with Christian faith. But as UNIP (United National Independence Party) rule became more oppressive, church leaders became more critical, attacking greed, 'laziness, inefficiency, lack of discipline, unfair distribution of wealth between rich and poor, dishonesty and theft in government offices, corruption and intimidation of non-Party members'.[48]

The position of the Catholic hierarchy in Mozambique illustrates the fact that in some contexts the churches stood

[44] Abraham Okoko-Esseau, 'The Role of Christianity in Congo's Quest for Democracy', to appear in Gifford, *The Christian Churches and Africa's Democratisation*.

[45] C. K. Omari, 'Church, Religion and the Democratization Process: Some Lessons from Tanzania', unpublished Leeds Conference paper, p. 6.

[46] *Ibid.*, p. 7.   [47] *Ibid.*, p. 8.

[48] *A Letter from the Leaders of the Church in Zambia to their Members about the President's Seminar on Humanism and Development*, Lusaka: Teresianum Press, 1982, p. 2. See also Gatian F. Lungu, 'The Church, Labour and the Press in Zambia: The Role of Critical Observers in a One-Party State', *African Affairs*, 85, July 1986, 399; Peter J. Henriot, SJ, 'Zambia – Analysis of a "Second Independence"', *Sedos Bulletin*, 25,9, 15 October 1993, 245f.

aloof from, or opposed, the struggle for independence, allied as they were to the various colonial administrations. It is not surprising then that, after independence in 1974, Mozambique's Marxist Frelimo government implemented a strongly anti-church and especially anti-Catholic policy, closing church buildings and using church assets for state programmes.[49] However understandable, this was counter-productive to nation-building, providing Renamo (Mozambique National Resistance or MNR) with much needed propaganda. It also meant that the churches 'came to represent the single largest and most influential voice and institution in the context where Frelimo demanded massive social control'.[50] State policy towards the churches began to change significantly for the better after 1982.

From the early 1970s the churches in Namibia provided the only 'solid institutional structures of opposition' to South Africa's apartheid rule, even though there was some division between them with regard to support for SWAPO and political strategy.[51] After the crucial /Ai-//Gams meeting of opposition groups in 1979 had 'redefined the political landscape in Namibia', the Christian Council of Namibia (CCN) and its member churches, especially the black Lutheran church, were the only institutions able to unite opposition groups in the struggle against South African rule. In the process the CCN virtually became the internal religious wing of SWAPO whose large Ovambo base was also solidly Lutheran. While this alignment was obviously crucial to the success of the liberation struggle, its uncritical nature became a liability after independence when the CCN, a product of the liberation struggle, became 'a major casualty of the peace'.[52]

In his assessment of the role of the churches in nation-

[49] See G. J. Rossouw and Eugenio Macamo, Jr., 'Church-State Relationship in Mozambique', *Journal of Church and State*, 35,3, Summer 1993, 536ff.

[50] Alex Vines and Ken Wilson, 'Churches and the Peace Process in Mozambique', to appear in Gifford, *The Christian Churches and Africa's Democratisation*.

[51] Philip Steenkamp, 'The Church and the Liberation of Namibia', to appear in Gifford, *The Christian Churches and Africa's Democratisation*.

[52] *Ibid.*, p. 17.

building in post-independent Africa, Richard Joseph has argued that, while there was no obvious overlap between Christian witness and resistance to authoritarian rule, certain structural attributes made the churches 'highly effective when the time came to move from partial to systemic opposition'.[53] The churches were the 'only tolerated countervailing power to that of the state' and were able to act 'as instruments of political substitution'.[54] This was often out of ecclesiastical self-interest. But in defending their own interests they were soon compelled to confront oppressive governments on a range of issues. While trade unions and the press, where they had some autonomy, were often more courageous in opposing corruption and tyranny, in many contexts the churches were alone in doing so. They also undertook tasks which the state failed to perform, and executed them far better, uniting people together in a common purpose.[55] Paradoxically, Joseph observes, it was because the new governments were unable 'to eliminate certain patterns of relations established during the colonial era that the Christian churches retained their capacity to challenge the decaying post-colonial state'.[56] No other organizations within civil society, such as it was, could really match the churches for autonomous action.

CHURCHES AND THE SECOND LIBERATION STRUGGLE

Ali Mazrui perceptively referred to the present process of democratization in Africa as 'the second liberation struggle'.[57] This second phase in the struggle for democracy may be traced back to the Portuguese Revolution in 1974, which led to the independence of Mozambique and Angola, but there can be little doubt that what happened in eastern Europe in 1989 was also decisive in reshaping the political development of sub-

---

[53] Richard Joseph, 'The Christian Churches and Democracy in Contemporary Africa', in Witte, *Christianity and Democracy*, p. 246.
[54] *Ibid.*, p. 232.   [55] Joseph referring to Bayart, *ibid.*, p. 233.
[56] *Ibid.*, p. 236.
[57] Ali A. Mazrui, 'Kenya Between Two Liberation Struggles', *West Africa*, 2–8 September 1991, p. 1450.

Saharan Africa as a whole.[58] One major reason for these changes was the fact that, as in eastern Europe, countries were forced to institute multi-party systems in order to attract western development assistance.[59]

The linkage of economic aid and democratization was a bitter blow for some countries where development was essential for the establishment of the necessary conditions for democracy. Yet the need to relate democratization to economic development was clearly critical to the success of both.[60] Africa cannot develop economically without developing democratically. Without that, as Larry Diamond argues, all the aid in the world will not suffice; with it, the promise of Africa's second liberation will not be wasted.[61] Not only does this require a change in the internal politics of African countries, it also requires changes in international politics and economics. Many sub-Saharan African countries have been so marginalized in the world economy, and have sought to develop new democratic political structures under such contrary conditions, that it is perhaps remarkable when any form of democracy is achieved. Quite apart from economic handicaps, fragile resources, social and cultural divisions, and poverty, African countries are often the victims of international power-play between the economically dominant nations. Hence the urgent need for a truly democratized global order which takes local needs seriously.

As in eastern Europe, the new wave of democratization has

---

[58] Multi-party systems of government were adopted between 1990 and August 1993 in Gabon, Ghana, Cote d'Ivoire, Madagascar, Cape Verde, Djibouti, Sao Tome, Kenya, Benin, Niger, Zambia, Lesotho, Burkina Faso, Burundi, Mauritania, Seychelles, Cameroon, Togo, Mali, Central African Republic, and Congo. There were ten multi-party states in Africa before 1990 which have held regular elections: The Gambia, Egypt, Botswana, Zimbabwe, Morocco, Tunisia, Mauritius, Comoros, Senegal, and in 1989 Namibia. *The Argus/Sowetan* Election supplement, 1 October 1993, p. 12.
[59] John Mukum Mbaku, 'Political Democracy and the Prospects of Development in Post-Cold War Africa', *The Journal of Social, Political and Economic Studies*, 17, 3 and 4, Fall/Winter 1992, 368.
[60] *Ibid.*, p. 345.
[61] Larry Diamond, 'The Second Liberation', *Africa Report*, 37,6, November–December 1992, 41.

affected virtually all sub-Saharan African countries, but in different ways. Each country, after all, has its own particular history, ethnic composition, and cultural ethos, as well as its own colonial and post-independence legacy. Moreover, what is understood by democratization also varies from one situation to another, though multi-party representative government, free and fair elections, and a free market economy are now widely regarded as basic to all else.

There remains, none the less, considerable resistance to democratization amongst many in power, even though pragmatic considerations elicit lip-service. The rhetoric of democracy is often co-opted as a means of controlling the process, both internally and internationally, in order to prevent meaningful change. Sometimes violence is even instigated, creating a nostalgia for authoritarian rule and ethnic nationalism. Tragically, Africa's second chance at democratization has already gone terribly wrong in several countries, notably in Togo, Nigeria, Burundi, and Rwanda. Even Zambia, widely regarded as the new model for democracy in Africa, has run into serious difficulties.[62]

What, we may then ask, is different about this second opportunity at democratic transformation in comparison to the first? Is there any reason for greater optimism? And how can the churches contribute better to the process? Obviously the general situation has changed dramatically since the ending of the 'cold war', and with the insistence of the international community and development funding agencies on the establishment of democratic forms of government. The abysmal record of many post-independent African countries has also been a sobering experience for many African politicians, and a disenchanting one for multitudes who are tired of policies and systems which do not work. There is also evidence of a greater sense of will and purpose not to repeat the mistakes of the past, even though this has yet to be proven over the long haul,[63] and

[62] Melinda Ham, 'History Repeats Itself', *Africa Report*, 38,3, May/June 1993, 13ff.
[63] Frank A. Kunz, 'Liberalization in Africa – Some Preliminary Reflections', *African Affairs*, 90, April 1991, pp. 223ff.

there is 'a voracious appetite in Africa for democracy'.[64] Furthermore, there is evidence of a new determination amongst many church leaders to be more active in facilitating the process of democratization.

Without denying the negative legacy of colonialism, African church leaders are aware that colonialism can no longer be held responsible for present corruption, mismanagement, and the abuse of human rights. There is also a greater awareness of the need to deal more decisively with potential conflict situations, to be more neutral in political alignments, and to be more deliberate in helping to create and nurture a democratic culture. All of this emerged at a symposium convened by the AACC, the Association of Member Episcopal Churches in East Africa, and the Nairobi Peace Initiative in July 1993.[65] Also indicative of this new determination on the part of church leaders was the revitalization of the work of the AACC. As Archbishop Desmond Tutu, speaking as its president, put it: 'The churches in Africa have now come into their own.'[66] Not only have they begun to assert their independence from the state and foreign control, but they have also discovered their indispensability in the democratic reconstruction of the continent. There is evidence that the key role which churches and Christian leaders have played in the various political transformations during the past twenty years, has significantly increased.[67] In some countries, such as Mozambique and Zimbabwe, where pressure from the movement for democracy has resulted in a legitimacy crisis for those in government, the state, it has been argued, 'now needs the church more than the church needs the state'.[68]

There are, however, strong divisions amongst the churches

64 Second Report of the Public Issues Committee, Central Committee of the World Council of Churches, January 1994.
65 Summary Statement from the Symposium on 'The Role of Religious Leaders in Peacemaking and Social Change in Africa', Nyeri, Kenya, 18–23 July 1993.
66 In a response at the Leeds Conference on the Churches and Democratization in Africa, September 1993.
67 Joseph, in Witte, *Christian and Democracy*, p. 231.
68 David J. Maxwell, 'The Church and Democracy in Zimbabwe', to appear in Gifford, *The Christian Churches and Africa's Democratisation*; Rossouw and Macamo, 'Church–State Relationship in Mozambique', p. 539.

with regard to political responsibility, particularly between those who are ecumenically open and involved, and conservative evangelical, fundamentalist, and Pentecostal groups. Just at the time when the AACC proposed its moratorium, and mainline Protestant missionary societies experienced a decline in funds and the number of candidates for foreign service, so these more conservative churches markedly increased their missionary programmes in the Third World,[69] often with massive financial and other support from conservative church groups in the United States. As a result they have expanded rapidly throughout the region. Whereas previously they shunned any political involvement, that is no longer the case, as seen, for example, by the extent of their support for Presidents Frederick Chiluba of Zambia and Daniel Arup Moi of Kenya.[70] They have also become involved at a time when some mainline churches, who were politically involved in support of previous governments, have been discredited, and are lacking in dynamism and vision. But history could well repeat itself. Ambitious politicians are only too ready to use the churches for their purposes, and church leaders find patronage a beguiling option. More seriously, such ideological support for democracy does not lead to the expansion of democratic participation, nor to the democratic transformation of society, but is really a mechanism 'to ensure one's group's own position *vis-à-vis* power and exclude others from its appropriation'.[71]

Mainline Protestant or Roman Catholic churches are however, not always more committed to democratic transformation than some more conservative evangelical churches. In some countries, they have consistently failed to take the lead, remained silent when they should have spoken, or spoken too generally when they have, and been far more circumspect in the criticism of the state and advocacy of human rights and

---

[69] E. M. Uka, *Missionaries Go Home? A Sociological Interpretation of an African Response to Christian Missions*, Berne: Peter Lang, 1989.
[70] See Paul Gifford, 'Christian Fundamentalism, State and Politics in Black Africa', in David Westerlund, ed., *Questioning Secularism*, Leiden: Brill, in press.
[71] Ruth Marshall, '"God is not a Democrat": Pentecostalism and Democratization in Nigeria', to appear in Gifford, *The Christian Churches and Africa's Democratisation*.

democracy than the press, human rights groups, or popular movements.[72] Even the stands which they have taken have sometimes 'been undermined by the public perception of their political sympathies and ethnic prejudices, and their close association with the current regime'.[73] As one inform-ant remarked before the eruption of civil war in Rwanda early in April, 1994: 'After years of helping the Tutsi, the Catholic church switched to supporting the Hutu when it looked like power was going to change hands. Now when it looks like democracy is inevitable, the church is supporting democracy.'[74] Tragically, democracy was by no means a foregone conclusion, and at the time of writing tens of thousands of people, including many priests and nuns, had been killed in what is, at least in part, an orgy of ethnic bloodletting.

None the less, in many countries, such as Zambia and Kenya, there has been considerable co-operation between the churches and other agents of civil society in opposing state abuse.[75] Church leaders have been outspoken in Zambia,[76] where the Catholic bishops, in their Pastoral Letter in July 1993, declared that the widening gap between rich and poor, 'is not only a moral scandal but a dangerous threat to our democratic stability'.[77] Likewise in Kenya, it has been pri-marily the churches which have kept a concern for democracy on the political agenda, even when 'it was anathema to discuss the subject'.[78] Here too, the Catholic bishops took the initiative in a pastoral letter in March 1992 which attacked the Moi government head-on.[79] The following year, targeting govern-ment corruption, the exploitation of ethnicity, and the encour-agement of violence, the Catholic bishops told Moi that all

[72] Lungu, 'The Church, Labour and the Press in Zambia', pp. 385ff.
[73] Longman, 'Rwanda: Church Responses to the Political Crises in the 1990s'.
[74] *Ibid.*   [75] Lungu, 'The Church, Labour and the Press in Zambia', pp. 385ff.
[76] Henriot, 'Zambia – Analysis of a "Second Independence"', p. 246.
[77] *Hear the Cry of the Poor*, A Pastoral Letter on the Current Suffering of the People of Zambia, Lusaka, 23 July 1993.
[78] Abuom, 'The Role of Kenyan Churches', p. 52.
[79] 'A Call to Justice, Love and Peace', 23 March 1992. See Paul Gifford 'Bishops for Reform', *The Tablet*, 30 May 1992.

'these abominations are done in your name'.[80] This reflects an important change which has taken place amongst both mainline Protestant and Catholic church leadership since independence.

Catholic bishops' pastoral letters have often been catalysts for ecumenical action, as was the case in Malawi where political protest on the part of the dominant Protestant churches was virtually unknown after independence in 1964. Opposition to one-party rule by the Catholic bishops began early in the 1980s, however, and reached a climax in March 1992 with the publication of the Lenten Pastoral Letter, *Living Our Faith*.[81] This demand for a return to democracy, so infuriated Dr Hastings Banda's Congress Party that there were demands for the death penalty to be exercised against the Catholic hierarchy.[82] Fortunately, wiser counsel prevailed, but the most vocal of the Catholic leaders, Monsignor John Roche, was deported, opposition figures were arrested, some disappeared, and there was general turmoil in the country. The leadership of the Catholic bishops in Malawi was followed soon after by the dominant Church of Central Africa Presbyterian (CCAP) to which Banda himself belonged.[83] Previously 'terrorized into silence', in June 1992 the CCAP addressed an open letter to the president which expressed similar concerns to those of the Catholic bishops, thus giving legitimacy to a growing groundswell for democratic change which eventually led to a democratically elected government in May 1994.

The relationship between Christianity and Islam has become an issue of considerable importance for the future of democracy in Africa.[84] Relations between Christians and

---

[80] Mark Huband, 'Kenya Trial Stirs Tribal Tensions', *The Guardian*, 12 November 1993, p. 12.

[81] See J. Chaphadzika Chakanza, 'The Pro-democracy Movement in Malawi: The Catholic Church's Contribution, 1960–1992, *Religion in Malawi*, 4, February 1994, 8f.

[82] *The Truth Shall Make You Free*, March 1992, published by the Catholic Institute for International Relations, London, September 1992.

[83] 'Malawi: A Moment of Truth', *Comment*, London: Catholic Institute for International Relations, July 1993.

[84] The issues were addressed at an AACC Consultation on 'Christians's Involvement in Minority Situations in Africa' held in Dakar, Senegal, January 1978.

Muslims are very difficult in some parts, such as the Sudan and Cameroon, and this impinges directly on the politics of the countries concerned. In some places, Christians and Muslims have worked together in helping to bring about mediation between warring factions, but in others the religious schism has added to the conflict between ethnic groups. In Christianity, as within Islam, there are different tendencies and it is not possible to generalize,[85] but where Islam insists that the political order should be in strict accordance with the *shari'a*, the kind of open society which democracy implies becomes problematic, if not impossible, and social transformation has different implications.[86]

There are both Christian and Muslim leaders who, in the interests of justice, human rights, and national reconciliation, have been able to transcend the divide which has traditionally separated the two faith communities. The nub of the matter was bluntly stated by Catholic Archbishop Okogie of Nigeria who, in response to the question whether religious affiliation should be a deciding factor in the election of a president, insisted that 'all Nigerians needed, were men and women of integrity, men and women who would not be tempted by filthy lucre, men and women who would work for justice with the fear of God in them'.[87] Democracy implies the acceptance of religious pluralism and tolerance at the very least, but it also requires that people of different faiths learn to co-operate in bringing about the just democratic transformation of society. The way forward is invariably not so much at the level of theological debate, but in practical co-operation, particularly in the area of human rights advocacy.

The churches fulfil different functions in democratization. The Kenyan symposium held in 1993, and to which we previously referred, highlighted consensus building, providing reliable information and expertise, peacemaking and recon-

85 Mazrui, 'Religion and Political Culture in Africa', p. 819.
86 Abdelwahab El-Affendi, '"Discovering the South": Sudanese Dilemma for Islam in Africa', *African Affairs*, 89, July 1990, pp. 371ff.
87 Matthew Hassan Kukah, 'Christians and Nigeria's Aborted Transition', to appear in Gifford, *The Christian Churches and Africa's Democratisation*.

ciliation.[88] Others refer to prophetic witness, clear social teaching, ecumenical action, challenging unjust economic policies
and justice within the church itself.[89] As in eastern Europe and
Latin America, many churches in Africa have become zones of
freedom, providing space for democratic education and action,
and becoming 'repositories of the very idea itself of the entitle-
ment to freedoms of conscience, association, assembly and
expression'.[90] The churches' struggle against the state's mono-
polization of a nation's resources, even if only in defence of the
churches' institutional interests, also limits the power and
influence of the state, pushing back its boundaries and creating
more space for NGOs.[91] In this way the churches often initiate
far-reaching changes, and, when the people lose confidence in
the credibility of national leaders, they turn to church leaders
as their guides.

The patent honesty and integrity of some church leaders,
and their impartiality and respect for legal procedures, have
often stood in marked contrast to the lack of moral fibre in
political leaders.[92] In Congo, for example, where the churches
became the key to democratization,[93] Catholic Bishop Ernest
Kombo was elected president of the Upper Council of the
Republic for precisely this reason, even though, for other
reasons, he was later forced to flee the country. Likewise in
Zaïre, the Catholic bishops, after succumbing to Mobutu's
patronage in the later 1980s, subsequently became key players
in the struggle for democratization.[94] The election of Lutheran
Bishop Diggs as vice-president of Liberia is another instance of
a church leader elected to high political office, though in this
instance his election reflected more an alliance between mainline churches and political leadership. One thing is clear,
however, if there had been no strong church leadership, the

---

[88] Summary Statement, items 27–39.
[89] Henriot, 'Zambia – An Analysis of a "Second Independence"', p. 251.
[90] Joseph, in Witte, *Christianity and Democracy*, p. 245.   [91] *Ibid.*, p. 245.
[92] Gifford, 'The Role of Liberian Christianity'.
[93] Abraham Okoko-Esseau, 'The Role of Christianity in Congo's Quest for
Democracy'.
[94] Paul Gifford, 'Endgame for Mobutu', *The Tablet*, 12 September 1991, p. 1110.

consequences would have been disastrous for many African countries.

The primary contribution of the churches to democratization has undoubtedly been their ability to mediate between warring factions, and to facilitate national reconciliation and reconstruction. In pursuing this role, church leaders throughout Africa today recognize that they can no longer be identified with a particular political party in the way in which they may have previously identified with liberation movements and post-independent governments. What was necessary in the struggle against colonialism is no longer helpful in building a democratic society where the separation of church and state is of fundamental importance if the church is to fulfil its *political* responsibility. There are many examples of the way in which churches have acted as mediators and reconcilers throughout Africa, and some instances where Protestant and Catholic action has been usefully complementary, as in Mozambique where their combined endeavours led to negotiations between the Frelimo government and Renamo.[95]

Churches are in a unique position to influence political developments, providing social cohesion at a time of national fragmentation and gathering international support in the struggle for justice and democracy. But even more, they are in daily touch with people, they often have a larger and more committed membership than political parties and, in many instances, their understanding of the situation on the ground is better than that of the politicians. While the witness of the church to central government is obviously critical, it is at the local community level that the church is often strongest and able to make the greatest difference in democratic transformation. A notable example is the emergence of the popular democratic movement in Uganda, where constitutionalism has developed from the grass-roots largely through the churches. Rural areas are of particular importance in this regard, for it is there that democratic structures will have to be adapted to local traditions, and in turn be shaped by them.

[95] Vines and Wilson, 'Churches and the Peace Process in Mozambique'.

The enormity of the problem facing those engaged in the transition to democracy in sub-Saharan Africa is daunting. What might be taken for granted in countries with a long experience of democratic government, with a well-trained civil service and adequate resources, an educated or at least literate population, and a vibrant civil society, cannot be assumed. The sheer logistics involved in voter education, organizing the ballot and ensuring free and fair elections, to say nothing of what then needs to happen, is often mind-boggling.[96] All of which points in the direction of the urgent need for people and politicians to be educated in the meaning of democracy if transitions are to be sustained and consolidated. As a vital part of this task it is essential that Africans discover the resources of their own traditions and do not simply rely on imported political systems and structures.

'UMUNTU NGUMUNTU NGABANTU'

The sorry tale of failed political orders in much of sub-Saharan Africa since independence indicates that systems of government, whether liberal democratic, socialist, or Marxist–Leninist, foisted on the people of Africa, cannot be expected to work. Democracy has to grow from within in ways appropriate to Africa and each nation's particular history and political tradition. This is precisely how democracy emerged in Britain, France, or the United States. Thus while attempts by western nations to prescribe democratic solutions for Africa have to be considered seriously, they also have to be treated with critical caution. Kwame Appiah rightly stresses that Africa will only solve its problems if they are seen as human problems arising out of an African context.[97]

Of particular significance in this regard is Basil Davidson's contention that democracy in Africa requires a synthesis rooted in its past yet able to deal with the challenges of the present.[98]

[96] Diamond, 'The Second Liberation', p. 39.
[97] Appiah, *In My Father's House*, p. 220.
[98] Basil Davidson, 'Questions about Nationalism', *African Affairs*, 76,302, January 1977, 44; see also Davidson, *Black Man's Burden*, pp. 76f.

What is necessary is the harnessing of resources which are part of African tradition, and their critical integration with those democratic values, institutions, and procedures which have developed more universally.[99] Democracy will not be a reality, nor can it be sustained in Africa, without the creation of a genuinely African form of democratic government, and an African civil society.[100] Without this, the gap between tradition and modernization will only widen, exacerbating the alienation between those governed and the elites who rule.

The importance of relating African traditional insights to contemporary political problems was recognized by those church leaders who met in Kenya in July 1993 to consider their role in peacemaking and social change. Reflecting on the extent to which competition and conflict are built into European political systems, they stressed the contemporary importance of the traditional African insistence on consensus-making. 'If', they argued, 'the goal of political change is harmonious community', then 'it does not necessarily follow that the politics of competition provides the means'. They urged the churches 'to become actively involved in the search for alternative democratic models appropriate to the respective countries, taking into account the African heritage, the colonial legacy, and post colonial-pressures'.[101]

With some notable exceptions, African political tradition prior to colonialism was communal rather than autocratic. Pre-colonial tribes, like those in Europe before the rise of nation-states, were 'organically structured' in such a way that they could take 'corporate decisions through well-defined procedures'.[102] Thus African societies were traditionally more akin to the organic type of society which characterized medieval Christendom. Organic societies are not democratic, but hierarchical, and authority is often sacralized. Traditionally,

---

99 Claude Ake, 'Rethinking African Democracy', *Journal of Democracy*, 2,1, Winter 1991, 33ff.
100 Lionel Cliffe and David Seddon, 'Africa in a New World Order', *Review of African Political Economy*, 50,3–11 1991, 10.
101 Summary Statement, item 35.
102 Klaus Nürnberger, 'Democracy in Africa – the raped tradition', in *A Democratic Vision*, p. 305.

chiefs were imbued with transcendent legitimacy and made whatever important decisions were necessary. There was little distinction between what we now refer to as political and civil society. But there was a tradition of participation and consultation without which rulers had little legitimacy. All adults had the right to participate and express their opinions; a system of checks and balances made rulers accountable; and an understanding of authority implied consent and responsibility.[103]

African societies did not always function according to such procedures and norms any more than pre-modern societies elsewhere. Many traditional African societies were oppressive, dictatorial, patriarchal, and, in some instances, imperialistic. There is even some justification for seeking a connection between traditional African society with its sacralized understanding of authority and a tendency towards one-party states and dictatorships. The difficulties 'encountered in the earlier endeavours with democratic constitutions in African post-colonial political life', Kwame Bediako writes, 'may have less to do with the unsuitability of "foreign conceptions of democracy" than the persisting weaknesses of the old order, only magnified within the conditions of the expansion of scale which Africa's entry into modern life has occasioned'.[104]

One of the problems with organic societies, and especially those with a sacralized notion of authority, is that they find it difficult to handle dissent and plurality. Traditionally, African communalism was not ethnically based; people from different communities could pass from one to another and be accepted without much difficulty. None the less, African communalism assumed a homogeneity, which is very different to the pluralism of modern nation-states. This may account in part for the ethnic conflict which has been such a feature of post-colonial Africa. In order for African societies to become democratic within a modern pluralist context, they have to retrieve com-

---

[103] M. Fortes and E. E. Evans-Pritchard, *African Political Systems*, London: Oxford University Press, 1963, pp. 11f.

[104] Kwame Bediako, 'Unmasking the Powers: Christianity, Authority, and Desacralization in Modern African Politics', in Witte, *Christianity and Democracy*, p. 213.

munal participation within a nation-state context. Christianity could play a critical and formative role in this process, challenging hierarchical domination, affirming community, stressing the importance of interpersonal relations rather than possessive individualism, and promoting an integrative spirituality.[105]

Fundamental to African culture is the understanding of human being (*ubuntu*) enshrined in the Xhosa proverb *umuntu ngumuntu ngabantu*: a person is a person through other persons.[106] *Ubuntu* in fact, provided the foundation for the legal code and customs which governed Xhosa society, and determined the way in which they were exercised.[107] Its contemporary reaffirmation is essential for the renewal of democracy in Africa and more universally. This does not imply the denial of individuals or individual political rights. On the contrary, a respect for each person as an individual is fundamental.[108] But it is very different from possessive individualism. The emphasis is on human sociality, on inter-personal relations, on the need which each person has for others in order to be herself or himself. This, rather than liberalism or Marxism, is the root of African humanism, and it relates well to biblical anthropology, trinitarian theology, and to the idea of Christian community.

During the past thirty years African theologians have made a significant contribution to the development of theologies in which African culture and Christianity have been creatively related.[109] However, although there has been courageous Christian opposition to unjust regimes, African theologians outside of southern Africa have not generally developed a critical political theology able to help the churches resist tyranny, overcome ethnic tension, and establish a just demo-

---

105 *Ibid.*, pp. 215f.
106 Augustine Shutte, *Philosophy for Africa*, University of Cape Town Press, 1993, p. 46.
107 See Noël Mostert, *Frontiers: The Epic of South Africa's Creation and the Tragedy of the Xhosa People*, London: Jonathan Cape, 1992, pp. 197f.
108 Kwesi A. Dickson, *Theology in Africa*, Maryknoll, N.Y.: Orbis, 1984, p. 135.
109 Kwesi Dickson and Paul Ellingworth, *Biblical Revelation and African Beliefs*, Maryknoll, N.Y.: Orbis, 1969; Kofi Appiah-Kubi and Sergio Torres, *African Theology en Route*, Maryknoll, N.Y.: Orbis, 1979; Kwesi Dickson, *Theology in Africa*; Mercy Amba Oduyoye, *Hearing and Knowing: Theological Reflections on Christianity in Africa*, Maryknoll, N.Y.: Orbis, 1986.

cratic order. The situation has been the reverse in South Africa where contemporary theologies have been honed in the struggle against apartheid and where, until more recently, theologians, wary of the abuse of ethnicity and culture by apartheid ideologists, have not engaged in the cultural task now incumbent on them.[110] The demise of apartheid has opened up fresh possibilities for an urgently needed dialogue between prophetic and culturally focussed theologies. Without the prophetic, there is no critical insight; without the cultural, there is no creative engagement. In both cases the dialectic between Christian faith and the creation of an African democratic culture breaks down. For the sake of democratic transformation, that dialectic needs to be sustained.

[110] John W. de Gruchy, 'South African Theology Comes of Age', *Religious Studies Review*, 17,3, July 1991.

CHAPTER 7

Midwives of democracy in East Germany and South Africa

The fall of the Berlin Wall in 1989 and the first post-apartheid democratic elections in South Africa in 1994, are now widely regarded as epoch-making events at the turn of the century and symbols of the emerging new world order. It is appropriate then that our two concluding case studies should take us back to the opening comments in our Introduction, and focus on the role of the churches as midwives of democratic transition and reconstruction in Germany and South Africa.[1]

Comparisons between Germany and South Africa have been made previously with regard to Nazism and apartheid.[2] In many respects the church struggle against apartheid was as inspired by the German *Kirchenkampf* against Hitler as it was by the Civil Rights movement in the United States. But, just as in those instances it was inappropriate to make simplistic comparisons, so it is with regard to the transition to democracy in Germany and South Africa today.

While in both Germany and South Africa there has been a rejection of totalitarian and authoritarian regimes followed by the attempt to establish democratic social orders, the two cases cannot be equated. In East Germany the revolutionary change was from an anti-Christian totalitarian Communism towards a liberal democratic capitalist social order in a relatively homo-

---

[1] See also Wolfgang Huber, 'The Role of the Church in Situations of Transition', *Journal of Theology for Southern Africa*, 74, March 1991, 14ff.

[2] Brian Bunting, *The Rise of the South African Reich*, Harmondsworth, Middlesex: Penguin, 1969; Patrick J. Furlong, *Between Crown and Swastika: the Impact of the Radical Right on the Afrikaner Nationalist Movement in the Fascist Era*, Johannesburg: University of the Witwatersrand Press, 1991.

geneous cultural context. In multi-cultural South Africa, by
way of contrast, the transition has been from a virulently
anti-Communist, right-wing racist social order, which was
overtly Christian in its claims, to a non-racial democracy in
which members of the Communist Party play an important
part in government. Ironically, the African National Congress
and its Communist Party ally were supported by the German
Democratic Republic in the struggle against apartheid.

Although both the Communist and the apartheid social
orders had much in common as authoritarian states, our cases
thus represent democratic revolutions against two fundamentally opposed ideologies and their respective political
structures – the one from the left and the other from right – and
two different programmes of democratic reconstruction – the
one categorically capitalist in orientation, the other seeking a
way in which socialist concerns will be met within a market
system. The two cases are thus complementary. They are
laboratories in which the future shape of democracy is being
contested; they are also test cases for the global future of
democracy as such – Germany, especially in terms of the future
of Europe; South Africa, both with regard to the rest of sub-
Saharan Africa and as a laboratory of the world in microcosm.[3]
Failure in either could be catastrophic for the 'third democratic transformation' of the world.

LUTHERANS AND THE GERMAN
DEMOCRATIC REVOLUTION

Of all the post-war, eastern bloc countries, East Germany was
the most uncompromising in its commitment to Marxist–
Leninism. Although the only state 'to guarantee religious
freedom to its members' from the time of its establishment in
1949, it was strongly anti-Christian.[4] Communist exiles who
returned from the Soviet Union and assumed positions of

---

[3] Heribert Adam and Kogila Moodley, *The Negotiated Revolution: Society and Politics in Post-Apartheid South Africa*, Johannesburg: Jonathan Ball, 1993, p. 12.
[4] Vera Wollenberger, 'The Role of the Lutheran Church in the Democratic Move-
ment in the GDR', *Religion in Communist Lands*, 19,3–4, Winter 1991, 207.

power were usually doctrinaire in their rejection of religion. Antagonism was also rooted in the long history of the alienation of the working class from the church in Germany, and the support which many Christians gave to Nazism. German Communists were among the first to suffer at the hands of the Nazis – their leader Ernst Thälmann died in Buchenwald in 1944, and many others were forced to flee into exile in the Soviet Union. Some returned after 1945 and became important figures in the new government. Erich Honecker, the president of the GDR from 1961 until its demise, was in a Gestapo prison for ten years.[5]

A 'church in socialism'

Prior to 1945 almost 90 per cent of the population of the GDR belonged to the various *Evangelische Landeskirchen*, and was overwhelmingly Lutheran. As a remnant of Nazi and bourgeois society, the church was perceived by the new regime as an integral part of a culture which had to be eradicated. Beginning in 1951, at the height of the Stalinist cold-war period, Walter Ulbricht, who was then General Secretary of the *Sozialistische Einheitspartei Deutschlands* (SED) persistently attacked the church, especially targeting work amongst students and young people (*Junge Gemeinde*).[6] Johannes Hamel, university chaplain in Halle and a leader of the student Christian movement (*Studentengemeinde*), was the prophetic theologian of those who rejected both the anti-Communism of Bishop Otto Dibelius and the atheism of the SED. In the tradition of Karl Barth, Hamel developed a dialectical theology of critical solidarity which was to be 'the hallmark of Christian witness in the GDR'.[7] Many of the leaders of the later democratic revolution

---

[5] Victoria Barnett, *For the Soul of the People: Protestant Protest against Hitler*, New York: Oxford University Press, 1992, p. 257.

[6] R. Solberg, *God and Caesar in East Germany: the Conflicts of Church and State in East Germany Since 1945*, New York: Macmillan, 1961.

[7] Paul Oestreicher, 'Christian Pluralism in a Monolithic State ; the Churches of East Germany 1945–1990', *Religion, State and Society*, 21,3–4, 1993, 267; See also Karl Barth and Johannes Hamel, *How to Serve God in a Marxist Land*, New York: Association Press, 1959.

were schooled in the student Christian movement. Just as 'Christian motives, together with moral-humanistic, liberal, socialist ideas of democracy, played a large part in the conspiracy of 20 July 1944',[8] so it was a combination of these elements which, in post-war East Germany, laid the foundations for later democratic developments.

Communist leaders were convinced that religion would disappear during one generation. As a result there was considerable tension between the church and the state, coinciding, so it happened, with growing conflict between the state and workers. This erupted in a workers' uprising in June 1953 which was brutally suppressed by Soviet intervention, revealing a growing gap between the Communist Party leadership and the workers whom they claimed to represent. It also marked the beginning of a recurring pattern 'in which a specific church–state conflict coincided with public unrest on other points, its effects rippling throughout the entire society'.[9]

During the years of Soviet *détente*, the situation changed for the better. But the relationship between church and state remained tense until Walter Ulbricht's 'Policy Statement' in 1960 in which it was acknowledged that Christianity and Communism shared the same humanitarian goals and were therefore not necessarily in contradiction. This was tacit recognition that the state had failed to destroy the churches, but it was also a shrewd political move to harness the influence of the Protestant churches in supporting GDR policies and giving them some international legitimation. In addition there were always those pastors who were fellow-travellers with the regime. Ironically, in East Germany the first major study on Bonhoeffer's theology was an attempt to use him to legitimate an uncritical solidarity with Marxist–Leninism.[10]

The Protestant church in the GDR had been part of the *Evangelische Kirche im Deutschland* (EKD) when the latter was established in 1948 to unite all the Protestant *Landeskirchen* in the two Germanies. The EKD was regarded by the East

---

[8] Bracher, *German Dictatorship*, p. 483.   [9] *Ibid.*, p. 261.
[10] Hanfried Muller, *Von der Kirche zur Welt*, Hamburg: Herbert Reich Evag. Verlag, 1961.

German leadership as a 'foreign body' seeking the unification of Germany, and therefore as unacceptable. Thus Ulbricht and then Honecker, who took over leadership of the Party in 1961, put pressure on the church to break its formal links with the EKD and become autonomous. Significantly, the Berlin Wall was erected in 1961 only a few weeks after the Berlin *Kirchentag* had brought East and West German Christians together in large numbers, providing a platform for expressing growing dissatisfaction with conditions in the GDR. It was only in June 1969 that formal ties with the EKD were severed and the *Evangelischer Kirchenbund* (Protestant Federation) was formed out of the eight *Landeskirchen* in the GDR.

At first, church opponents of Nazi totalitarianism found it difficult to contemplate any co-operation with a Communist one-party state, but during the sixties a new church–state relationship was worked out by the Protestant leadership, and a decision was taken to be a 'church in socialism'. This did not mean being in uncritical solidarity with the regime, but searching for ways of serving *within*, rather than *against*, socialism. Central to this policy was a pastoral commitment to the people of the GDR, and a concern to bring about much needed social reform. This also meant encouraging people to stay in the GDR and work for change, rather than fleeing to the West. In fact the EKD in West Germany made it very difficult for East German pastors to find parishes in the West for this very reason.[11] The immense 'brain-drain' from the GDR was an important reason why the Berlin Wall had been erected.

The Protestant 'church in socialism' policy was in contrast to that of the Roman Catholic hierarchy which distanced itself from the state, only involving itself in political issues when its own interests were threatened. While some Catholic bishops were convinced that the GDR would not survive very long, the Protestant leadership made their decision on the contrary assumption that the socialist system would endure. It was also assumed, incorrectly in hindsight, that the GDR leadership was willing and capable of undertaking the necessary reforms

[11] Barnett, *For the Soul of the People*, pp. 263, 265.

needed to transform society. The Protestant decision was recognized as a risky one by its own leadership, as it could so easily lead to compromise. Yet it prevented the church from becoming trapped in a ghetto, and helped create an unusual place for the church in a socialist society, recognized officially by the state yet used by dissidents within an 'ideologically free space'.[12]

Many Protestant church leaders and theologians conceived the task of the 'church in socialism' on the basis of the experience of the Confessing church. Christian resistance to Hitler remained vividly alive in the collective memory of the church. Bonhoeffer's theology, in particular, enabled them to walk the tightrope between compromise and irrelevancy.[13] Albrecht Schönherr, a former student of Bonhoeffer and the bishop of Berlin-Brandenburg after the Protestant Federation was formed, later described the task of 'the church in socialism' as preserving its freedom in order 'to fulfil its task as Jesus Christ's "community of witness and service", and as far as possible to secure freedom for individual Christians to live in accordance with their faith'.[14] Schönherr went on to say that it 'was also the duty of the church leadership in a state ruled by party dictatorship, to preserve or win as many human rights as possible for all citizens'.[15] Together with his legal adviser, Manfred Stolpe, Schönherr was responsible for doing precisely this, ever seeking to maintain the crucial balance between irrelevance and compromise.[16]

The Communist Party permitted the Protestant church to participate in international ecumenical organizations, notably the World Council of Churches, the Lutheran World Federation and especially the pro-socialist Prague Christian Peace

---

[12] *Ibid.*, p. 269.

[13] See John P. Burgess, 'Church-State Relations in East Germany: the Church as a "Religious" and "Political" Force', *Journal of Church and State*, 32,1, Winter 1990.

[14] Albrecht Schönherr, 'Dietrich Bonhoeffer under der Weg der Kirche in der DDR', in Albrecht Schönherr and Wolf Krötke, eds., *Bonhoeffer-Studien: Beitrage zur Theologie und Wirkungsgeschichte Dietrich Bonhoeffer*, Berlin: Evangelische Verlagstalt, 1985, pp. 148ff.; Albrecht Schönherr 'Church and State in the GDR', *Religion in Communist Lands*, 19,3–4, Winter 1991, 197.

[15] *Ibid.*   [16] Oestreicher, 'Christian Pluralism in a Monolithic State', p. 270f.

Conference. This was a two-edged sword for the GDR authorities. It helped project an image that the church was not being persecuted, and that it even approved of socialist policies, while providing an opportunity to express criticism of western human rights violations as well as strengthen ties between the GDR and Third World countries. Yet such contacts also provided a window on the world, and eventually led to the criticism of human rights violations within Soviet bloc countries themselves.[17] During the seventies such criticism became more explicit. What is also of significance is that the GDR regime, because of its own desperate need for foreign money, allowed the church to receive considerable financial aid from the EKD in West Germany, without which the church might not have had the resources to achieve what it finally did.[18]

Creating space for a revolution

The catalysts for criticism were the introduction of compulsory military service and especially the introduction of defence studies in the school system. Overnight the Protestant church became the 'champion of parents, both Christian and non-Christian, who were opposed to defence studies for their children'.[19] Soon after this, the focus of criticism shifted to the Warsaw Pact decision to station nuclear rockets in the GDR, and this led in turn to the birth of the peace movement, the first major opposition coalition in the country.[20] The Helsinki Conference on Security and Co-operation in Europe, held in the middle of 1975, then 'gave the Church the opportunity to link international peace issues with internal civil rights questions'.[21]

Inspired by the non-violent Civil Rights movement and anti-Vietnam protests in the United States in the sixties, peace

[17] John A. Moses, 'The Church's Role in the Collapse of Communism in East Germany 1989–1990', *Colloquium*, 23,3, 1991, 128.
[18] Oestreicher, 'Christian Pluralism in a Monolithic State', p. 274.
[19] Wollenberger, 'The Role of the Lutheran Church', p. 208.
[20] *Ibid.*   [21] Moses, 'Church's Role', p. 128.

groups were formed in Protestant parishes, attracting Catholics[22] as well as non-Christians, a significant number of whom became conscientious objectors. By 1979 the churches in Dresden were holding special prayer services for peace, anticipating what would later happen in Leipzig. Thus the churches began to provide a protective space in which other issues concerning human rights and the environment could be discussed. The churches also provided leadership, theological and ethical insight, and other resources. In turn, the churches gained growing moral support even from beyond their membership. At a more official level, the Synod of the Federation of Protestant Churches made clear statements, notably in 1982 and again in 1987, 'opposing "the spirit, logic and practice of deterrence"'.[23]

After meeting with Schönherr in March 1978, Erich Honecker set out a new policy for church–state relations in which the state recognized a positive role for the church, and not just individual Christians, within society. This made it possible for the church authorities to put their own concerns on the agenda in a new way, and 'intercede for individual citizens – even those who were not church members – and often help them effectively'.[24] The authorities were willing to talk as long as the socialist system as such was not being criticized. So church leaders had 'to weigh up whether helping individuals or criticizing the system was more important'.[25] This became increasingly tricky the more it became apparent to church leaders that the GDR leadership was really unable to bring about desperately needed socio-economic reforms. By the end of the seventies the GDR had entered a period of serious economic stagnation, paralysis, and decline, and, despite Honecker's promises and statements, the church was placed under 'horrendous surveillance' as tension began to mount within society at large.[26]

Criticism of the state became unavoidable on a range of

[22] Hans-Friedrich Fischer, 'The Catholic Church in the GDR: a Look Back in Anger', *Religion in Communist Lands*, 19, 3–4, Winter 1991, p. 217.
[23] Schönherr, 'Church and State', p. 203.   [24] *Ibid.*, p. 202.   [25] *Ibid.*
[26] *Ibid.*, p. 199.

issues, especially on matters of militarization. In an astonishing act of harmony in mid-1987, members of the state youth movement, the Protestant *Junge Gemeinde*, and many peace groups, joined together in the Olaf Palme March for Peace, which criss-crossed the GDR. This proved too much for the state and led to an escalation in police security action.[27] An environmental library in Berlin was raided that November and members of the staff arrested. Likewise arrests were made at a rally of remembrance for Rosa Luxemburg and Karl Liebknecht, Marxist heroes who were murdered in 1919. They had been especially critical of totalitarianism, maintaining that there could be no socialism without democracy. These events sparked off the first big public demonstration of solidarity, a four-day vigil in the Zionskirche in Berlin. As a result the prisoners were released. Continued police action led to further services of solidarity in churches round the country, and in turn to the formation of a human rights group in the Nikolaikirche in Leipzig which held public prayers for peace every Monday.[28] Thus began the Monday demonstrations which spread to other churches in Leipzig and elsewhere, and eventually led to massive public demonstrations outside church buildings despite a heavy police presence. The way was prepared for 'the revolution before whose non-violent power the SED regime was compelled to capitulate'.[29]

Several Lutheran and ecumenical developments gave direction and stimulation to the process: the synod of Berlin-Brandenburg's decision in April 1988 to welcome the democratization process begun under President Gorbachov in the Soviet Union, expressing the hope that the same might happen in the GDR, despite Honecker's wishes; the publication of twenty theses for social renewal, 'a courageous

[27] The Stasi files were made public in January 1992. They included six million names, the names of 100,000 paid agents and a further 180,000 informers, many of whom had infiltrated the church or been pastors within it. Information based on discussions with the Assistant Director of the office charged with processing the Stasi files, Berlin, May 1992.

[28] Wollenberger, 'The Role of the Lutheran Church', p. 210.

[29] Schönherr, 'Church and State', p. 204.

demand for democracy',[30] written by Friedrich Schorlemmer, a theologian from Wittenberg, and presented at a church conference in Halle in June; and the widespread grass-roots participation in the European Ecumenical Assembly on 'Justice, Peace and the Integrity of Creation' in May 1989. The state found it impossible to marginalize the church, and at least three years before the end Honecker was 'unable to take any political decision without considering how it would be received by the opposition and the church'.[31]

The end came swiftly, as more and more people escaped to the West from 1987 onwards, and as protest meetings grew in size and scope. The final straw was the electoral fraud in May 1989 which indicated that there was no chance of democratic reform within the system, and that the only way forward was through non-violent revolution. New Forum groups criticized church leadership for not acting more forthrightly and even trying to control events.[32] Their criticism had some validity, although they failed to acknowledge that throughout the previous decade Protestant church leaders 'had prepared the way in a long conciliar process – year after year offering an alternative worldview and way of life'.[33] Peace and human rights had long been their concern.

Perhaps above all else, the churches kept hope alive in a situation of growing despair and hopelessness, and they 'nurtured civil society in a totalitarian era when others could not or would not'.[34] It was precisely because the church had engaged in dialogue with socialism, honouring the ideals of peace and justice for which it stood but which it had failed to practice, that it could provide leadership in the crises of 1989.[35] For once in German history, the church was not part of a reactionary movement, but an enabler of social change. Instead of Luther's doctrine of the 'two kingdoms' preventing prophetic praxis, as

[30] Moses, 'Church's Role', p. 130.
[31] Wollenberger, 'The Role of the Lutheran Church', p. 209.
[32] Ascherson, in Dunn, *The Unfinished Journey*, p. 225.
[33] Niels Nielsen, *Revolutions in Eastern Europe*, New York: Orbis, 1991, p. 29.
[34] *Ibid.*, p. 16; Wollenberger, 'The Role of the Lutheran Church', p. 207.
[35] Nielsen, *Revolutions in Eastern Europe*, p. 34.

was traditionally the case, it gave the church the necessary freedom to become an agent of dissent and the handmaid of revolution.

The democratic revolution in the GDR was about the restoration of human rights in a civil society, but it was also, in the tradition of the Civil Rights movement, 'a victory of non-violence over violence, of spirituality over the debasement of human beings'.[36] Those in authority had failed to recognize how much their suppression of Christianity had run counter to the Lutheran tradition and culture of the majority of the people. Economic factors were obviously fundamental in forcing change in the GDR, but the country also imploded through the collapse of moral values.[37]

Communist society, out of touch with reality and out of ideas, lacked credibility and meaning. It could promise, but not deliver; it could try and control the media, but it could not suppress the truth. Materialist dogma and substitute rituals had not sufficed, and even those who were truly committed to Marxist and socialist ideals were themselves disillusioned by the totalitarian means and mind-set of those in power, as well as by their inability to respond creatively to criticism. East Germans had lived under totalitarian regimes since 1933, and previous to that under an authoritarian Prussian monarchy. For decades almost everyone had been leading a double life, unable to utter or live the truth in public. Liberation began when some, including many Christians and some church leaders, dared to think within the framework of a 'post-totalitarian mind'.[38] In the end, the percentage of committed Christians and committed Marxists in relation to the rest of the population was small, but the Christians proved to be the creative minority because they had long since learnt not to be dependent on the state and to assert an inner freedom.

Twenty-one Protestant pastors won seats in the first demo-

---

[36] *Ibid.*, p. 7.
[37] A comment made to the author during a discussion in May 1992 with Christians in Berlin who had been participants in the events of 1989.
[38] Walter Sawatsky, 'Truth Telling in Eastern Europe: the Liberation and the Burden', *Journal of Church and State*, 33,4, Autumn 1991, 726.

cratically elected parliament in 1990, a testimony to their leadership in the struggle for democracy,[39] and possibly a previously repressed desire to become politicians at a time when this was impossible.[40] In the absence of any other non-governmental organizations, they were amongst the few people available who had any real knowledge of democratic procedures.[41] This did not mean 'a seizure of power by the church', as New Forum charged, but a case of the churches 'having to take over the thankless task of liquidating the GDR at a time of political and moral collapse'. Many Christians had retained their integrity in a corrupt society, and had more understanding of democracy than most other people.[42] Indeed, the churches' establishment of Round Tables throughout the country after the Honecker government collapsed prepared the way for the first elections and prevented anarchy.[43]

The East German experience suggests at least three contributions which the church can make to the process of democratization in such situations.[44] The first is the development of an appropriate theology of a church 'open to the world', concerned about the marginalized, and committed to a more inclusive and participatory society.[45] The second is a willingness to provide 'free space' for alternative groups working for social change. The third is the need for the church to be in 'critical solidarity' with such groups, and not allow itself to be misused in giving legitimacy to acts or policies which are unjust.

---

[39] See John S. Conway, 'How to Serve God in a Post-Marxist Land? East German Protestantism's Contribution to a Peaceful Revolution', *The Journal of Religious History*, 16,2, December 1990, 138; Richard V. Pierard, 'Religion and the East German Revolution', *Journal of Church and State*, 23,3, Summer 1990, 509.

[40] Beth Cantrell and Ute Kemp, 'The Role of the Protestant Church in Eastern Germany: Some Personal Experiences and Reflections', *Religion, State and Society*, 21,3–4, 1993, 281.

[41] Huber, in Witte, *Christianity and Democracy*, p. 47.

[42] Schönherr, 'Church and State', p. 204.

[43] Wollenberger, 'The Role of the Lutheran Church', p. 210.

[44] John B. Burgess, 'Preparing for the Fall of 1989: Religion and Democratization in East Germany, *Soundings*, 74,1–2, Spring/Summer, 1991.

[45] The significance of this theology for the church in a reunited Germany is a matter of considerable debate. See the discussion by Friedrich Wilhelm Graf and Wolfgang Huber in *Zeitschrift für Evangelische Ethik*, 36, 1992, 179ff., 303f.

There is also a sobering lesson to be learnt. The revolution of 1989 only led to the 'incomplete liberation' of the GDR.[46] With the reunification of Germany, the revolution was, in a sense, hijacked by the architects of 'liberal, capitalist democracy' who, in many ways, proceeded to strip the country of its assets and undermine some of its achievements. In the process, the church was sidelined to the periphery of society and beholden to the church in West Germany, which, it must be said, only made a formal statement on democracy as late as 1985.[47] 'Thirty-five years earlier', comments Wolfgang Huber, the present bishop of Berlin, 'this memorandum would have doubtless been something of an event'.[48] Hence the urgent need for the church to redefine its public role in the reunified Germany in terms of the new victims of injustice, and not succumb either to disillusionment or to the temptation to retreat into its pre-1933 parochialism as Bonhoeffer feared it would. This would mean that the vision of the 'church in socialism' and the church as an agent of democratic revolution would be surrendered, and its role in the ongoing democratic transformation of Germany and Europe seriously impaired.

THE CHURCH AND DEMOCRATIC RECONSTRUCTION IN SOUTH AFRICA[49]

The story of the long and painful struggle against apartheid by the African National Congress and other partners in the liberation movement,[50] and the role of the churches within it, has been told many times.[51] We will begin our case study by briefly

---

[46] Huber, in Witte *Christianity and Democracy*, p. 47.

[47] *Evangelische Kirche in Deutschland, Evangelische Kirche und Freiheitliche Demokratie: Eine Denkschrift der Evangelischen Kirche in Deutschland*, 1985.

[48] Huber, in Witte, *Christianity and Democracy*, p. 46.

[49] For a comprehensive theological discussion of the issues involved in democratic reconstruction in South Africa, see Charles Villa-Vicencio, *A Theology of Reconstruction: Nation-Building and Human Rights*, Cambridge University Press, 1992.

[50] For a recent account see John Pampalis, *Foundations of the New South Africa*, London: Zed Books, 1991.

[51] John W. de Gruchy, *The Church Struggle in South Africa*, Grand Rapids: Eerdmans, second edition, 1986; Charles Villa-Vicencio, *Trapped in Apartheid*, Maryknoll, N.Y.: Orbis, 1988.

recounting the final phase of that struggle which began with the student uprising in Soweto in 1976. This led to the 1977 banning of the Black Consciousness Movement (BCM) as well as the Christian Institute, led by Beyers Naudé, which had previously been in the forefront of Christian resistance to apartheid.[52] As a result, ecumenical leadership in the struggle was increasingly located within the South African Council of Churches (SACC), especially after Bishop Desmond Tutu became its General Secretary in 1978. The Roman Catholic church, an observer member of the SACC, and the South African Catholic Bishops' Conference (SACBC), co-operated closely with the SACC throughout this period.[53]

The work of the SACC and its affiliated regional councils was varied, but its major concern was to spearhead the churches' participation in the struggle against apartheid, and at the same time to care for and assist the victims of apartheid.[54] Without that solidarity, and the international ecumenical support which made it possible, it is highly unlikely that the resilience and hope of those who suffered so greatly in prison, under house arrest, and in many other ways, could have been sustained.

The rejuvenation of the liberation movement outside South Africa as a result of the Soweto uprising, the renewal and intensification of the armed struggle, and growing international and ecumenical solidarity with the anti-apartheid movement including economic sanctions, put enormous pressure on the white-minority South African government. This was especially so because of the dramatic changes which

[52] Peter Walshe, *Church Versus State in South Africa: the Case of the Christian Institute*, Maryknoll, N.Y.: Orbis, 1983; Charles Villa-Vicencio and John W. de Gruchy, *Resistance and Hope*, pp. 3ff.

[53] Peter Walshe, 'South Africa: Prophetic Christianity and the Liberation Movement', *The Journal of Modern African Studies*, 29,1, 1991, 45f.

[54] On the work and witness of the SACC during this period see, for example, M. Nash, ed., *Your Kingdom Come*, Papers and Resolutions of the Twelfth National Conference of the SACC, Hammanskraal, 5–8 May 1980; *The Divine Intention*, Presentation by Bishop D. Tutu, General Secretary of the SACC to the Eloff Commission of Enquiry, 1 September 1982; Hans Brandt, ed., *Outside the Camp: A Collection of the Writings by Wolfram Kistner*, Braamfontein: SACC, 1988; Sol Jacob, ed., *Hope in Crisis*, SACC National Conference Report, 1986.

were in process in southern Africa due to the liberation of Mozambique and Angola from Portuguese colonial rule in 1974. As a result the liberation struggle for Zimbabwe and Namibia intensified, with Zimbabwe gaining independence in 1980 and Namibia a decade later.

After the Soweto uprising, internal resistance and dissent had been kept in check by an increasingly powerful national state security system. At the same time, the war in Namibia and the intensification of the liberation struggle both externally and internally forced the South African government to introduce some changes in order to gain international legitimacy and prevent a full-scale revolution. However, President P. W. Botha's attempt to broaden 'white democracy' to include Coloureds and Indians, but not Africans, in a segregated tricameral parliamentary system in 1983, simply meant the perpetuation of white power. This set off a new wave of resistance to apartheid under the leadership of the United Democratic Front (UDF), launched in 1982.

'Kairos': judgment and opportunity

A broad coalition of anti-apartheid organizations, the UDF was in effect the internal wing of the ANC, and had the support of many Christian activists around the country.[55] A key figure was Dr Allan Boesak, a minister of the *NG Sendingkerk* (Dutch Reformed Mission Church), who began to play an increasingly important role in the ecumenical church's resistance to apartheid. Partly under his influence his own church, and a broader coalition of black-led Reformed churches (Dutch Reformed, Presbyterian, and Congregational), initiated a frontal attack upon the attempt to provide theological justification for apartheid by declaring it a heresy.[56] Archaic as this may appear in the modern world, within the context of 'Christian' South Africa it was a direct

---

[55] For a detailed account see Walshe, 'Prophetic Christianity', pp. 34ff.
[56] See John W. de Gruchy and Charles Villa-Vicencio, *Apartheid is a Heresy*, Grand Rapids: Eerdmans, Cape Town: David Philip, 1983.

challenge to the moral legitimacy of the state at precisely the moment in which it was seeking such legitimacy.

In response to growing resistance, P. W. Botha intensified efforts to destroy the liberation movement. Rejecting appeals by the world community to negotiate, Botha opted for a state security solution to his dilemma with the declaration of a general state of emergency in 1986, a situation which was to last until 1990. Part of Botha's strategy was to co-opt whatever church groups he could, and to try to discredit and destroy the witness of those he could not. Direct security police action against Christian activists was supported by a continuous propaganda attack on 'radical Christians' and 'liberation theology' by the state-controlled media, all of which created division and polarization within the member churches of the SACC, weakening further an already inadequate witness. Right-wing fundamentalist groups, financed by the state, engaged in a vociferous war on the ecumenical church as part of the state security's offensive against what it referred to as the 'total onslaught' on South Africa by Communism and the liberation movements.[57]

One response to the deepening crisis in South Africa was the National Initiative of Reconciliation (NIR) which was launched in Pietermaritzburg in 1985.[58] Sponsored by Africa Enterprise, an evangelical para-church organization, the NIR managed to gather together a wide range of Christian leaders, including white Dutch Reformed church leaders and SACC representatives. In a display of unity on political issues remarkable for that period, the NIR issued a statement which called for the release of all political prisoners, the return of exiles, and talks between the government and the 'authentic leadership of the various population groups with a view toward equitable power sharing in South Africa'.[59]

[57] On 'right-wing' Christian movements in South Africa, see the *Journal of Theology for Southern Africa*, 69, December 1989.

[58] The general stance of the NIR may be ascertained from Klaus Nürnberger and John Tooke, eds., *The Cost of Reconciliation*, Cape Town: Methodist Publishing House, 1988; Klaus Nürnberger, John Tooke, and Bill Domeris, *Conflict and the Quest for Justice*, Pietermaritzburg: Encounter, 1989; and Nürnberger, *A Democratic Vision*.

[59] 'NIR Statement of Affirmation', *Journal of Theology for Southern Africa*, 54, March 1986.

A more radical response was expressed in the *Kairos Document* a few weeks later.[60] While the NIR recognized the connection between justice and reconciliation, and called for an end to apartheid, the 'Kairos theologians' argued that the notion of reconciliation was being widely abused in the church as a means to obviate the need for fundamental change. Recognizing that the basic difference between Christians in South Africa was not primarily denominational or confessional, but political and economic, the *Kairos Document* rightly perceived that the church itself was a site of the struggle against apartheid, and identified three conflicting groups within it which, in certain respects, are in continuity with those which we have previously identified within the history of Christianity as reactionary, reformist, and radical.

Under the rubric of 'state theology' the *Kairos Document* placed those who supported the apartheid status quo and gave it theological legitimacy; under 'church theology' it placed those who emphasized the need for reform and reconciliation without the fundamental restructuring of society; and in opposition to both it spoke of a 'prophetic theology' of resistance and democratic transformation. Heated controversy ensued within the churches, and state repression against Christian activists intensified. Recognizing a moment of judgment as well as opportunity, the 'Kairos theologians' called for direct Christian participation in the struggle, including acts of civil disobedience in resistance to government tyranny.

The influence of the *Kairos Document* can be seen in 'The Harare Declaration' adopted by a conference of ecumenical church leaders from around the world which met in the Zimbabwean capital in December 1985.[61] Amongst its recommendations, the Declaration called on the ecumenical church to

---

[60] *The Kairos Document*, Grand Rapids: Eerdmans, 1986; See also John W. de Gruchy, 'From Cottesloe to the "Road to Damascus"': Confessing Landmarks in the Struggle against Apartheid', in G. Loots, ed., *Listening to South African Voices*, Proceedings of the Theological Society of South Africa, Port Elizabeth, August 1990; de Gruchy, 'The Church and the Struggle for South Africa', in Buti Tlhagale and Itumuleng Mosala, eds., *Hammering Swords into Ploughshares: Essays in Honor of Archbishop Mpilo Desmond Tutu*, Johannesburg: Skotaville, 1986, pp. 198ff.
[61] 'The Implications of Harare', *ICT News*, March 1986, pp. 3ff.

give its support to the liberation movements, and on the international community to apply comprehensive sanctions against South Africa immediately. It also called for prayer 'to end unjust rule in South Africa'. In response, services of prayer were held during 1986 in some, though not many, churches.[62] These anticipated the prayer vigils in East Germany in 1989, and constituted a frontal challenge to the legitimacy of the state.

Long-standing personal relations and a common commitment to the anti-apartheid struggle had ensured that there had always been contact between some church leaders and the liberation movement in exile. This relationship developed and deepened in the late seventies and early eighties as the ecumenical church in South Africa, together with the trade unions, assumed the leadership of the struggle. Quite apart from ecumenical contact and consultation, there were also meetings between denominational leaders and representatives of the liberation movements in exile. In 1986, for example, the executive of the United Congregational Church met ANC leaders in Bulawayo, Zimbabwe, and that same year the Catholic bishops sent a delegation to meet with ANC leaders in Lusaka, the Zambian capital.[63] Anglican and Methodist leaders had similar contact. And then, in May 1987, ecumenical church leaders gathered again, also in Lusaka, with leaders of trade unions, women's and youth organizations, and anti-apartheid groups from around the world.[64] In continuity with the Harare Declaration, 'The Lusaka Statement' called upon the churches to support the liberation struggle, both in Namibia (which was not yet independent) and South Africa, and declared that the South African government was illegitimate.

In May 1988 a concerted programme of mass Christian action was launched by the SACC after a convocation of church leaders entitled the 'Standing for the Truth Cam-

[62] Allan A. Boesak and Charles Villa-Vicencio, eds., *When Prayer Makes News*, Philadelphia: Westminster, 1986.
[63] Walshe, 'Prophetic Christianity', p. 48.
[64] *The Churches Search for Justice and Peace in South Africa*, Geneva: WCC, 1987.

paign'.[65] This campaign failed to achieve its full potential. Yet, as Frank Chikane, General Secretary of the SACC later noted, it did contribute significantly, within the context of the Mass Democratic Movement spearheaded by the UDF, to the events which led to the unbanning of the liberation movements in February 1990.[66] In the end, apartheid could not withstand the challenge of truth and the legitimacy of the struggle for justice. Although the witness of the church was sometimes sullied by compromise, and while there were other important players in the process, there can be little doubt that the church played a key role in the ending of apartheid.

A redefining of roles

The unbanning of the liberation movements on 2 February 1990, and the subsequent release of Nelson Mandela from prison after twenty-seven years, signalled the beginning of the 'negotiated revolution' which followed. An immediate consequence was that church leaders who had been at the forefront of the struggle became less prominent. Some, like Archbishop Tutu, were the first to recognize that they were no longer the political representatives of the oppressed. As in Germany, there was a need to redefine the role of the churches. Yet, as subsequent events unfolded, there was no time for any retreat from the public arena. With the eruption of political violence in many parts of the country the political task of the churches, though now different, remained as crucial as ever.[67]

Two ecumenical conferences were of particular importance in helping the churches rethink their role. The Rustenburg

---

[65] See the mimeographed Report of the Convocation of Churches in South Africa, 30–31 May 1988; comprehensive preparatory material was published under the title *Emergency Convocation of Churches in South Africa*, SACC, 1988, and a brochure, 'The Standing for the Truth Campaign', published subsequently, detailed possible lines of action.

[66] Frank Chikane, Foreword to *Standing for the Truth*, published by the Southern Transvaal region of the campaign, 1991. See also Charles Villa-Vicencio, *The Spirit of Hope: Conversations on Politics, Religion and Values*, Johannesburg: Skotaville, 1993, p. 67.

[67] See Frank Chikane, 'The Church's Role During a Period of Transition', an address given on 12 August 1992, published by Diakonia, Durban.

Conference, held in November 1991, brought together an extraordinary cross-section of church leadership representing more than 90 per cent of South Africa's Christians, and more than 70 per cent of the population.[68] Given the range of theological, denominational, and ideological opinion, it was remarkable that a consensus could be reached on a range of significant issues. These included a confession of guilt for the sins of apartheid; the need to work for justice, especially economic justice; restitution in health, education, housing, employment, and land ownership; the need for the exclusion of 'racial, gender, class and religious discrimination in the implementation of justice'; the 'acceptance of the Rule of Law under an independent judiciary' and the 'entrenchment of a Bill of Rights'; and the 'establishment of a democratic elective process based on one-person, one-vote ... in a multi-party democracy in a unitary State'.[69]

The second conference was convened by the South African member churches of the WCC in Cape Town the following October (1992). Recognizing the important changes which had happened since February 1990, the Cape Town Conference was nevertheless mindful of the crisis facing South Africa as reflected in the escalating violence and the general instability of the country. The Statement adopted by the Conference listed five dimensions to the task of the church in the process of democratic transformation.[70] The first was the exposure and eradication of all persisting forms of apartheid, exploitation, and discrimination; the second was the liberation of church and society from an obsession with apartheid, to deal with the urgent and life-threatening issues facing the country (poverty, development, education, pollution, AIDS, and technological challenges); the third was to participate in the reconstruction of society on the basis of values determined by the kingdom of God and in solidarity with others committed to those values;

[68] Louw Alberts and Frank Chikane, eds., *The Road to Rustenburg: The Church Looking Forward to a New South Africa*, Cape Town: Struik, 1991, p. 10.
[69] *Ibid.*, pp. 275ff.
[70] 'Cape Town Statement', October 1991, *Journal of Theology for Southern Africa*, 77, December 1991, 84f.

the fourth was to express solidarity with those who suffer in other parts of the world; and the fifth was the need to transform the structures of the churches themselves. The Statement then went on to challenge the churches to become involved in peacemaking and the monitoring of the violence; in working for reconciliation, restitution, reconstruction, and justice, including justice for women and the enabling of young people to participate more fully in the democratic process. The Cape Town Statement also expressed the need for multi-cultural respect and tolerance, as well as for the renewal of the church, its unity and ongoing ecumenical solidarity.

Despite important achievements, Rustenburg had several shortcomings, most particularly in the way in which it failed to deal with sexism and gender issues,[71] and some compromises watered-down some of the prophetic demands of radical Christianity.[72] By the time of the Cape Town Conference all the hopes for an early negotiated settlement and elections had been dashed by the eruption of violence throughout the country. This was one reason why the Cape Town Conference was less euphoric than Rustenburg. It was also more prophetically focussed, reflecting the fact that those involved were united in their social analysis and their theological convictions. Yet, taken together, and also with the many other documents which subsequently emerged on the witness of the church in democratization,[73] both Rustenburg and Cape Town helped church leadership to redefine the prophetic and pastoral responsibilities of the church in a transitional

---

[71] Sheena Duncan, 'Some Reflections on Rustenburg', in Denise Ackermann, Jonathan A. Draper, and Emma Mashinini, *Women Hold up Half the Sky*, Pietermaritzburg: Cluster, 1991, pp. 386f.

[72] Malusi Mpumlwana, 'The Road to Democracy: The Role of Contextual Theology', Opening Address to the AGM of the Institute for Contextual Theology, May 1993.

[73] See, for example, 'Democracy and Voting in South Africa', An Information Manual, SACC, n.d.; 'Democracy and the Churches', the Pastoral Letter of the South African Catholic Bishops' Conference, April 1993; David Venter, ed., *Towards a Democratic Future: The Church and the Current Situation*, Johannesburg: Institute for Contextual Theology (ICT), 1993; 'The Road to Democracy', ICT, May 1993; *Christianity and Democracy*, Lenten Lectures, 1992, published by the Justice and Peace Commissions of the Roman Catholic dioceses of Johannesburg and Cape Town.

situation which was proving to be far more violent than anticipated.

Between February 1990 and the election in April 1994, the country was plunged into a cycle of violence which threatened to tear it apart. The causes of the violence were several, and varied from one part of the country to another.[74] Undoubtedly a 'third force' with links to the right-wing and elements in the security forces was partly, if not largely, responsible.[75] It was within this context that the churches once again became directly involved in the political arena.[76] Addressing the issue at the beginning of 1992, the Roman Catholic bishops noted that violence was part of the evil heritage of the past. 'Violence', they said, 'was used to impose apartheid and violence was used to resist it. Still today – violence wastes lives, destroys property, separates families and blights our very souls'. They also referred to the alarming extent to which 'people are being attacked and even killed for disagreeing about political parties or ideas'.[77]

Many church leaders, congregations, and Christian activists played an indispensable role in seeking to deal with the violence, not least through the various national and regional peace structures which were established. Methodist Bishop Mmutlanyane Stanley Mogoba and the General Secretary of the SACC, Frank Chikane, for example, played key roles in the leadership of these initiatives. Without the intervention of church leaders as mediators in many situations of conflict, it is doubtful whether South Africa would have been able to hold

---

[74] See Adam and Moodley, *The Negotiated Revolution*, pp. 121ff; *South Africa: Half-Hearted Reform*, published by Africa Watch, New York, May 1993.

[75] The Institute for Contextual Study took this position in identifying violence as 'the new kairos'. *Violence: The New Kairos: Challenge to the Churches*, Braamfontein: ICT, n.d.

[76] Ironically, some church leaders and theologians who became involved in seeking to bring about peace were held responsible by right-wing analysts for having sown the seeds of the violence. See Rachel Tingle, *Revolution or Reconciliation: The Struggle in the Church in South Africa*, London: Christian Studies Centre, 1992. In response see 'ICT Replies to Accusations', in *Challenge*, September 1992, pp. 8f.; Brian Brown, 'The Churches and Violence in South Africa', *CCSA Occasional Paper*, no. 1, 1993, published by Christian Concern for Southern Africa, London.

[77] *A Call to Build a New South Africa*, Pastoral Letter of the South African Catholic Bishops' Conference, January 1992, 2.7.

its first democratic elections. In preparation for these, various denominations and ecumenical agencies also became involved in extensive voter education programmes.[78] During the elections themselves, assisted by international ecumenical monitors established by the SACC with the help of overseas partners, they also acted as monitors.

As is already apparent, the churches have played a variety of roles in the process of democratic transition in South Africa, and they have a full agenda of tasks for the immediate as well as long-term future in the consolidation of democracy and democratic transformation. We will focus, however, on what may be regarded as three key responsibilities which derive directly from their pastoral, evangelical, and prophetic mandate.

Exorcizing the past

Apartheid has long been regarded by the United Nations as a crime against humanity, and there is a widespread sense of obligation to investigate and punish those responsible.[79] The issues are, however, extraordinarily complex, and if mishandled they could undermine any attempt to build a government of national unity and pursue the much-needed policies of reconstruction.[80] In the words of Albie Sachs, 'We're not simply dealing with a criminal generation, but with a criminal system that goes back deep into the past.'[81]

Some countries in post-Communist eastern Europe, such as Hungary and Czechoslovakia, aware of the threat to reconciliation and reconstruction posed by opening an investigation into past crimes, have tried to avoid the issues through amnesty

---

[78] Sheena Duncan, 'The Church's Role in Preparing for Free and Fair Elections', *Diakonia*, Durban, 1992; amongst the many documents being prepared by the churches for use in educating voters, see 'Democracy and Voting in South Africa', An Information Manual, no. 2, published by the SACC as part of its Education for Democracy Programme.

[79] See 'South Africa: Accounting for the Past', *Africa Watch*, 4,11, 23 October 1992, 19f.

[80] For a detailed discussion of the issues in South Africa and other similar contexts today, see Alex Boraine, Janet Levy, and Ronel Schaffer, eds., *Dealing with the Past: Truth and Reconciliation in South Africa*, Cape Town: Idasa, 1994.

[81] Albie Sachs, 'Amnesty not Amnesia', *New Era, Summer 1991*, p. 19.

legislation. Others, particularly Latin American countries such as the Argentine, Chile, and Uruguay, have instituted Commissions of Truth to bring to light the political crimes of previous regimes, without necessarily instituting legal proceedings against those responsible. In Germany, the approach has been directed far more at bringing those responsible for past crimes in the GDR to justice.[82] Each of these approaches is understandable and reasonable given their specific contexts. But what about South Africa and the role of the church in dealing with the past?

Many leaders in the struggle against apartheid have cautioned against a Nuremberg-type trial,[83] and some are now as wary of even the establishment of a truth commission to bring past crimes into the light. Certainly, the issues are far more difficult to deal with than in post-Nazi Germany, or even after the demise of the GDR, when the victors were in a position to determine what should be done. What might be morally right is not always politically feasible, and may even threaten the democratic process. This would then lead to even more suffering. Yet there is a counter-argument which, from a Christian perspective, must carry considerable weight. If a just democracy is to be established in South Africa, the truth about the past has to be established, guilt acknowledged, and forgiveness extended. Only in this way will the demons which have caused such suffering be exorcized. A concern for the victims of apartheid must be more important than the danger of unfairly victimizing the perpetrators of past crimes, and a concern for the rule of law must be as important for the future of democracy as the danger of alienating the military and police. The victims of apartheid need that hope which is 'born from the knowledge that justice has been done and will continue to be done'.[84]

---

[82] For a comparison of the issues see Konrad Raiser, *Democratization in Germany and South Africa: A Challenge to the Church*, published by the Ecumenical Foundation of Southern Africa (EFSA), 1993, pp. 12f.

[83] *Bishopscourt Update*, no. 7/1992, 17 November 1992.

[84] Kadar Asmal, 'Victims, Survivors and Citizens – Human Rights, Reparations and Reconciliation', Inaugural Lecture, 25 May 1992, University of the Western Cape, p. 29.

To enter this arena of personal and national soul-searching must of necessity open up many deep wounds, and lay bare the fact that even those who have struggled against injustice and oppression have also been tainted, compromised, and even corrupted in the process. Yet the aim is the restoration of the humanity of a nation which has been torn apart by racism, greed, and violence. As Karl Jaspers saw so clearly in post-war Germany on the eve of the Nuremberg trials, only a genuine confession of guilt can restore a nation's humanity.[85] To repress the demons of the past inevitably means the bedevilment of the future.

The pastoral responsibility of the church in South Africa in this regard parallels that of the Catholic church in Latin America where the rite of penance is being related by liberation theologians to structural sin and the creation of community.[86] The church's pastoral responsibility means that it will help everyone to recognize the nature and extent of his or her guilt, and confess it in appropriate ways; it will therefore oppose false accusations, scapegoating, and witch hunts; and it will help the victims of oppression to exercise forgiveness rather than vengeance.[87] The aim of any truth commission or confession of guilt must always be forgiveness, healing, and reconciliation.

The reality of this process does require, however, a further step – not punishment and vengeance, but appropriate reparation.[88] Reparation means affirmative action on behalf of all who have been unjustly disadvantaged, including the just restoration of land. This is the nub of the matter. Liberation and equality without reparation will not bring about justice. While it will be impossible to redress all the wrongs that have been perpetrated against the victims of colonial injustice and

[85] Karl Jaspers, *Die Schuldfrage: Zur politischen Haftung Deutschland*, Heidelberg: Verlagen Lambert Schneider, 1946; John W. de Gruchy, 'Guilt, Amnesty and National Reconstruction', *Journal of Theology for Southern Africa*, 83, June 1993. pp. 3ff.

[86] Michael Sievernich, '"Social Sin" and its Acknowledgment', *Concilium*, Edinburgh: T. & T. Clark, 1987.

[87] See 'Statement on Amnesty', issued by the Western Province Council of Churches, *Journal of Theology for Southern Africa*, 81, December 1992.

[88] *The Road to Damascus*, chapter 4.

apartheid, concrete steps have to be taken which will lead to a more equitable distribution of, and sharing in, the resources of society. It is not a question of retribution, but of healing and reconstruction, of restoring faith in the due processes of the law and thus nurturing a democratic culture.

Nurturing a democratic culture

Addressing the Free Ethiopian Church of Southern Africa, one of the oldest African Independent churches in the country, in December 1992, Mr Mandela called on the churches in South Africa 'to join other agents of change and transformation in the difficult task of acting as a midwife to the birth of our democracy and acting as one of the institutions that will nurture and entrench it in our society'.[89] As one of the main institutions within civil society, and especially as one deeply concerned about those values which are fundamental to the well-being of a just democratic society, the church has a particularly important responsibility and role in nurturing a democratic culture without which democracy cannot be sustained.

Just as totalitarianism in the GDR led to moral collapse, so apartheid has led to the subversion of fundamental human values: a denial of free speech and the subversion of the truth with lies; intolerance for the views of others; a disrespect for the rule of law and the exercising of authority; the cheapening of life and the undermining of family life; the manipulation of natural cultural differences; the abuse of human rights; the strengthening of the rich through corruption and at the expense of the poor.[90] If a just democracy and genuinely civil society is to be born and nurtured, it will require considerable effort to cultivate those core moral values which are essential for its existence and success. With this in mind, the Roman Catholic bishops in 1992 called on their membership 'to be good democrats' by evaluating political parties and policies in

---

[89] Speech to the Free Ethiopian Church of Southern Africa, 14 December 1992.
[90] John Aitchison, 'The Conflict in Natal – Prospects for Democracy', in Nürnberger, *A Democratic Vision*, p. 369; Stanley Mogoba, 'The Role of the Church in the Formation of Democratic Assumptions and Behaviour', in *ibid.*, p. 569.

terms of justice and the gospel, promoting democracy by providing 'an example of justice, respect and equality',[91] and encouraging the building of a civil society 'without domination by either the market or the state', and the empowerment of 'the poor and handicapped, the aged and youth, and women from every group'.[92]

With some justification, some analysts might well argue that no real culture of democracy exists in South Africa, and that this will make it impossible for democracy to be sustained even after a democratically elected government has been inaugurated. But this is not the whole truth. South Africa has a relatively strong civil society, especially in comparison with the rest of sub-Saharan Africa or the former GDR, despite concerted attempts by the apartheid state to undermine and destroy it. In building a democratic culture which will be able to sustain the transition to democratic rule and achieve social transformation, it is important to identify those strands of civil society in the country's social history which can be critically retrieved and woven into the tapestry of a new multi-cultural, democratic nation.[93]

Four such strands may be identified. Firstly, the traditional African communal and participatory understanding of society, *ubuntu*, which we discussed in the previous chapter; secondly, the liberal democratic tradition which, for all its faults, has none the less sought to uphold democratic values and principles;[94] thirdly, the democratic experience within the liberation struggle, and especially its grass-roots formations;[95] and

---

[91] *A Call to Build a New South Africa*, 3.13–15.

[92] *Ibid.*, 4.26.

[93] There are a number of organizations engaged in developing a democratic consciousness in South Africa, for example, the Institute for Democracy in South Africa (Idasa) which sponsored the Dakar, Senegal, meeting between the ANC and Afrikaners, as well as meetings with other South African groups, prior to February 1990.

[94] Jeffrey Butler, Richard Elphick, and David Welsh, eds., *Democratic Liberalism in South Africa: its History and Prospect*, Cape Town: David Philip, 1987; Paul B. Rich, *Hope and Despair: English-speaking Intellectuals and South African Politics 1896–1976*, London: British Academic Press, 1993.

[95] Mizana Matiwana, Shirley Walters, and Zelda Groener, *The Struggle for Democracy: A Study of Community Organizations in Greater Cape Town from the 1960s to 1988*, Centre

fourthly, democratic tradition and practice within religious communities, including the church, which is our particular focus.

The vast majority of South Africans claim some connection with one or other church. This does not imply strong commitment to Christian faith on the part of all, but the fact that the church embraces a wide spectrum of society means that it has considerable potential in helping to create a stronger civil society than most other institutions. Church organizations (women, youth, para-church, local churches) as well as denominational synods and ecumenical councils, have provided many people, not least those previously excluded from political participation in the government of the country, with expertise in democratic values and procedures at national, regional, and local levels. The churches are of key importance not only because of their prophetic role at a national level, but perhaps more importantly because of their potential to create participatory communities at the grass-roots.

This task is obviously not one which can or should be undertaken by the church in isolation from other religious communities. Hence the significance of the *Declaration on Religious Rights and Responsibilities* which was produced by the South African chapter of the World Conference on Religion and Peace in 1992, after two years of broad consultation. The declaration not only affirms the freedom of conscience and the equal rights of religious communities, which are fundamental to any truly democratic society, but it also calls on all religious communities to exercise their moral responsibility in society in ways which are essential for the nurturing of a just democracy.[96]

There are obvious similarities in the way in which the

---

for Adult and Continuing Education: University of the Western Cape, 1989; Molefe S. Tsele, 'Education for Democracy – a Case Study: The National Education Co-ordinating Committee (NECC)', in Nürnberger, *A Democratic Vision*, pp. 460f; and Malusi Mpumlwana, 'African democracy and grass roots conflict resolution', in *ibid.*, pp. 376f.

[96] *Declaration on Religious Rights and Responsibilities*, adopted by the National Inter-Faith Conference, Pretoria, 22–24 November 1992, under the auspices of the World Conference on Religion and Peace.

churches in the GDR and in South Africa acted as midwives in the democratic revolutions which have taken place in their respective countries. It is far too early to assess these roles in any depth. What is more important now is to focus on the role of the churches in enabling the process of democratic transition to move forward towards democratic transformation. The problems facing both Germany and South Africa in this period of reconstruction are immense. The legacies of a failed Communism and a failed apartheid will remain for generations. There is a long, hard road from transition to transformation, but it does appear that the church in South Africa will not be pushed onto the periphery of public life in the way in which this has happened in Germany.

Just as it is problematic to interpret the struggle against apartheid solely from the perspective of the Civil Rights struggle in the United States or the German *Kirchenkampf*, so it is equally problematic to assume that secularization will occur in the same way in which it has in Europe or North America since the Enlightenment. Even the term 'secularization' has to be used with care, given the ethnic, cultural, and religious complexity of the country, and the fact that vast sections of the population live in rural areas. This does not mean that the process of secularization as experienced elsewhere in the world is not a similar reality, or that most sections of the population are untouched by its impact. But South Africa remains a profoundly religious country, not least because of the underlying holistic character of African culture. The separation of the religious and the political, and the consequent privatization of piety, so fundamental to modernity, is countered by a very different cultural ethos in South Africa. Christianity will undoubtedly undergo significant changes in the future, but democratization will not necessarily mean that its public and prophetic role will be lessened.

Critical solidarity

The indispensable role of the churches and other religious communities in South Africa in the process of democratization is widely recognized.[97] This was emphasized by Mr Mandela on several occasions shortly before the elections in April 1994, and it was symbolically affirmed later at his inauguration as president. Addressing ANC supporters in Cape Town, many of them religious leaders, he even suggested that churches and other religious communities should play a direct role in government in order to ensure that moral values were respected in the new administration, to foster national reconciliation, and to help implement the ANC programme of national reconstruction.[98] The churches must surely provide such support. But what does this mean for the traditional insistence on the separation of church and state within a democratic society?

As in the case of the East German 'church in socialism', so the prophetic task of the church in post-apartheid South Africa must be redefined in terms of critical solidarity. The struggle is no longer to be understood primarily in terms of resistance and liberation, but in terms of reconstruction and transformation. Being in critical *solidarity* means giving support to those initiatives which may lead to the establishment not only of a new, but also a just, social order. It means that the church remains prophetic in its stance towards a new democratically elected government, that it must continue to stand for the truth, but now on the basis of a shared commitment to the realization of national reconstruction. Being in *critical* solidarity means continued resistance to what is unjust and false, and continued protest on behalf of what is just and true. In this regard the church has to be alert to the fact that liberation movements which come to power are not exempt from the temptation to resort to authoritarian rule.[99] No one has put this more sharply than Frank Chikane:

---

[97] Contrast Adam and Moodley who give little credit to the churches or the SACC for the ending of apartheid, nor anticipate them having a significant role in the building of a democratic society. See *The Negotiated Revolution*, p. 164, where they speak of the 'absence of strong religious communities' in South Africa!

[98] Speech at Zonnebloem College, Sunday 17 April 1994.

[99] Marina Ottaway, 'Liberation Movements and Transition to Democracy: the Case of the ANC', *Journal of Modern African Studies*, 29,1, 1991, 61ff.

It is important that the Church of Christ say it now – we stood for justice and we will continue to do so in the new era that is coming. Even if we eventually have a legitimate system in South Africa the struggle for the ideals of the reign of God will not stop.[100]

Critical solidarity means taking sides with all who remain oppressed in one form or another in a new democratic society, and participating with them in their never-ending struggle for justice, human dignity, and liberation. The church has to take seriously Mr Mandela's call that it warn against the 'danger of superficial changes that may leave power and privilege in the hands of whites and a sprinkling of affluent blacks'.[101] Critical solidarity also means the defence of the human rights of all people, especially minority cultural and religious groups, and taking the side of those who may be the new victims. Liberalization is not democratic transformation; adoption of the democratic *system* is not the realization of the *vision*.

The danger of the church being ignored by the government in South Africa, as it has been in the former East Germany, is far less than the danger of being co-opted. For this reason, the church has to avoid becoming the uncritical moral legitimator of the new order, and ensure that it keeps the government accountable and faithful to its promise of a just democracy. The continuing relevance of the church will therefore be determined not by the freedoms or status which the state may give it, but by the extent to which it engages in prophetic witness, pastoral care, and the nurturing of moral values in ways relating to circumstances which will continue to change. Hence the vital importance of ongoing critical theological reflection, the task to which we will shortly turn.

Twenty million South Africans of all races went to the polls for the first non-racial election held 26–29 April 1994. Against all expectations, the election was virtually free of violence. The election proved to be a cathartic experience in turning from the past, and a nation-building, consciousness-raising event in turning to the future. Many hardened secular observers

---

[100] Chikane, 'The Church's Role During a Period of Transition', p. 6.
[101] Speech delivered by Nelson R. Mandela, President of the ANC to the Free Ethiopian Church of Southern Africa, Potchefstroom, 14 December 1992.

labelled it a miracle, and some may even have pondered on the power of prayer. There remains, none the less, a long road ahead before the promise of a non-racial, non-sexist, and just democratic society is fulfilled.

PART IV

Critical theological reflection

CHAPTER 8

A theology for a just democratic world order

The Enlightenment, it has been said, 'was the original liberation movement'[1] of the modern age. Spawning the American
and French Revolutions, it ushered in a new world order in
which the people governed, set free from the hierarchies of the
past. In the New World, the new order was distinctly Protestant, liberal, and capitalist. In the Old World it was predomi-
inantly secular, and, in some respects, more socialist in orientation. Hence the definition of modernity as that historical
project, linked to both capitalism and socialism, which has
made democracy its chosen polity, the nation-state its form of
political sovereignty, and the bourgeoisie its creative vanguard.[2]

The Russian Revolution in 1917, also a product of modernity, was an attempt to break the hegemony of the bourgeoisie
and institute a new world truly governed by the people without
any distinction of class. Marxist–Leninism was, however, a
detour in the development of democracy, not its fulfilment.[3] In
the end, the Party not the people ruled with totalitarian
thoroughness. Hence the contemporary claim that the collapse
of Communism has heralded the victory not only of democracy, but more specifically of liberal democratic capitalism.
According to Fukuyama, modernity is back on track; Hegel's

---

[1] Albert Borgmann, *Technology and the Character of Contemporary Life: A Philosophical
Inquiry*, University of Chicago Press, 1984, p. 35. Quoted in Larry L. Rasmussen,
Moral Fragments & Moral Community, Minneapolis: Fortress, 1993, p. 27.
[2] *Ibid.*
[3] Neil Harding, 'The Marxist–Leninist Detour', in Dunn, *The Unfinished Journey*,
pp. 155ff.

prediction that the emancipatory promise of the Enlightenment and the French Revolution would be fulfilled has come
true. From a different perspective some would argue that we
are now already at the end of project-modernity, and are
searching for ways to understand what it means to be post-
modern.

Whether we regard the present time in the cultural history of
the world as the dying moments of modernity, or the birth of
post-modernity is unimportant. At the same time it is clear that
we are in a period of global transition in which significant
elements in the paradigm of modernity are being replaced by
others. As is the nature of paradigm shifts, there is both
continuity and discontinuity with the legacy of the past. All of
which is of considerable importance for our attempt to discern
the relationship between Christianity and democracy, and to
develop a theology for a just world order. For, if democracy
was wrenched from its Christendom matrix by the Enlightenment and the social movements it generated, thus becoming
the polity of modernity, it is now possible to renew the connection fruitfully on the basis of experience. After all, the world is
a very different place to what it was when, to use Berman's
metaphor again, the divorce between Christianity and democracy occurred. Hopefully, both are wiser.

Ecumenical Christianity, as we have seen, now recognizes
democracy as the best available option for the establishment of
a just social order, whether in individual countries or world-
wide. And there are those engaged in the struggle for democratic transition and transformation who recognize their need
for the support of religious communities, including the Christian church, both as instruments of enabling the process to take
place, and as nurturers of a culture of democratic moral value.
We now wish to take this discussion one step further as we
consider the theological basis for a just democratic world order.

At the outset we noted Niebuhr's contention that democracy
needs a firmer theological foundation than that which has been
provided for it by liberal culture. The same is true for the
Christian church if it is to participate in critical solidarity in
the process of global democratization. It is unsatisfactory, even

dangerous, for the church to become involved unless it under-
stands why, and in what way, this is consonant with its faith
and integral to its mission in the world. As our point of
departure for our theological response, we turn once again to
the claim made by Francis Fukuyama and others that the end
of Communism in eastern Europe, and the 'victory' of liberal
democratic capitalism, has ushered in a new world order.

THE REIGN OF GOD AND A JUST WORLD ORDER.

Like Fukuyama, many contemporary theologians have found
Hegel helpful in affirming the Enlightenment's emancipation
of the human spirit, while at the same time overcoming some of
its negative, rationalistic consequences.[4] Although aware that
whatever may be said in contradiction of Hegel's system probably has already been subsumed within it,[5] most theologians
have none the less expressed critical reserve even when affirming Hegel's achievement.[6] One major problem has been an
awareness of the danger of Hegelianism becoming a dialecti-
cally determined, and therefore closed system which, instead of
enabling human freedom as Hegel intended,[7] undermines it as
in nineteenth-century right-wing Hegelianism, or in contemporary neo-conservative adaptations of Hegel.[8] Nothing
could better illustrate this danger than Fukuyama's own
appropriation of Hegel in arguing that the dialectic of history
has been resolved in the victory of liberal democratic capitalism – the *telos* to which all of history has been moving –
signalling the end of ideology and the arrival of a lasting new
world order.

[4] See Wolfhart Pannenberg, 'The Significance of Christianity in the Philosophy of
Hegel', in *Basic Questions in Theology*, vol. 3, London: SCM, 1972, pp. 144ff.; Hans
Küng, *The Incarnation of God: An Introduction to Hegel's Theological Thought as a
Prolegomena to a Future Christology*, New York: Crossroad, 1987.

[5] Karl Barth, *Protestant Theology in the Nineteenth Century*, London: SCM, 1959, p. 396.

[6] See, for example, Milbank, *Theology and Social Theory*, pp. 148ff.

[7] Peter C. Hodgson, *New Birth of Freedom: A Theology of Bondage and Liberation*,
Philadelphia: Fortress, 1976, pp. 276f.

[8] For a critique of neo-conservative readings of Hegel, see Jürgen Habermas, *The
Philosophical Discourses of Modernity*, Cambridge: Polity Press 1987, pp. 68f.

But, it may well be asked, is not Christianity itself an ideology which hinders rather than helps the process of human emancipation and the creation of a just world order? Or, from a different perspective, does not Christianity engender a dangerous utopianism which is unrelated to reality and achievable social goals?

Ideology, utopia, and liberation

All systems of thought, including theologies, are ideological in the broad sense and may also become ideological in its pejorative sense – uncritical rationalizations of a closed worldview which claims ultimacy in the protection of self- or group interest.[9] As a social construction prone to such rationalization,[10] Christian theology has to remain continually on guard in order to serve the reign of God rather than ecclesial and other self-interests. The unmasking of ideologies, whether secular or religious, Marxist–Leninist, Fascist, or liberal democratic capitalist, is the task of prophetic witness and the necessary first step towards human emancipation and social transformation. The Enlightenment might be the first modern liberation movement; but human emancipation has its roots in the biblical Exodus and the prophetic denunciation of idolatry, as recognized in both the Barmen Declaration and in theologies of liberation.

Just as we can distinguish between two uses of ideology, so we can also distinguish, as does Karl Mannheim, between 'abstract utopianism', which is a form of escapism, and 'concrete utopianism', which engenders socially transformative action and enables the achievement of penultimate anticipations of what may be ultimately unattainable.[11] Part of the struggle within the church is between those for whom the reign of God is an abstract utopia ('the kingdom of heaven') beyond this 'vale of tears', and those for whom it is concretely related to

---

[9] Juan Luis Segundo, *Faith and Ideologies*, vol. 1, Maryknoll, N.Y.: Orbis, 1984, p. 97.
[10] Nicholas Lash, *Theology on the Way to Emmaus*, London: SCM, 1986, pp. 136f.
[11] Karl Mannheim, *Ideology and Utopia: an Introduction to the Sociology of Knowledge*, New York: Harcourt, Brace & World, 1936, pp. 192ff.

God's justice in this world ('your kingdom come on earth as in heaven'), and therefore hope for this world.

The loss of concrete utopian vision would make the realization of a just world impossible. For this reason Pope Paul VI called for a 'rebirth of utopias' without which it is impossible to overcome the domination of authoritarian, bureaucratic, and technocratic social orders, whether capitalist or socialist.[12] By relinquishing utopias human beings lose the ability to imagine new possibilities for the world, or the will to shape history.[13] The concrete utopian vision of reality is the only way whereby we can break free of the circularity of a closed ideology, express judgment upon it,[14] and pursue the goal of a more just world order. Without a vision of what a just democratic society should be, it is not possible to unmask its ideological pretenders, create the necessary democratic culture, nor empower its agents. Moreover social and political movements are unlikely to transcend their own self-interests in the struggle for justice unless goaded by that utopian vision to which biblical hope bears witness. 'Utopian unconditionality', as the neo-Marxist philosopher Ernst Bloch perceived, 'comes from the Bible, and from the idea of the kingdom that remained the apse of each New Moral World.'[15]

There is, then, a teleological utopianism at the heart of Christian eschatology, yet it is fundamentally different to the historical determinism propounded by Fukuyama.[16] The prophetic proclamation that in Jesus Christ the reign of God's righteousness and justice was inaugurated within world history in a decisively new way, promises an omega-point in history with the arrival of God's gift of human liberation and justice, not the victory, or supposed triumph, of any ideology. Unlike Fukuyama's scheme of things, the end of history does not mean

[12] See D. A. Lane, *Foundations for a Social Theology: Praxis, Process and Salvation*, New York: Paulist, 1984, p. 137.

[13] Mannheim, *Ideology and Utopia*, p. 263.

[14] Paul Ricoeur, *Lectures on Ideology and Utopia*, New York: Columbia University Press, 1986, p. 173.

[15] Ernst Bloch, *Man on his Own*, New York: Herder and Herder, 1971, p. 141.

[16] Steven Schroeder, 'The End of History and the New World Order', *Union Seminary Quarterly Review*, 46, 1–4, 1992.

boredom,[17] nor does it mean the universal homogenization of culture,[18] nor does it require Nietzschean 'will-to-power' and human aggression to get the cycle of history moving again.[19] The reign of God means *shalom* – it opens up the future for justice, peace, and the restoration of the integrity of creation.

Christian faith in the reign of God thus anticipates the ultimate transformation of all things, but it is also about the relating of ultimate hopes to penultimate struggles and achievements.[20] No social order *en route* to the goal of history should be confused with the ultimate. Likewise, liberating utopias need to be translated into feasible 'topias' as we noted previously, otherwise they cannot help bring about social transformation. They may well be counter-productive. A false utopianism, or radicalism, with its unrealistic expectations is a serious danger in situations of democratic transition, just as an unrestrained utopianism is a denial of the mystery of Christian faith and hope. The end may be full of surprises (Matthew 25:31–46), and is a gift of God's grace alone. It is not something which can be planned through social engineering, but something which can be anticipated only through prayer and participation in the struggle for its realization. The establishment of a more just society in a particular country does not mean the arrival of the reign of God. But, if it expresses in some meaningful way God's justice and *shalom*, it is a sign of that new world for which Christians hope. Hope, after all, is not knowledge of future events, but living out of the conviction that there is meaning in history and that our actions do in fact make a difference.[21]

The proclamation of the good news of God's reign in Jesus Christ addresses situations of social crisis and political transition with a peculiar directness. This accounts in part for the world-wide impact of the *Kairos Document*. Perceived as historical crises, such 'kairotic moments' are moments of God's judgment as well as God's grace; moments in which the reign of

[17] Fukuyama, 'The end of History?', p. 18.
[18] Fukuyama, *The End of History and the Last Man*, p. 338.
[19] *Ibid.*, p. 330.   [20] See Bonhoeffer, *Ethics*, pp. 125f.
[21] Davis, *Religion and the Making of Society*, p. 193.

God breaks afresh into history, judging human injustice, but also creating opportunities for liberating and redemptive response. Moments such as these reveal the interconnectedness between the penultimate and the ultimate. They remind us that human history is located 'between the times', not only between the dying of old orders and the birth of new ones, but between God's inauguration of a just new world order in Jesus and its fulfilment. That is why Christian faith and theology seem more immediately relevant within situations of historical crisis than they do within more stable political environments. It is also why we should not confuse any moment of historical transition with the 'end of history', as though everything converges on our time and place.

It is increasingly apparent that political stability, like normalcy, is a relative concept. The notion of the inevitability of progress is one of modernity's heresies which has been discredited by historical experience. 'Even a superficial look at history', Martin Luther King Jr. declared, 'reveals that no social advance rolls in on the wheels of inevitability'.[22] The whole created order is always in a state of transition. This is as true of penultimate approximations of the coming just world order as of any others. Political stability is something which societies continually seek rather than something they can permanently embody. There is, therefore, no guarantee that this present wave of democratization will last, that 'Berlin Walls' will never be erected again, that racism will not perpetuate itself in apartheid social structures, or that the American Empire built on the ideology of liberal democratic capitalism will not suffer the same fate as all empires of the past.

Not only has Christian 'abstract utopianism' led to an escapism from political responsibility in the history of Christianity, but it is also the case that a misconceived 'concrete utopianism' has sometimes produced an ideological triumphalism. Post-Constantinian Christendom increasingly equated the expansion of the church and its influence with the extension of God's kingdom until eventually the Roman *Curia* became its univer-

---

[22] Martin Luther King Jr., *Stride Towards Freedom*, p. 197.

sal vanguard; a role and status which the Communist Party would later claim within Marxist–Leninism, and which now the western capitalist powers and their elites assume.[23]

The identification of Christianity with the triumphalism of the western world is essentially in continuity with the heresy at the heart of Constantinianism. But the history of Europe affords no reason for such triumphalism.[24] Without denying for a moment that the state belongs to God, Christianity does not advocate political theocracy, nor should it claim any special privileges and prerogatives for itself over and against other religious traditions. However, this does not mean that Christianity has no responsibility in the formation of democratic societies.[25] Indeed, this task has become urgent because democracy as a product of modernity has been subject to the corrosive effect of its acids. In short, liberal democratic capitalism and Communism are ideological expressions of modernity gone wrong. The pathos of modernity, Colin Gunton observes, is to be discerned in both 'the failed experiments of modern totalitarian regimes and the insidious homogeneity of consumer culture'.[26]

The contradictions of modernity

The achievements of modernity either in the realm of natural science and technology, or in human understanding, must not be denied. The refusal by dominant forms of Christianity to respond more positively to such Enlightenment values as tolerance, rationality, and human autonomy, has seriously impaired its life and witness. But this does not imply an uncritical acceptance of all the values of modernity, especially as represented by 'positivism, relativism and a purely calcula-

[23] See Andre Gunder Frank, 'Nothing New in the East: No New World Order', *Social Justice*, Spring 1992, 19, 1, pp. 49f.

[24] Huber, in Witte, *Christianity and Democracy*, pp. 49f.

[25] Claude Geffré and Jean-Pierre Jossua, eds., *The Debate about Modernity, Concilium*, London: SCM, 1992.

[26] Colin E. Gunton, *The One, the Three and the Many: God, Creation and the Culture of Modernity*, Cambridge University Press, 1993, p. 13.

tive rationality'.[27] As we consider the negative consequences of modernity, then, it is important that we stress from the outset that this does not mean an unequivocal rejection of its emancipatory values. 'Contempt for the age of rationalism', Bonhoeffer reminds us, 'is a suspicious sign of failure to feel the need for truthfulness'.[28] And, as Charles Taylor has rightly argued, modernity has vital resources necessary for retrieving and revitalizing democracy today.[29]

None the less, modernity is an incomplete project and, as such, is shot-through with contradictions. Many of its resources have been squandered in ways which are destructive of human community and the environment. 'Modernity', writes Gunton, 'is the realm of paradoxes: an era which has sought freedom, and bred totalitarianism; which has taught us our insignificance in the vastness of the universe, and yet sought to play god with that same universe; which has sought to control the world, and yet let loose forces that may destroy the earth'.[30] This has resulted in three detrimental consequences pertinent to our discussion. The first is the undermining of relationality. By separating human beings from creation and from God, persons have become alienated and disengaged individuals, and this has had far-reaching negative social and ecological consequences. The second is the reduction of meaningful particularities ('the many') to a meaningless homogeneity ('the one'). Claiming to champion both individuality and plurality, modernity has paradoxically ended up by denying the rich diversity of creation and culture. The third has been the displacement of God in the interests of human emancipation, though emancipation at best has only been partial. This has not meant the abolition of those functions attributed to God, but the shifting of those functions to human reason and will. The result has often been the dictatorship of technocrats and bureaucrats, not human freedom and fulfilment. 'Where the true one is displaced false and alienating gods rush in to fill the vacancy.'[31]

[27] Davis, *Religion and the Making of Society*, p. 31   [28] Bonhoeffer, *Ethics*, p. 97.
[29] Charles Taylor, *Sources of the Self: The Making of Modern Identity*, Cambridge, Mass.: Harvard University Press, 1989.
[30] Colin E. Gunton, *The One, the Three and the Many*, p. 13.   [31] *Ibid.*, p. 38.

Thus, in exalting individual autonomy, modernity has undermined community; in exalting reason, it has undermined faith, hope, and love, and created dehumanizing collectivities – whether capitalist or socialist; in exalting humanity as the source of moral value, it has undermined the foundations of ethical endeavour. The separation of God from the world, and the strong emphasis on creation as being contingent on the divine will, rather than creative and redemptive presence, has led inexorably to the conclusion that God is no longer a necessary working hypothesis with regard to science, ethics, or art.[32] And western Christianity in particular itself must take a large share of the blame for this development because of the neoplatonic dualism which has permeated much of its theology and praxis for so long, especially under the influence of Augustine. As a result, creation and the material world have been sundered from redemption and the spiritual, making nonsense of the doctrine of the Incarnation and contradicting the witness of Scripture. All of this has reinforced the Cartesian and Newtonian dualisms which have been so fundamental to modernity, and yet so contrary to the biblical worldview.

Biblical faith begins with the liberation by Yahweh of the Israelite slaves from the bondage of Egypt. Yahweh, by definition, is the God who emancipates slaves, liberates the oppressed and leads them to the land of promise (the original, biblical 'concrete utopia'). The creation narratives, which post-date the Exodus account, go further and declare that Yahweh is also creator of heaven and earth. Faith in God the creator derives from faith in the liberating God of history.[33] But the history of redemption and liberation is located within a cosmic context in which human culture and nature are given coherence and significance as creation. Creation becomes 'the framework of history'.[34] The utopian, prophetic *vision* of a 'new

[32] Bonhoeffer, *Letters and Papers from Prison*, London: SCM, 1967, especially pp. 359f.
[33] George S. Hendry, *Theology of Nature*, Philadelphia: Westminster, 1980, pp. 18f.
[34] Jürgen Moltmann, *God in Creation: A New Theology of Creation and the Spirit of God*, New York: Harper & Row, 1985, p. 56. See also J. Richard Middleton, 'Is Creation Theology inherently Conservative? A Dialogue with Walter Brueggemann', *Harvard Theological Review* 87, 4, 1994.

creation' gives history its meaning and purpose. All of this is socially structured (i.e. as a political *system*) in the covenantal relationship between God and Israel, with its very precise codes of personal, social, political, and environmental behaviour as embodied in the Torah.

The biblical interconnectedness of liberation, creation, and the development of social structures which are meant to enable the flourishing of human community and embody God's justice, reflects a holism that is fundamental to the future of Christian witness and of civil and political society in the contemporary world. Various dimensions of this holistic worldview will be explored as we proceed, but the reconnecting of redemptive history and the creative matrix of all life in nature is basic to everything else. This requires the reaffirmation of the dignity of the created order. Concomitantly, it means that the building of a just and democratic world order is inseparable from the proper stewardship of the earth and its resources.[35]

Cynics, especially those captivated by the ideology of 'liberal capitalism' question the wisdom or possibility of putting a break on technological expansion convinced that 'a progressive modern natural science is irreversible'.[36] Though this may seem to indicate a hard-nosed realism, it actually betrays a fundamental lack of realism, and ignores 'the chief challenge to democratic capitalism as an enduring arrangement – fragile eco-systems and limits that industrial society and high levels of consumption have flouted with abandon'.[37] If modern society does not become a great deal more concerned about the environment, it will not have any future. A concern for a democratic order in which people achieve their liberation and govern themselves cannot be considered in isolation from issues affecting nature and the environment. The affirmation of human equality, the struggle for liberation and a just demo-

---

[35] Wolfgang Huber, 'Rights of Nature or Dignity of Nature?' in *The Annual*, Society of Christian Ethics, 1991, pp. 43ff.
[36] Fukuyama, *The End of History*, p. 88.
[37] Rasmussen, *Moral Fragments & Moral Community*, p. 62 n.1.

cratic society, are, in the end, dependent upon the struggle to
restore the integrity of creation.[38]

THE TRIUNE GOD AND HUMAN SOCIALITY

The metaphors and models used to describe the meaning of
God in relation to the world of human experience invariably
reflect social values, norms, and interests.[39] As David Nicholls
and others have demonstrated, 'successive concepts and images
of God have been related to political rhetoric' and 'have to
some degree echoed, or at times heralded, changes in the social
structure and dynamics – in the economic, political and cultural life – of given communities'.[40] The idea that God may be
a democratic ruler who welcomes human participation in the
unfolding of the divine purpose, rather than an absolute
monarch who is solely responsible for providence, might
appeal to twentieth-century sensibilities, but it is undoubtedly
shaped more by western liberal culture than the Bible.[41] How
we understand humanity – ourselves – invariably reflects our
understanding of God, and, in so far as most political questions
also have to do with our understanding of what it means to be
human,[42] the anthropology of modernity is an appropriate
starting-point for our discussion of God.

All that was previously attributed to God by Christian
tradition – reason, power, will – was attributed by the
Enlightenment to man (the choice of gender here being quite
specific). As central to the modernity project, 'man' became
the measure of all things. The will of God became the will of
those who had the vote. The result was the birth of a new type
of individual, the self-made man, the bourgeois of modern

---

[38] See 'Entering into Covenant Solidarity for Justice, Peace and the Integrity of
Creation', adopted by the World Council of Churches sponsored conference at
Seoul, Korea, 5–12 March 1990.

[39] Sallie McFague, *Models of God: Theology for an Ecological, Nuclear Age*, Philadelphia:
Fortress, 1987.

[40] David Nicholls, *Deity and Domination*, vol. 1, *Images of God and the State in the Nineteenth
and Twentieth Centuries*, London: Routledge, 1989, pp. 2f.

[41] *Ibid.*, pp. 14f.

[42] Nathaniel Micklem, *The Theology of Politics*, London: Oxford, 1941, p 38.

which the distinctness of each person is affirmed and therefore within which the other remains a significant other. At the same time, God is one, but not the monolithic, patriarchal sovereign of the universe remote from human history, relationships, struggles and suffering.

If God is to be understood in this way, then, in the first place, being in the image of God cannot possibly refer to atomistic individuals. When advocates of democratic capitalism claim that individual self-interest reflects what is meant by the triune image of God, they have resorted to twisted logic.[51] The divine persons (*personae*) are not individuals; by definition they only exist in relationship to each other. And it is this which defines what it means to be a person 'in the image of God' not post-Enlightenment anthropology.[52] At the same time, trinitarian theology cannot support a collectivist understanding of human nature.[53] Collectivism is simply 'atomism packed tight', the pursuit of selfish interests on the part of the group, the class, the nation, or the race.[54] Individualism and collectivism are both Christian heresies;[55] they are mirror images of each other which represent destructive half-truths about humanity, and fail to meet those needs which enable human beings to be truly human. Both the self-centred individualism of liberal democratic capitalism and the collectivity of Communism fail to acknowledge that human beings are more than the natural and historical processes in which they are involved.[56] Democracy is not about self-interest, but arises out of 'respect for the human person and the vocation for liberation rooted in human personality'.[57]

---

[51] Michael Novak, *The Spirit of Democratic Capitalism*, New York: Simon & Schuster, 1982, p. 338.

[52] Gunton, *Promise of Trinitarian Theology*, pp. 13, 116.

[53] *Ibid.*, p. 117.

[54] V. A. Demant, *Religion and the Decline of Capitalism*, London: Faber & Faber, 1952, p. 195; see Niebuhr, *Children of Light*, p. 59.

[55] Demant, *Religion and the Decline of Capitalism*, p. 195; see Villa-Vicencio, *A Theology of Reconstruction*, pp. 154ff.

[56] Niebuhr, *The Children of Light*, p. 59.

[57] Maritain in a letter to Yves Simon, quoted in John Hellman, 'The Anti-Democratic Impulse in Catholicism, Jacques Maritain, Yves Simon, and Charles de Gaulle during World War II', *Journal of Church and State*, 33, 3, Summer 1991, 458.

Whether or not we accept Barth's understanding of the *imago Dei* as referring specifically to the relationship between man and woman, he is surely correct in recognizing that sociality is essential to the structure of being human.[58] This is not an exclusively Christian view. It is fundamental to the African notion of *ubuntu*: a person is a person through other persons.[59] It is universally true that life itself derives from, and is sustained by, people living in community, in groups and families. Human beings only find their true fulfilment in relationships, not in pursuing selfish individual interests. Even John Locke's 'autonomous individual' was, in the context of eighteenth-century society, 'embedded in a complex moral ecology that included family and church on the one hand, and on the other a vigorous public sphere in which economic initiative, it was hoped, grew together with public spirit'.[60] Thus Cornel West speaks of a 'creative democracy', which enhances human individuality in the process of seeking the good of society as a whole.[61] This is fundamental to the renewal of civil society.

There is a further anthropological insight of fundamental importance in the doctrine of the *imago Dei*. The Hebrew prophetic tradition democratized the 'image of God' by rejecting the established notion that the king alone bore the divine image. It was not only the monarch, but every human being who was created in the image of God. Understood in this way, the *imago Dei* is essentially an egalitarian concept. The Hebrew prophets were the first to proclaim 'the unconditional dignity of human beings, simply as human beings' in the history of western thought.[62] To say that every person is created in the image of God means that everyone, irrespective of race, gender, or religion, has an unconditional God-given dignity which no one can rightly deny. Human beings belong to God. This is the basis for a Christian doctrine of human rights.

[58] Karl Barth, *Church Dogmatics*, vol. 3, part 1, *The Doctrine of Creation*, Edinburgh: T. & T. Clark, 1958, pp. 183ff; for a critical feminist retrieval of Barth's view see Elizabeth Frykberg, *Karl Barth's Theological Anthropology: An Analogical Critique Regarding Gender Relations*, Princeton Theological Seminary, New Jersey, 1993.
[59] Shutte, *Philosophy for Africa*, p. 46.   [60] Bellah, et al. *The Good Society*, p. 265.
[61] West, reflecting on John Dewey, in *American Evasion of Democracy*, p. 72.
[62] Kaspar, *Theology and Church*, p. 58.

When true to its trinitarian credo,[63] which stresses that 'the Father is not the Son, and the Son not the Spirit', Christianity not only affirms human equality, but also promotes the rights of difference. Egalitarianism thus does not mean a denial of particularity any more than difference implies subordination. Human beings are not simply equal irrespective of their identities as women or men, they are also equal in terms of such identities. Yet there is an important qualification necessary if we take the analogy of the divine trinity seriously. The distinctness of persons has to do with serving the purposes of creation and redemption. Difference does not mean division and conflict, but the enhancing of community and the healing of the world. Freedom is not freedom from others, but freedom for others. It is a covenantal freedom of rights and responsibilities, a freedom which 'proves itself in love'.[64] Human rights are both social and individual in character. This means, moreover, that human beings are called to be in covenant with the generations to come. Being created in the image of God is therefore to be regarded as a task and responsibility rather than just a status.[65]

Freedom, power, and love

The struggle for liberation from oppression achieves its immediate goal when those who have been oppressed have overcome the source of their oppression. The tyrant has been dethroned, the dividing wall has been broken down, or apartheid is no more. Throughout the struggle for liberation, however, many have demonstrated that despite their bondage they were more profoundly free than their oppressors or captors. Their freedom derived from an awareness of their

---

[63] This implies more than simply the formal confession of God as triune, which can, as was the case during the negotiations for democratic transition in South Africa, become more a matter of political argument than one of theological praxis. This is the background to Deputy President F. W. de Klerk's statement – 'so may the triune God help me' – when taking the oath of office at his inauguration.

[64] Kaspar, *Theology and Church*, p. 70.

[65] Douglas John Hall, *Imaging God: Dominion as Stewardship*, Grand Rapids: Eerdmans, 1987.

God-given dignity and from their moral commitment to the struggle for justice irrespective of the personal cost involved. Their freedom was demonstrated in a commitment to living and acting as responsible human beings, and even in loving their enemies. By the same token, after political liberation there is still a massive task ahead before all, whether oppressed or oppressor, are truly free, and therefore responsible human beings, people who have discovered their dignity before God and each other.

Our speaking about democracy and freedom must therefore be more nuanced. Democracy as a *system* is intended to protect certain liberties (of speech, of assembly, human rights, and so forth) which are ours by right. But if democracy is to expand and become inclusive, if it is to realize its *vision* more fully, then the notion of freedom has to include being responsible for others. This is not something which democracy itself can produce; it is a spiritual virtue of redemptive love which no political system can manufacture. For such reasons, Christianity must be critical of a democracy which encourages an individualism free of social responsibility. This inevitably produces 'an atomization of society which is false to the nature of human existence'.[66] It is a sign of the crisis of modernity and a symptom of human sinfulness.

Secular philosophies unite in rejecting the Christian doctrine of original sin.[67] Yet it is precisely this doctrine which provides us with profound insight into the human predicament. The biblical narrative of the Fall (Genesis 1–11), on which the doctrine has been based, accounts for the brokenness of human relationships – the alienation of male and female and of humanity from creation, and the collapse of society (the Tower of Babel represents the antithesis of a just, communicative global community) – in terms of the human desire to be like God. Like a meteor torn away from its nucleus, society seeks to discover its way apart from God,[68] and in the process

---

[66] Demant, *Religion and the Decline of Capitalism*, p. 195.
[67] Niebuhr, *The Children of Light*, p. 16.
[68] Dietrich Bonhoeffer, *Creation and Fall: A Theological Interpretation of Genesis 1–3*, London: SCM, 1959, p. 77.

fragments into warring factions. Instead of accepting the dignity of being in the image of God, human beings desire to be God in the exercise of power and the determination of value. Human brokenness is a consequence of the will-to-power, and its result is not freedom, but the 'bondage of the will' (Luther). Human wholeness, by way of contrast, is dependent upon the will-to-love, for it is this which sustains relationships and engenders responsible freedom.

The doctrine of original sin owes much to Augustine's pondering on the fates and fortunes of history, and the limited extent to which we have rational control over our environment, in the light of the biblical Fall. With the best of intentions, how free are we to act responsibly? This question and responses to it, have, as Peter Brown noted, 'revolutionized political theory'.[69] Marx, Freud, and their disciples discerned the answer in forms of historical or psycho-social determinism. Those imbued with the spirit of modernity have generally believed, to the contrary, that we can resolve our problems through rational thought and action, and that we are capable of doing so if we could only put our minds and wills to the task, freeing ourselves from prejudicing particularities.

For Augustine, as for St Paul before him, the problem is far more complex. Human nature is turned in upon itself. In its egocentricity it cannot think rationally, nor does it have the will to act responsibly. This is not a denial of the importance of reason and rationality, but a recognition of the human predicament. Hence, by way of example, the economic problems facing humankind today could be dealt with rationally if only there was the will to do so; the will to put the interests of the world community above those of the self and the nation.[70]

Rather than being an outdated concept, a revisioned doctrine of original sin is then, in Niebuhr's words, 'more adequate for the development of a democratic society than either the optimism with which democracy has become historically associated or the moral cynicism which inclines human communi-

[69] Peter Brown, *Religion and Society in the Age of Saint Augustine*, London: Faber and Faber 1972, p. 28.
[70] See chapter 1 above, p. 33.

ties to tyrannical political strategies'.[71] In so far as democracy is built on optimism, rather than realism, about human nature, it is always in danger of being rejected.[72] The consequences are anarchy or tyranny. This is one reason why Christianity has tended to be politically conservative, and was so opposed to the idea of human emancipation in post-revolutionary Europe.

An acute sense of human fallibility has also prevailed amongst political philosophers from Plato to Machiavelli and Hobbes through to our own day, leading to the belief that, if society is to function efficiently at all, human beings must be 'enticed by gain or fitted with a collectivist strait-jacket'.[73] And yet it is really such a view of society, whether Christian or secular, which allows power to become absolute with all its attendant dangers. If unrealistic optimism about human nature is a recipe for anarchy or totalitarianism, pessimism 'must despair of politics altogether',[74] and likewise lead to authoritarianism. But democracy need not be a weak form of government. Genuine democracy in a way consonant with the doctrine of original sin acknowledges the human will-to-power through its system of checks and balances whereby it seeks to limit political power and ensure accountability.

Christianity recognizes that justice requires order in society, even though order does not always, nor necessarily, imply justice. But Christianity does not regard human sin, or will-to-power, as the only determinant of human behaviour. There is more to human nature than simply its brutishness. The doctrine of original sin tells us about human self-will, the will-to-power, and self-interest, but this is only the prolegomenon to the doctrine of redemption, the possibility of human transformation, and the re-birth of the will-to-love in responsible freedom. At this point Christianity is unashamedly utopian and moves firmly beyond the political cynics.

There is a strange paradox, theologically speaking, in the anthropology which underpins the arguments of the advocates of the new world order. On the one hand, the collapse of

[71] Niebuhr, *The Children of Light*, p. xv.   [72] *Ibid.*, p. xii.
[73] Demant, *Religion and the Decline of Capitalism*, p. 155.
[74] Micklem, *Theology of Politics*, p. 158.

Communism is attributed to the fact that it failed to allow individuals to assert their freedom. As a former president of the United States, George Bush, was reported to have told a Moscow audience: 'Socialism could not create human nature anew.'[75] On the other hand, a major argument put forward for the success of capitalism is that people are selfish by nature and that human nature cannot change. How this makes a new world order possible is not explained, for, if human nature is beyond transformation, social structures must be even more so.

An alternative, produced by modernity in its rediscovery of the human subject, is the cult of self-realization in and through which individuals no longer value anything beyond the self. But, Charles Taylor reminds us, when nothing is important other than self-fulfilment, nothing counts as fulfilment.[76] Either way, the 'victory' of liberal democratic capitalism is a Pyrrhic one. Citizens, as captives of boredom, cease to participate in any meaningful way in shaping the *polis*. The new world order is not a victory for the moral agents of history, but for bureaucratic and technocratic government driven by free market forces under the pretence of democracy. This is the price of modernity gone wrong, and links up directly with one of the fundamental premises of this book, namely that democracy cannot survive without the spiritual basis which gives meaning to life. The boredom of those who are captives to a mono-cultural consumerist society would be relieved if they underwent the catharsis of conversion from self-interest to service of God's justice, and began to participate responsibly in the life of the *polis*. They would thereby also help to overcome the much more debilitating struggle for life of those who are the victims of grinding poverty and unemployment.

It has been assumed for too long that democratic systems will produce morally responsible citizens as a matter of course, but the reverse is equally if not more true – only people who have been morally formed and empowered are able to make democracy work. Both the achievement of social justice and the

---

[75] Reported by Christopher Wright, 'Whose New World Order?' *Themelios*, 17, 3, April/May, 1992, p. 3.
[76] Taylor, *Sources of the Self*, p. 507.

fulfilment of human life require participation in meaningful relationships and therefore in institutions which foster and enable such relationships. Hence the need for the creation and sustenance of institutions which enable persons to fulfil their social responsibilities, and without which neither human fulfilment nor genuine democracy is possible. If our understanding of God as triune is to be more than notional, 'we must have experienced co-operation and community here on earth, from which the divine analogy may come alive'.[77] Hence the importance of the role of the church and other religious communities in the process of democratization.

THE PEOPLE OF GOD AND PARTICIPATORY DEMOCRACY

From the outset we have noted an intrinsic connection between the Christian *ekklēsia* and political society or the *polis*. The choice of the word *ekklēsia* by the first Christians, so we argued in chapter 2, was politically pretentious. Those early Christians were a small minority, often situated on the periphery of public life, but they did not regard their mission as a private affair – it had to do with the transformation of the world. The church was not a religious club established for the purpose of spiritual self-gratification, but a sign and model of God's new world order established in Jesus Christ. From the beginning of Christianity, then, a connection was made between the life and structure of the church, and God's will and purpose for the world.

Modernity willed that the public role of the church should be replaced by the civil religion of nation-states. The necessary separation of church and state, and the need for tolerance within religiously plural societies, required that this be so. In so far as the church had a public role, it was to give its support to those in authority. But its primary task was in the private sphere. This dualism has often been rationalized on the basis of Luther's doctrine of the two kingdoms, and as such the doctrine gave theological legitimation to secularization. For secu-

---

[77] David Nicholls, *Deity and Domination*, p. 237.

larization required and led to a privatized Christianity, a development which fitted in well with the liberal Christian and democratic emphasis on the individual. The kingdom or reign of God was likewise located within the individual human heart rather than in the public square. If, however, we are to take seriously the meaning of the reign of the triune God, then we have to return also to the original significance of the Christian *ekklēsia* and its public and prophetic mission.

Patriarchy, hierarchy, and democracy

The majority of Christian denominations are not democratic in polity. Even within more democratic church traditions, however, there is a strong sense that the church should not be governed by the will of the majority. Christianity, after all, 'is not individualism tempered by the ballot box'.[78] Each Christian tradition claims that the ultimate authority in the church is Jesus Christ. In what sense can the church, which claims to be the 'body of Christ' with Christ himself as head, be democratic? The question must also be raised as to whether an organization, such as the church, which may seek to contribute to a just democratic social order, has to be run along democratic lines.

The question of the democratic character of the church is relevant to all Christian denominations, but it obviously affects them in different ways, because some, like the Roman Catholic, are essentially hierarchical in structure, those within the Reformed tradition are governed through representative democratic procedures, and others, like the Baptists, are, in theory at any rate, more like participatory democracies. In fact the various denominational polities mirror the different ways in which political society itself has been structured within different historical contexts.[79] This is a reminder that denominational polities are as much the products of history as of theology. With justification, Hans Küng argues that it is

---

[78] John Oman, *The Church and the Divine Order*, London, 1911, p. 318.
[79] Everett, *God's Federal Republic*, pp. 64ff.

'modern democracy' which has led in part to a new participatory understanding of the church,[80] in which all the baptized participate in the decision-making processes of the church. This ensures that the gifts of the Spirit given to all may contribute fully to the life and mission of the 'people of God'.[81]

There can be little doubt, however, that in the history of the church, ecclesial practice has usually contradicted that which was envisaged in the New Testament. Christendom led to the increasing clericalization of the church. On the basis of Augustine's Platonic distinction between the visible and the invisible church it also led to an understanding of the church as God's vehicle of individual salvation for the next life, rather than a community of *koinonia* of believers in which the life of God's reign was expressed. As a result, biblical texts subversive of hierarchy and patriarchy were made subservient to the interests of hierarchical power relations, for it was the hierarchy which became the custodian of the means of saving grace. For example, Paul's insistence that there is 'neither slave and freeman, male or female; for you are all one person in Christ Jesus' (Galatians 3:28) has been distorted so as to deny the importance and validity of gender and other differences in the interests of maintaining male power. This too, it may be argued, fits in well with the modernity paradigm. 'Man', so the Enlightenment decreed, became the measure of all things. But this did not mean all human beings – slaves, women, and 'nonwhite' males were excluded from the vote, just as they were discriminated in, if not excluded from, the church. Thus there has been an intrinsic connection within modernity between all forms of domination – class, race, gender, clerical, and colonial – with patriarchy being the nerve-centre.[82] Just as there has been an intrinsic link between a denial of the triune nature of God and patriarchy.[83]

---

[80] Hans Küng, *Theology for the Third Millennium*, New York: Doubleday, 1988, p. 163.
[81] Alberigo, 'Ecclesiology and Democracy', in Provost and Walf, *The Tabu of Democracy*, p. 17.
[82] Rosemary Radford Ruether, 'Feminists Seek Structural Change', *National Catholic Reporter*, 20, 13 April 1984, pp. 4f.
[83] Boff, *Trinity and Society*, p. 21.

The question of the equality of women, and what that actually means, has become critical both for democracy and the public witness of the Christian faith today.[84] Hence the importance of Elizabeth Schüssler Fiorenza's studies on Christian origins, and the exegetical foundation she has provided for 'the *ekklēsia* of women,' that is, communities comprised of 'women who have acted and still act in the power of the life-giving Sophia-Spirit'.[85] This recognition of gender-difference in the life of the church is of fundamental importance, paralleling as it does the political debate about democratic equality and difference. But it is also important in raising questions about the relationship between patriarchy and hierarchy. Is it possible to overcome patriarchy without undermining the hierarchical structure which is fundamental to much traditional Christianity? If not, can there be any integrity in the ecumenical church's declared support for democracy?

The rediscovery of the church as the 'people of God' at Vatican II did not mean a rejection of hierarchy, but it did pave the way for the fuller participation of all Catholics in the life of the church at various levels.[86] Essentially it was rediscovery of the medieval notion of subsidiarity and the representative aspects of conciliarism. But this provided an opening for some to take further steps towards the democratic transformation of the church. This has been most notably the case in the 'base communities' in and through which participation has been more meaningfully expressed at a grass-roots level. As noted previously, the development of local communities of participatory democracy is a key contribution which the church can make to democratic transformation. In the words of Jon Sobrino:

In the Church of the poor the age-old barriers between hierarchy and faithful, priests and workers, peasants and intellectuals have been broken down. They have been broken down not by a process of formal democratization in which all are made equal, but by the rise

---

[84] Ruether, *Disputed Questions*, p. 125.   [85] Fiorenza, *In Memory of Her*, p. 350.
[86] Herbert Vorgrimler, ed., *Commentary on the Documents of Vatican II*, vol. 1, New York: Herder and Herder, 1966, pp. 98f.

of solidarity in the form of 'bearing one another's burdens', being 'one' ecclesial body, and thus making the Church 'one'.[87]

Yet, as we noted in the case of Cardinal Obando in Nicaragua, *comunidades eclesiales de base* have been regarded as a threat to the hierarchical order and control of the church. The charge of 'congregationalism' was amongst the chief reasons used by the Vatican to silence the Brazilian liberation theologian Leonardo Boff.[88]

Latin American Catholic 'base communities' undoubtedly reflect a congregational polity because of their particular understanding of the witness of the church within Latin America. But this is not generally regarded by liberation theologians or members of the communities as antithetical to episcopal authority or the teaching magisterium of the church.[89] The claim that they are antithetical is based on 'false reasoning and a magical and ideological use of the word "hierarchy"'.[90] If hierarchy were an expression of ministerial representation within the church understood as the whole people of God (*laos*), then many would agree with P. T. Forsyth, the Congregationalist theologian, who argued that there is 'no ultimate incompatibility between episcopacy and Congregational principles'.[91]

Vatican II achieved a great deal, but its promise has not been fully realized, not least because of a conservative reaction on the part of the Vatican during the past decade. The theological rationale for this reaction to the democratization impulse, or, better, the greater participation of the whole people of God, has been the claim that the church is a divine mystery which cannot be reduced to a sociological phenom-

---

[87] Jon Sobrino, *The True Church and the Poor*, London: SCM, 1981, p. 103.

[88] V. Messori, *The Ratzinger Report*, Hertfordshire: Fowler Wright, 1985; Leonardo Boff, *Ecclesio-genesis: The Base Communities Reinvent the Church*, London: Collins, 1986; Harvey Cox, *The Silencing of Leonardo Boff*, London: Collins, 1988.

[89] Juan Luis Segundo, *Theology and the Church: A Response to Cardinal Ratzinger and a Warning to the Whole Church*, San Francisco: Harper & Row, 1987, p. 156.

[90] Edward Schillebeeckx, *Church: The Human Story of God*, New York: Crossroad, 1991, p. 220.

[91] P. T. Forsyth *The Church and the Sacraments*, p. 12; *The Principle of Authority*, pp. 226, 235f., 380.

enon. This recourse to ecclesiological mystery-discourse is really a smoke-screen based on a dualistic understanding of the church, as though its divine nature can be separated from its historical existence.[92]

Ecclesial polity has legitimacy in so far as it reflects and enables a faithful witness to the reign of the triune God in Jesus Christ in relation to its particular historical context. The rule of Christ in the church is not juridical, it is the rule of truth, justice, and love through the Spirit. There is no reason, then, why an authoritarian church ruling 'from above' should be able to discern the mind of Christ better than the whole people of God listening to the Word of God. Hence Karl Rahner's opinion that the Catholic church should now 'grow quite differently from the past, from below, from groups of those who have come to believe as a result of their own free, personal decision'.[93] This also applies to other denominations which, despite their stated polity, have succumbed to rule by bureaucracy.

'Koinonia' as witness

One of the fundamental New Testament images for the church which expresses the dialectic of mystery ('body of Christ') and sociological reality (institution) is that of 'fellowship' or 'community' (*koinonia*). It is an image rooted in the activity of the Holy Spirit as the action of God bringing unity and giving life to the body. The first Christians regarded themselves essentially as a fellowship of believers 'in Christ' who worshipped God together 'in the fellowship of the Holy Spirit' (II Corinthians 13:13), a phrase which refers both to sharing *in* the Holy Spirit and to the community which is its result. In other words, the church was experienced as participation through the Spirit in the life of the triune God. For this reason, Eastern Orthodox theologians continually remind us that the essence of the church is communion – it exists in the interrelatedness of

---

[92] Schillebeeckx, *Church*, pp. 210f.
[93] Karl Rahner, *The Shape of the Church to Come*, New York: Crossroads, 1983, p. 121.

human beings, God and society.[94] As such it is called to reflect the sociality of the triune God in which each person is equal yet distinct; a community of persons in and through which Jesus Christ is present, rather than an assemblage of individuals or a collectivity.[95]

On this understanding, *koinonia* is not to be regarded as something 'spiritual', separate from daily concerns and life. Rather, as in Acts, it was exemplified in the sharing of possessions: 'they had all things in common (*koine*)' (2:44–5). It was this life as a community, in which all members participated equally, which characterized the first Christian churches. The Christian community was called to be a counter-culture (Romans 12:1–2) in which the normal divisions of society were overcome (Galatians 3:26–9); a 'new creation', which was the beginning and sign of God's reconciled humanity (II Corinthians 5:17f.; Ephesians 2–3). All of this is well expressed in the World Council of Churches' statement:

The purpose of the church is to unite people with Christ in the power of the Spirit, to manifest communion in prayer and action and thus point to the fullness of communion with God, humanity and the whole creation in the glory of the kingdom.[96]

The integral connection between the structures of the church and political society have been noted several times in the course of our discussion. The 'great church' of Constantinian Christendom, for example, patterned much of its life on the structures of Roman provincial government. In like manner, Hooker's discussion of ecclesiastical polity (the Anglican *via media*) was mirrored in English political society. Far too often, however, the church has taken its cue from the dominant culture in which it has existed rather than the other way round. Yet it is the mission of the church to transform the world, not to become conformed to its norms. For this reason it is important to recognize the connection between ecclesial

---

[94] John D. Zizioulas, *Being as Communion*, New York: St Vladimir's Press, 1985.
[95] Dietrich Bonhoeffer, *The Communion of Saints: A Dogmatic Inquiry into the Sociology of the Church*, New York: Harper & Row, 1963, p. 135.
[96] Michael Kinnamon, ed., *Signs of the Spirit*, Official Report of the Seventh Assembly, Geneva: World Council of Churches, 1991, p. 172.

structure and witness both at the local and the ecumenical levels.

Barth, Bonhoeffer, and other leaders within the Confessing church in the Third Reich rightly insisted that the order of the church was not something peripheral to its witness against Nazism. Similarly, in the church struggle against apartheid in South Africa, as in the Civil Rights struggle in the United States, racial segregation within the church was rejected as a denial of the gospel. For this reason, as Barth put it: 'the decisive contribution which the Christian community can make to the upbuilding and maintenance of the civil consists in the witness which it has to give it and to all human societies in the form of the order of its own upbuilding and constitution.'[97] The prophetic witness of the church to the reign of God against injustice and discrimination of all kinds, has to be addressed first of all to its own life and structures.

If political democracy means the way in which justice is structured on the presupposition of equity and for the sake of freedom, then it reflects by analogy what should be even more true within the life of the Christian *ekklēsia*. If genuine democracy should enable human fulfilment and flourishing, how much more should the life of the church enable its members to discover an even deeper fulfilment and freedom in Christ? If democracy is about political participation in which difference is respected and which contributes to the well-being of the whole, how much more should the church as the *koinonia* of the 'people of God' embody and express true human sociality, reflecting the restored image of the triune God? This being so, 'the most authentic support that the church can give to a democratic order of society remains that of an effective and increasingly profound praxis of communion within itself'.[98]

THE POWER OF GOD AND HUMAN ACCOUNTABILITY

The logic of our theology for a just world order thus far has been as follows: First of all, we located our discussion within

---

[97] Karl Barth, *Church Dogmatics*, Edinburgh: T. & T. Clark, 1961, vol. 4, no. 2, p. 721.
[98] Giuseppe Alberigo, 'Ecclesiology and Democracy: Convergences and Divergences', in Provost and Walf, *The Tabu of Democracy within the Church*, p. 23.

the prophetic tradition by considering the much heralded new world order in relation to the reign of God. We then proceeded, secondly, to a consideration of Christian anthropology based on the doctrine of the triune God, which enabled us to enter into the contemporary debate about democracy from a Christian perspective. Thirdly, we related our discussion to the church as the sign and model of the new age of God's justice inaugurated in Jesus Christ, and considered the implications which this had in terms of its structure and witness within the process of democratization. We now turn more specifically to the Christian witness to political society, beginning with the question of the sovereignty of people and nations in relation to their accountability before God and to one another.

Sovereignty of God and nations

The concept of 'sovereignty' has been fundamental to political philosophy and constitutional law since the Middle Ages, and the sovereignty of the nation-state has been fundamental to the project of modernity. It is not surprising, then, that the doctrine of the sovereignty of God became so important in the theology of the Reformation. The notion of God as self-sufficient sovereign was particularly evident in the theologies of those Germans, such as Friedrich Schleiermacher, who were concerned about the unity and sovereignty of Prussia.[99] Bismarck, one of Schleiermacher's confirmation candidates, later applied this theology with considerable force in the power struggles of German nationalism. At the other end of the spectrum, the language as well as the notion of the sovereignty of God have been challenged by contemporary theologians in the United States, where the model of God as sovereign has conflicted with federal republicanism, liberal democracy, and, more recently, feminism.[100]

Although Christian rhetoric abounds with sovereignty-language – 'Lord of lords, and King of kings' – 'sovereignty' is a concept which has become as ambiguous for many con-

---

[99] Nicholls, *Images of God*, pp. 20f.   [100] McFague, *Models of God*, pp. 63f.

temporary Christians as it has for citizens within the body political.[101] However appropriate such language may have been, it has to be asked whether it remains so, not only because of the serious criticisms raised by feminist and other forms of theology, but also because of the need to relate Christianity to democracy. Sovereignty language about God, it is argued, reinforces that kind of monotheism which legitimates patriarchal hierarchy and triumphalism.

The abuse of the 'sovereignty of God' metaphor is undoubtedly an argument against its use, and calls for at least its qualification if not rejection. It has been used to reduce human beings to the status of puppets at the mercy of the inscrutable decrees of God, as well as to justify political and social tyrannies of various kinds. The problem is to find an adequate alternative. Despite its problematic character, sovereignty helps us focus on 'the ultimate sources of power'.[102] As H. Richard Niebuhr argued, when we think about the sovereignty of God we often do so in negative terms because we are confusing it with the triumphalism of the church or the theocratic rule of Puritan preachers. But the sovereignty of God stands in critical contrast to such claims.[103] In any case, in speaking about the 'sovereignty of nations', or the 'sovereignty of parliament', or the 'sovereignty of people', is it inappropriate to speak about what Christians believe to be the ultimate authority in terms of the sovereignty of God?

Sovereignty is not only a royal metaphor which separates God from the world, thereby legitimating hierarchy and paving the way for a theocratic-style tyranny; it is also a prophetic metaphor which, when applied to God, de-absolutizes and relativizes all other claimants to absolute power. The idea of the sovereignty of God has probably been employed more often as a weapon against tyranny than it has been used to support it. For that reason, it has been 'a particularly

---

[101] Clyde Binfield, 'Collective Sovereignty? Conscience in the Gathered Church c. 1875–1918', in Diana Wood, ed., *The Church and Sovereignty c. 590–1918*, Oxford: Basil Blackwell, 1991, p. 479.

[102] J. Philip Wogaman, *Christian Perspectives on Politics*, Minneapolis: Fortress, 1988, p. 19.

[103] Niebuhr, *Radical Monotheism and Western Culture*, p. 72.

relevant theological entry point in the era of the totalitarian state'.[104] But it is also of relevance more broadly in terms of putting moral limits on the state and its use of power.[105] Thus, whatever the inadequacy of sovereignty as a divine attribute, we dare not surrender the theological claim which is being made. If we had to extract 'sovereignty' or 'lordship' language from the Hebrew prophets or the New Testament we would end up with a very strange text!

The way through this dilemma is to locate the doctrine of the sovereignty of God more clearly and conscientiously within that of the doctrine of the trinity. God's power is not that of naked omnipotence, but the power revealed in the resurrection of the crucified Christ, and in the redemptive activity of the Spirit in the world. Understood in this way, the sovereignty of God – if we are to use the term for the sake of political discourse – cannot be used to legitimate hierarchy, patriarchy, and other forms of authoritarian government. It means that all that we have said about the triune God in terms of human sociality is sovereign. Trinity defines sovereignty, not the other way round; the doctrine of the sovereign triune God thereby becomes the basis for a theological critique of authoritarian regimes, while at the same time providing the theological grounds for a democratic social order. The sovereignty of God thus becomes the precondition of human freedom rather than the source of human bondage. The sovereign triune God does not close off history, but opens it up through the Spirit in order that its goal of justice and *shalom* might be realized. From this perspective, the sovereignty of God is God's predestined determination to bring a human community into being in which equality, freedom, and justice flourish.[106] It is a doctrine of liberation, especially the liberation of the oppressed: it is also a doctrine of liberated community. Other claims to sovereignty, whether that of the church, the nation, or the people, have to be evaluated in terms of whether they enable the realization of such freedom and community.

---

[104] *Ibid.*, p. 114.   [105] Bonhoeffer, *Ethics*, p. 104.
[106] De Gruchy, *Liberating Reformed Theology*, pp. 125f.

The question of sovereignty invariably raises the enduring
and complex problem of church–state relations.[107] What we
can learn from the history of church–state relations is important, but the issues have to be considered afresh in every
context and generation in the light of Scripture and praxis, and
cannot simply be dealt with according to traditional formulae
which were themselves historically conditioned.[108] This is particularly true in a post-Christendom context. Even the time-
honoured notion of the separation of church and state, which
has been fundamental to modern democracy, has to be critically reformulated. Lip-service to the doctrine can mask
unholy alliances or prevent prophetic witness.

The point of departure for any understanding of the political
task and responsibility of the church must be its primary
obligation to witness to the reign of God in Jesus Christ. From
the outset of the Christian era, this confession has been a
problem for the sovereignty of the state. Authoritarian and
totalitarian regimes have always sought to control or smash the
church, for its very presence, despite its compromises and
failures, is a sign which contradicts the all-embracing claims of
the state. But the church would cease to be the church if it
failed to remind the state of its responsibility to govern justly,
and the parameters of its power. This 'protects the state from a
religious or quasi-religious self-misunderstanding and thereby
serves it in the best possible way'.[109] It sets the state free to be
the state. So it is that theology today, as Moltmann reminds us,
must continue its critical task of 'desacralization, relativization
and democratization'. The churches must overcome political
idolatry, as well as the mystique of political and religious
systems which produce apathy, and 'build up the political
liveliness of each individual'.[110]

Popular sovereignty, or the power of the people, is essential

[107] *Church and State: Opening a New Ecumenical Discussion*, Faith and Order Paper no. 85,
Geneva: World Council of Churches, 1978, pp. 173f.
[108] Helmut Thielicke, *Theological Ethics*, vol. 2, Philadelphia: Fortress Press, 1969,
p. 6.; Rudolf Schnackenberg, *The Moral Teaching of the New Testament*, New York:
Seabury, 1965, p. 236.
[109] Jüngel, *Christ, Justice and Peace*, p. 62.
[110] Jürgen Moltmann, *The Crucified God*, pp. 328f.

to any real understanding of democracy. Yet Christianity is not populist in its understanding of political power. If the people are not subject to a moral law which transcends them, and especially to the norms of equality, freedom, and justice, genuine democracy is an impossibility. In Maritain's words: 'The people are not God, the people do not have infallible reason and virtues without flaw, the will of the people or the spirit of the people is not the rule which decides what is just or unjust.'[111] In so far as the sovereign will of the people has been linked traditionally with the sovereignty of nation-states – that particular form in which modernity has found political expression – what Maritain says is equally applicable.

Addressing the ecumenical conference on Life and Work at Oxford in 1937, the Marquis of Lothian spoke of the demonic influence of national sovereignty on world order in 'producing war and in making impossible fidelity to the moral law or to Christian principle both in international, and in increasing spheres of national, life'.[112] Like his hearers, Sir Philip Henry Kerr was fearful of the way in which national sovereignty was threatening the future of Europe in the late 1930s, and of the impotence of the world community to do much about it. The only hope, Kerr argued, lay in the potential of the church as a universal community to overcome 'the political and economic divisions of which the national state is the most ruthless and powerful' and which, then as now, tears 'human society to pieces'.[113] For Kerr, it was part of the essential ecumenical vocation of the church to keep the nations accountable.

In his reflections on African independence, Basil Davidson, reminds us that nationalism has both 'a capacity for enlarging freedom' and a 'potential for destroying freedom'.[114] African movements of liberation had to be nationalist in order to achieve freedom from colonial rule, but nationalism can also devour its own children. As E. J. Hobsbawm has argued,

---

[111] Maritain, *Christianity and Democracy*, p. 39.
[112] Philip Henry Kerr, 'The Demonic Influence of National Sovereignty', in *The Universal Church and the World of Nations: Church, Community, and State*, vol. 7, London: George Allen & Unwin, 1938, p. 3.
[113] *Ibid.*, p. 23.   [114] Davidson, *Black Man's Burden*, p. 52.

nationalism precedes the historical construction of nation-states, but, unless critically checked, it leads to an obligation to the nation which 'overrides all other public obligations'.[115] When this happens, nationalism takes on the character of a religious faith and becomes one of the most destructive powers imaginable, undermining and inevitably destroying democracy.[116] This is particularly true of 'ethnic nationalisms' which undermine the plurality and tolerance necessary for the creation of democratic order.[117]

To speak of the sovereignty of a nation-state does not mean, then, that there are no limitations or boundaries to its power and authority.[118] Just as the power of the people is not absolute, but is derived from God, so the sovereignty of the nation-state is not absolute or independent of God or the people of which it is comprised. Under God, the people give to the state its authority, and therefore its sovereignty. As such, it is not inalienable or beyond criticism. All of which raises acutely the need for institutions within society which, while committed to nation-building, are none the less able to rise above and express criticism of nationalism. In particular, it requires that the church resist nationalization as much as it resists privatization, and affirm its universality even as it seeks to be critically and creatively engaged in its particular context.

There is another dimension to national sovereignty, however, which has to be taken into account by the church. Many small nations, such as Nicaragua, which have their own *de iure* sovereignty, are under the economic domination of other more powerful nations. Unless checked, international exploitation will destroy democratic order and sow the seeds for ongoing international conflict and war, as has been the case in many Third World countries.[119] Thus, both as a means to curb

---

[115] E. J. Hobsbawm, *Nations and Nationalism Since 1780: Programme, Myth, Reality*, Cambridge University Press, 1992, pp. 9, 15.

[116] Niebuhr, *Radical Monotheism and Western Culture*, p. 27.

[117] See Maré, *Ethnicity and Politics in South Africa*, p. 43.

[118] Wogaman, *Christian Perspectives*, p. 18.

[119] See, for example, Horacio Morales, 'The Third World's Struggle for Development and Economic Sovereignty: Problems and Prospects', Catholic Institute for International Relations, January 1991.

destructive nationalism and national policies which are globally detrimental (such as those relating to the environment), and to protect weak nations from the aggression and interference of more powerful nations, international control mechanisms are needed.

All of this emphasizes the necessity for such international institutions as the World Court and the United Nations. But for such agencies to fulfil their role, nations have to recognize the relative character of their sovereignty. The 'sovereignty of parliament' is undoubtedly an essential ingredient in British democracy, but, by way of example, it can also become a means to prevent the process of democratization from being broadened into a more just European and world community. The democratization of one nation is of considerable concern both to its immediate neighbours and to the world community.

Just as it is necessary to develop a strong civil society within every nation, it is equally important to develop an international civil society comprising a network of agencies and institutions committed to a just democratic order. In this respect the ecumenical church, as we have seen numerous times in our case studies, has a crucial role to play in the international arena in co-operation with people of other faiths. While it is misleading to regard the World Council of Churches as the United Nations at prayer, there is a relationship between the ecumenical church and organizations such as the United Nations, the European Community, or the Organization of African Unity, which is analogous to that of the relationship between church and state within particular nations. The strength and value of that relationship is dependent upon a critical solidarity in which the church is free to speak prophetically to the nations in terms of God's justice, and yet is committed to the same task of building a world community in which peace and human flourishing become more of a reality for more people and nations. This is what the doctrine of the common good within Catholic social teaching, and the covenant tradition within the Reformed tradition, have sought to ensure.

The common good

If a democratic society is not to fall prey to the ravages of national or individual self-interest, it requires a broad acceptance of a common set of values which binds its members together in mutual accountability. This is the intention of the doctrine of the common good, defined at Vatican II as 'the sum of those conditions of social life which allow social groups and their individual members relatively thorough and ready access to their own fulfillment'.[120] The common good, thus understood, is more a process, something to be struggled for and attained, than something which, as in earlier Catholic teaching, is understood as a static set of principles which can be applied directly to social issues irrespective of context. The common good has even been described as a 'necessary vision of a just social order that progressive movements need to sustain themselves'.[121] In the words of *Gaudium et Spes*, it is a vision of a social order 'founded on truth, built on justice, and animated by love'.[122]

The common good is the antithesis of the notion underlying atomistic individualism, namely, that the liberty of individuals is the highest good. It insists that human beings are not only responsible for their own personal welfare and fulfilment, but for the welfare and fulfilment of society as a whole. The aim of political power should therefore be the achievement of the common good.[123] Contemporary Roman Catholic theologians would certainly now acknowledge with Robert Bellah that, whereas the good of some individuals may be achieved even by a benevolent tyranny, only a just democracy can enable a society to achieve this goal.[124]

Fundamental to the pursuit of the common good, then, is the need to ensure that human rights are maintained and

[120] *Gaudium et Spes*, 26, in Walter M. Abbott, *The Documents of Vatican II*, London: Geoffrey Chapman, 1966, p. 225.
[121] Dorrien, *Reconstructing the Common Good*, p. 4.
[122] *Gaudium et Spes*, 26, in Abbott, *Documents of Vatican II*, p. 225.
[123] *Octagesimo Adveniens* 46.1, in Michael Walsh and Brian Davies, *Proclaiming Justice and Peace: Documents from John XXIII to John Paul II*, London: Collins, 1984, p. 184.
[124] See Bellah, *The Good Society*, p. 81.

broadened; that there is development of institutions in and through which people can both express their concerns in publicly significant ways, and experience solidarity with others; that there is distributive justice in the economic sphere; and that these goals cannot be confined to nations but must be sought at an international level.[125]

The fact that the common good is to be understood in international terms is of considerable importance, tying in with what we have already said about the need to establish criteria by which national sovereignty is subject to international checks and balances. Hence the pertinence of Bellah's observation that 'unlike many other groups, religious communities are often concerned not only with the common good of the nation but also with the common good of all human beings' because they regard their ultimate responsibility to a transcendent God. To forget that, Bellah continues, 'is to obscure perhaps the most important thing we need to understand about the role of religion in society'.[126]

Despite its self-evident appeal, there has been much debate about the appropriateness of the notion of the common good in a modern pluralistic society.[127] A. P. d'Entréves levelled three criticisms which remain pertinent to the debate.[128] The first is the danger, as argued by liberals from Jeremy Bentham onwards, that the good of individual persons can be sacrificed in the interests of some greater more noble cause which is identified as the common good. The protection of individual rights is often the best protection of society as a whole, thus to seek the common good should be to seek the welfare of each member of society. The second is the problem of who should define the common good within a modern pluralist and secular state. The danger is that the state will take this responsibility upon itself, or delegate it to experts, as in Plato's *Republic*.

---

[125] A. Nemetz, 'Common Good', *New Catholic Encyclopedia*, New York: McGraw Hill, 1967, vol. 4, pp. 18f.

[126] Bellah, *The Good Society*, pp. 181f.

[127] See Dahl, *Democracy and its Critics*, pp. 28off.; Wogaman, *Christian Perspectives*, p. 134; see Held, *Models of Democracy*, p. 147; J. Schumpeter, *Capitalism, Socialism, and Democracy*, London: Allen & Unwin, 1976, pp. 251f.

[128] d'Entréves, *The Notion of the State*, pp. 225f.

Related to that is the third problem, namely that 'a description of the common good implies the indication of a choice already made'.[129] Although it may be claimed that certain values are 'given', the question remains: Who says so, on what grounds, and in whose interest?

These difficulties notwithstanding, the doctrine of the common good remains an important challenge to the possessive individualism which lies at the heart of liberal democratic capitalism, and to the sacrifice of human rights on the altar of social collectivism. It is a way of ensuring that the biblical injunction to 'love one's neighbour' remains a challenge to personal responsibility for others, rather than the motto of a social welfare programme, but, at the same time, that it finds expression in the development of just social structures. Like all visions of a just social order it is a challenge and a guide rather than the dispenser of infallible prescriptions cast in concrete.

Covenantal solidarity

The nearest Protestant approach to the common good has been the Reformed (or Calvinist) use of the doctrine of the covenant. Within the covenant, rulers and ruled alike are held accountable before God for the public good determined by the concrete commandments of God. Although covenantal theory has been misused in the service of the exclusive interests of particular groups,[130] the original biblical covenants were inclusive (cf. Genesis 9:9f.,12:1f.). Reflecting on this within the North American context, William Everett has called for the recovery of 'the fullness of the ancient covenant, in which the claims of God, the land, social groups and individuals' are recognized 'within a complex web of mutual obligation'. A purely secular state is clearly inadequate 'if the claims of transcendent loyalty are not mediated to it at least in some indirect way'.[131]

Covenantal language may be inappropriate within con-

---

[129] *Ibid.*, p. 228.   [130] De Gruchy, *Liberating Reformed Theology*, pp. 264ff.
[131] Everett, *God's Federal Republic*, p. 121.

temporary political discourse – though it has begun to resurface – but the doctrine still offers important insights for a Christian contribution to the public debate, and for the development of a contemporary social creed.[132] This was recognized at the ecumenical conference in Seoul in 1990 at which representatives of many churches throughout the world entered into 'covenant solidarity' with regard to justice, peace, and the integrity of creation, and invited others, including people of other faiths, to join with them in doing so: 'through the Spirit a new community is being gathered out of the dispersion and division of nations, religions, classes, sexes, ages and races.'[133] This is the ecumenical vision to which the Hebrew prophets bore testimony (cf. Joel 2:28).

The broadening of the covenant in this way is essential if it is to have any political relevance for global democratization in our contemporary multi-cultural environment. Co-operation with people of other faith communities in working for justice and creating a global democratic culture does not mean indifference to truth, but respect for the opinions and beliefs of other people. Loyalty to one's own tradition does not mean being closed to the insights of others. Christians are called to respect differences and share together with all people of good-will and moral commitment in upholding those values which affirm human dignity, equality, freedom, and justice without which genuine democracy is impossible. Instead of religious pluralism being a problem for the building of common democratic values, it could become a source for the renewal of the democratic vision, as well as for human survival and world peace.[134] It is essential to discover ways whereby the richness and harmony of the whole community will be enhanced by religious and other forms of cultural diversity, rather than destroyed by them.[135]

---

[132] *Costly Unity: Koinonia and Justice, Peace and the Integrity of Creation*, Geneva: WCC, 1993, p. 16.

[133] 'Entering into Covenant Solidarity for Justice, Peace and the Integrity of Creation', the Final Document of the Seoul Conference, March 1990, published in D. Preman Niles, ed., *Between the Flood and the Rainbow*, Geneva: WCC, 1992, p. 166.

[134] Hans Küng, *Theology for the Third Millennium*, p. 227.

[135] Niebuhr, *Children of Light*, p. 124.

Our consideration of the question of sovereignty has led us to consider the basis upon which political power can be held accountable according to Christian tradition – the common good and the covenant. In doing so we have raised the questions concerning who should decide what is good and just for society, and what the criteria should be on which they must base their decisions. Clearly the decisions cannot be left in the hands of an elite, whether religious or academic, however important their role may be in the process of clarifying the issues and providing insight. Neither can such decisions be left to the vote of a majority bent on protecting self-interest, as though the majority by definition are always right. From a biblical, and therefore Christian, perspective, political ethics is, in the first instance, a response to the cry of the victims of injustice and the needs of the powerless and poor. The significance of democratization in many Third World countries today is precisely the fact that those cries and needs can be heard in ways which have previously been denied, but which now have the potential to transform the conditions under which the victims of society are living and thus help provide a better quality of life.

THE GOD OF THE POWERLESS AND POOR

If the first obligation of the church is to keep those in power accountable, its second responsibility is to enable those who are powerless to become empowered so that they can participate as equals in the exercise of power. For understandable reasons, those who have been engaged in the struggle against the power of an unjust regime, and who have seen the way in which the church can be seduced by its identification with those in power, have become wary of political power. This wariness is healthy, but also dangerous. While absolute power may corrupt absolutely, the exercise of power is fundamental to the ordering of society. Understood as legitimate authority and the ability to put policies into practice, power is not sinful or evil, nor does it necessarily corrupt. Politicians who have no will-to-political-power seldom rule. What is of vital importance is the way in which power is understood and used.

The relationship between power and powerlessness has been at the centre of the struggle for democracy historically, and it remains so today, not least with regard to gender relationships. Power is the ability to control the political process: when exercised for self-advantage it is in danger of becoming corrupt. Powerlessness is the condition of those who have no meaningful way of participating in the process, and therefore no ability to protect what is justly theirs. Yet, right from the beginning of the evolution of democracy, groups have been excluded from democratic participation and therefore from sharing in the exercise of power, not least when their own interests have been most at stake. A primary task of Christian political witness is, therefore, to enable those who have previously been excluded from the corridors of power to gain access, and to ensure that power is exercised in such a way that it works for the good of society as a whole. This is fundamental to the move from democratic transition to transformation.

The church has a particular responsibility to help those with power to act responsibly, but in solidarity with those who are powerless. The humiliation of Jesus Christ at the hands of those in power, from Herod to Pilate, remains paradigmatic in locating the church within society, even if political rulers may not always be as ruthless or fickle. Political witness from the perspective of the 'weakness of the cross' (*theologia crucis*) is not powerlessness. The cross is not a sign of God's powerlessness, but of the way in which God's power is exercised for the sake of human redemption and wholeness.

Economic justice

The prophetic understanding of justice is not the impartial administration of law, but the overcoming of the gap between rich and poor; it is economic justice.[136] From the perspective of the gospel, the care for, and the empowerment, of the poor and other social victims is the chief criterion by which to evaluate social structures and to become involved in them. Christian

---

[136] See also Villa-Vicencio, *A Theology of Reconstruction*, pp. 231ff.

political thought should be determined, under the impulse of the gospel, 'by a disinterested will to serve and to attention to the very poorest'.[137] This is the permanent test of the authenticity of Christian witness, and the basis upon which critical theology must evaluate all social and political structures. It is also the critical test for democracy. The failure of Communism in eastern Europe, and the inability of capitalism to really solve the immense economic problems now facing the world, are indicative of the crisis of modernization and the need to go beyond the dichotomy which has hitherto separated global economic systems.[138]

Democracy cannot be sustained and flourish where there is large-scale poverty, especially where this co-exists with considerable wealth. Poverty, not the poor, is an enemy of democracy and incompatible with a just world order. If the vote does not bring about access to clean water, adequate housing, health-care, employment, and a decent education, democracy will lose its legitimacy. Likewise, there can be no real global democratization without redressing the balance between rich and poor nations, the North and the South.[139] The gap between rich and poor, threats to the environment, the question of land distribution, gender relations, unemployment, and the continual eruption of conflict, are all interrelated. Perhaps symptomatic of everything else is, however, the debt crisis which threatens to destroy the already fragile fabric of democracy in many Third World countries.[140] Clearly, without the development of sustainable economies, the problem of debt will increase. Hence the urgent need to relate democracy and development. The question is whether there is an efficient alternative to capitalism which is true to the democratic vision and able to deal with the enormity of the problem.

---

[137] *Octogesima Adveniens* 42, in Walsh and Davies, eds., *Proclaiming Justice and Peace*, p. 182.
[138] Wolfgang Huber, 'Bonhoeffer and Modernity', *Union Seminary Quarterly Review*, 46, 1–4, 1992, p. 7; Davis, *Religion and the Making of Society*, p. 176.
[139] See *Christian Faith and the World Economy Today*, A Study Document, Geneva: WCC, 1992, pp. 17ff.
[140] 'Entering into Covenant Solidarity', in Niles, *Between the Flood and the Rainbow*, p. 170.

Many of the major figures in Christian theology in the twentieth century 'have vigorously criticized liberal capitalism'.[141] Some have regarded the notion of 'Christian capitalism' as an oxymoron,[142] and the reduction of democracy to something simply bourgeois as a betrayal of its essence.[143] This has become progressively the case in Catholic social teaching since *Rerum Novarum*, and especially Pope John XXIIIs summons at Vatican II for a 'church of the poor'.[144] Catholic teaching has distanced itself from capitalism in the matter of ownership,[145] called for a more just economic ordering of North–South relationships,[146] warned against the danger of basing human freedom on the autonomy of the individual,[147] and recommended dialogue with socialism 'as a means of overcoming the serious limitations of the collectivist economies of the East and the capitalist economies of the West'.[148] In their celebrated pastoral letter, *Economic Justice for All*, the bishops in the United States appealed for 'a new experiment in economic justice and participatory democracy',[149] and, more recently, John Paul II has related the dignity of the individual to the common good, made the defence of private property subordinate to human sharing, and suggested that the socialization of the means of production can best serve to protect the rights of the individual and the common good.[150]

[141] Dorrien, *Reconstructing the Common Good*, p. vi; See William Temple, *Christianity and Social Order*, London: SPCK, 1976, pp. 46f.

[142] Davis, *Religion and the Making of Society*, p. 179.

[143] Maritain, *Christianity and Democracy*, p. 23.

[144] The foundation for this development was laid especially by John XXIII in *Mater at Magistra* (1961) and in *Pacem in Terris* (1963). Paul VI spoke about the possibility of a Christian socialism. See John J. Mitchell, 'Embracing a Socialist Vision: The Evolution of Catholic Social Thought, Leo XIII to John Paul II', in ed. James E. Wood, Jr., *Readings on Church and State*, Waco, Texas: Baylor University 1989, p. 244, Enrique Dussel, *Ethics and Community*, Maryknoll, N.Y.: 1988, p. 208.

[145] *Magister et Magistra*, 104–9, in Walsh and Davies eds., *Proclaiming Justice and Peace*, p. 20.

[146] *Magister et Magistra*, 171, in *ibid.*, p. 30.

[147] *Octagesimo Adveniens*, 35, in *ibid.*, p. 179.

[148] Mitchell, 'Embracing a Socialist Vision', p. 235; Dussel, *Ethics and Community*, p. 209.

[149] *Economic Justice for All: Pastoral Letter on Catholic Social Teaching and the U.S. Economy*, Washington D.C.: National Conference of Catholic Bishops, 1986.

[150] *Centesimus Annus*, 30–43; see also Matthew Habiger Papal Teaching on Private Property, New York: University Press of America, 1990.

In view of this tradition of opposition to liberal capitalism, it is perhaps surprising that a leading Christian social ethicist steeped in the tradition of Christian socialism, Ronald Preston, has called for a reassessment of the market 'as the only alternative on offer to deal with the fundamental economic problems which any society has to solve'.[151] In a spirited response to the challenge, John Atherton has gone even beyond Preston in his new-found enthusiasm for 'the market'. Acknowledging the validity of many of the traditional Christian criticisms of capitalism, and distancing himself from the idolatry of free-marketers, Atherton argues that Christianity has none the less failed to understand the market and its contribution 'to the development of necessary civic virtues in the modern context'.[152] Convinced that the market-related values of self-interest, efficiency, freedom in competition, and the independence of the individual can be morally redeemed, he calls for their affirmation not rejection.

Atherton identifies three major interconnected challenges to the modern market system, namely poverty, participation, and the environment, each of which shares a concern for human dignity and equity.[153] But, he argues, they must not be allowed to become the 'governing principle' of society, for this only leads to 'economic inefficiency and a greater political oppression'.[154] The market is ambiguous, but the only viable economic model today is one which is fashioned through the interaction of these great challenges with the market economy.[155] But economics, he continues, must be kept as free from political interference as possible. The subordination of the economy to political ideology was precisely what happened in command economies.[156] For both the economy and democracy to function properly, they need to be kept relatively autonomous. Justice is important, but without efficiency the economy 'is a moral lame duck'. [157]

---

[151] Ronald H. Preston, *Religion and the Ambiguities of Capitalism*, London: SCM, 1991, p. 128.
[152] Atherton, *Christianity and the Market*, p. 219.   [153] *Ibid.*, p. 238.
[154] *Ibid.*, p. 258.
[155] *Ibid.*, p. 224.   [156] *Ibid.*, p. 72.   [157] *Ibid.*, p. 212.

Atherton's attempt to overcome the impasse in Christian social ethics raises certain critical questions. The first is whether the market can be regarded quite as autonomously and scientifically as he claims. Does it not assume a particular social philosophy oriented towards the individual consumer rather than towards the needs of the community as a whole?[158] Does it not value efficiency above all else?[159] Its success is dependent not just on economic laws, but, as Adam Smith himself recognized, on the acceptance of a general moral law which guides the behaviour of those engaged in it. 'Without this sacred regard to rules', Smith wrote, 'there is no man whose conduct can be much depended on'.[160] The fact is, the market cannot survive unless it is based on some accepted moral norms and commitments. Material incentives and profits alone, without recognized behaviour codes, would be self-defeating. Adam Smith warned of the need to be suspicious of any legislation which originated with profit-makers, because they generally have 'an interest to deceive and even oppress the public'.[161]

Secondly, is it possible or desirable to keep politics out of economics anymore than out of religion? Are not economic issues and policies of general public concern, and, if so, should they be removed from public debate and decision-making? Economics does not function outside of the body politic, but within, and as such it is inevitably subject to political decisions. At least some market-economists recognize the possibility of redistributing resources and correcting 'market failures in ways that move towards "just" outcomes viewed in terms of equality of outcomes or of equality of opportunities while preserving the essential efficiency of market incentives'.[162] It seems to be of paramount importance to ensure that the right decisions are

---

[158] Preston, *Religion and the Ambiguities of Capitalism*, p. 24.   [159] *Ibid.*, p. 23.
[160] Adam Smith, *The Theory of Moral Sentiments*, Oxford: Clarendon Press, 1988, p. 163.
[161] Adam Smith, *An Inquiry into the Nature and Causes of the Wealth of Nations*, New York: Random House, 1937, p. 250.
[162] G. A. Hughes, 'The Economics of Hard Choices: Justice and the Market', in *Justice and the Market*, Occasional Paper no. 21, Centre for Theology and Public Issues, New College, Edinburgh, 1991, p. 17.

made both on the basis of good economic sense and in the light of ethical and theological critique. If we decide to let the market sort things out, it is likely that the end-product will be neither justice nor efficiency.[163] The market, Preston argues, is superior to any alternative, 'but it needs to be set in a firm framework of controls, involving redistribution of income and wealth by public policy in order to achieve a mutuality between citizens in dealing with the basics of life, and the crippling uncertainties with which any one of us may be faced from time to time'.[164] Moreover, politicians need the moral will to do what they already can with the resources at their disposal.

The third question is whether the market has been as successful as Atherton suggests in dealing with the problems facing the economies in countries which are in democratic transition. This has by no means been proved, and there are indications which suggest that earlier optimism in this regard will not be sustained. Can there be one economic model which works equally well in every context? Certainly the validity and value of economic systems look very different depending on where we live, and on our experience of the prevailing system. Thus, just as eastern Europeans have rejected Communism because it failed to deliver on its economic promises, so many Latin Americans and others in the Third World have experienced capitalism in a way which has exacerbated their poverty.[165] Despite Atherton's critique of Preston, the latter's perception of the issues remains compelling:

the issue is not between the free market and the central, planned economy, but how far we can get the best of what the social market and democratic socialist models propose; and by democratic I mean a system whereby the government is removable by free elections, so that the policies it pursues must enable it to win power and retain it.[166]

The relationship of the market and capitalism to democracy has been a thread running throughout our discussion, and it is clearly of fundamental importance both for determining Chris-

---

[163] Tom D. Campbell, 'Markets and Justice', in *Justice and the Market*, p. 27.

[164] Preston, *Religion and the Ambiguities of Capitalism*, p. 46.

[165] Dussel, *Ethics and Community*, p. 193.

[166] Preston, *Religion and the Ambiguities of Capitalism*, p. 15.

tian witness in the political arena, and for working towards a just democratic social order. Perhaps the debate between socialism and capitalism has been misguided, as Charles Davis suggests, because they are 'essentially incompatible'. Socialism, Davis argues, 'is a political vision of a moral and religious character', whereas capitalism 'is a self-regulating system that has established itself as autonomous in relation to the rest of the social structure'.[167] Socialism is not about state-ownership and central planning, but about justice and human relationships, about whether people are reduced to labour units or whether they have meaningful control over their lives and labour. In order to deal with the immense problems of poverty and the scarcity of resources we need market efficiency, but we also need just distribution and the participation of all concerned in the means of production. Just distribution implies the rediscovery of genuine human relationships beyond individual and group interests.[168] It requires a commitment to the realization of the ecumenical vision.

THE 'SHALOM' OF GOD; THE ECUMENICAL VISION

From the outset we have made a distinction between democracy as a *system* of government, and democracy as a *vision* of a just society which is inclusive of the whole human family. A society in which all are respected as equals, in which difference is enriching not divisive, and in which human beings discover freedom and fulfilment. This 'concrete utopia' is always beyond full realization, and yet every victory for human equality, freedom, justice, peace, and the integrity of creation, is a step towards its fulfilment. Once democracy settles down into the rut of its past achievements, uncritically embodied in one or other of its historic forms, then it degenerates into an ideology which must eventually petrify. It may still be described in technical terms as democracy, but it has lost its dynamism. In order for democracy to be retrieved it has to be revitalized by being reconnected to the driving force of a vision of a fully inclusive and just world order.

[167] Davis, *Religion and the Making of Society*, p. 173.   [168] *Ibid.*, p. 185.

It may be argued that while the democratic *system* has derived from the liberal trajectory in the development of democracy, the prophetic *vision* has been best expressed in the socialist trajectory. But whatever their past relations there is today the clear need to embody the best of both and move beyond them in search of new models of a just and democratic world order. Pressure to do so has come from different quarters – feminists, secular humanists, non-western nations, and the ecumenical church, often joined together in a coalition in the struggle for justice, peace, and the integrity of creation.

The Christian contribution to the development of democracy has been manifold. As we have shown, Christianity provided the matrix within which the democratic system evolved in the western world. In doing so it experimented with proto-democratic forms of church and social life, providing analogies and antecedents for the future and generating key concepts. Furthermore, in various places and at various times, churches have been directly involved in the practicalities of democratic transition and transformation, especially during the latter half of the twentieth century. Yet, however much Christianity provided the matrix for the gestation of democracy, or, through its praxis has enabled its birth in different contexts, it has been its witness to the prophetic vision as interpreted through the reign of God in Jesus Christ that has been its lasting contribution. We have argued that the democratic *vision* as such owes more to the prophets of ancient Israel than it does to the journey which began in ancient Athens and which eventually led to democracy becoming the polity of modernity. Moreover, it is the eschatological message of the prophets, their concrete utopianism in which hope and justice have been inseparably related, which has provided Christianity with its resources in the public sphere and enabled it to remain in critical tension or solidarity with political systems.

The radical break between Christianity and modernity which occurred in Europe as a result of the French Revolution and conservative Christian reactions to it, meant that the vision of *egalité*, *liberté*, and *fraternité* was separated from its theological foundations with disastrous results for both church

and society. Yet there have always been those Christians and
churches which have recognized that the Revolution – without
its atheism or the terror which followed – was in many ways the
historical outworking of the prophetic vision. Thus during the
past century there has been a growing attempt to reunite that
which belongs together in the interests of a just and democratic
world. In our century, the ecumenical movement has fulfilled a
key role in pursuit of this task. Vatican II and the 1966 Church
and Society Conference in Geneva are symbolic of this endeavour, and we have noted many other contributions of the
ecumenical church in different places to the process. At the
same time, people of other faiths as well as secular men and
women have, in their often greater efforts to achieve justice,
peace, and democracy in the world, challenged Christians and
the church to become more faithful to their own prophetic
vision. In participating together in the struggles for such a
world order they have discovered a solidarity in which some of
the dichotomies created in the course of historical struggle have
been overcome.

There is today, then, a convergence between the democratic
system and its *vision*, and the ecumenical *koinonia*, its holistic
missionary paradigm,[169] and its vision of *shalom*. The two
traditions, separated by the distortions of modernity, have
rediscovered each other in theory and in praxis. Their convergence is not one of synthesis or assimilation. Democracy
remains a form of political organization – the best option
available for embodying penultimate expressions of the vision
of *shalom* – but it is not the kingdom of God. Christianity, as we
stressed at the beginning, cannot be equated with any political
order even though it may express a strong preference for
democracy today as the best way of structuring equality,
freedom, and justice. The prophetic vision itself, however,
demands critical solidarity, and that means a creative and
constructive tension expressing the dialectic between Christian
faith and culture, between the reign of the triune God and the

---

[169] For the emerging holistic ecumenical missionary paradigm which parallels our
discussion, See David J. Bosch, *Transforming Mission: Paradigm Shifts on Theology of
Mission*, Maryknoll, N.Y.: Orbis, 1991.

sovereignty of the people. This dialectical relationship is a two-way process, for the global struggle for a just democratic order has forced complacent churches to re-examine their own prophetic roots and rediscover the vision which is at the heart of Jesus' proclamation of the reign of God. If faithful to that vision, Christianity will continue to contribute to the ferment for democratic transformation and the pursuit of a world order which is not only new but also just, and therefore one in which God's *shalom* will become a reality.

As we have suggested, the vision of God's *shalom* – the 'ecumenical vision' – is no longer solely the prerogative of particular religious traditions (Jewish and Christian), but one which is global and multi-cultural in its influence and scope. Ecumenism is, after all, far more than the attempt to reunite the Christian church in the pursuit of its mission. In the words of Konrad Raiser, present General Secretary of the WCC:

Oikoumenē is a relational, dynamic concept which extends beyond the fellowship of Christians and church to the human community within the whole of creation. The transformation of the *oikoumenē* as the 'inhabited earth' into the living household (*oikos*) of God – that remains the calling of the ecumenical movement.[170]

The *oikoumenē* thus refers to the 'whole inhabited universe', and therefore the ecumenical vision is one in which the unity and mission of the church is inseparably related to the restoration of the unity of the whole of humankind and the integrity of the creation itself, through the establishment of God's reign of justice and *shalom*. That is why it is impossible to conceive of the mission of the church apart from the struggle for a just world order, or to consider the role of the church except in relation to the needs and concerns of humanity and creation as a whole. This is, indeed, the vision of the prophets and the hope of the world. Nowhere is this expressed better than in the words of the prophet Isaiah:

---

[170] Konrad Raiser, '*Oikoumene*', in Nicholas Lossky, José Míguez Bonino, John S. Pobee, Tom. F. Stransky, Geoffrey Wainright, and Pauline Webb, eds., *Dictionary of the Ecumenical Movement*, Geneva: WCC, 1991, p. 742.

Then the wilderness will become garden land
and garden land will be reckoned as common as scrub.
Justice will make its home in the wilderness,
and righteousness dwell in the grassland;
righteousness will yield *shalom*.[171]

---

[171] Isaiah 32:15f. A passage read at the inauguration of Nelson Mandela as President
of South Africa on 10 May 1994.

Select bibliography

Atherton, John, *Christianity and the Market: Christian Social Thought for Our Times*. London: SPCK, 1992.

Bellah, Robert; Madsen, Richard; Sullivan, William M.; Swidler, Ann; and Tipton, Steven M., *The Good Society*. New York: Alfred A. Knopf, 1991.

Berman, Harold J., *Law and Revolution: the Formation of the Western Legal Tradition*. Boston: Harvard University Press, 1983.

Boff, Leonardo, *Trinity and Society*. London: Burns & Oats, 1988.

Bonhoeffer, Dietrich, *Ethics*. New York: Macmillan, 1965.

Chomsky, Noam, *Deterring Democracy*. New York: Verso, 1991.

Cochrane, Charles Norris, *Christianity and Classical Culture: a Study of Thought and Action from Augustus to Augustine*. London: Oxford University Press, 1944.

Coleman, John A. ed., *One Hundred Years of Catholic Social Thought: Celebration and Challenge*. Maryknoll, N.Y.: Orbis, 1991.

Cort, John C., *Christian Socialism*. Maryknoll, N.Y.: Orbis, 1988.

Costly Unity: Koinonia and Justice, Peace and the Integrity of Creation. Geneva: WCC, 1993.

Dahl, Robert, A., *After the Revolution: Authority in a Good Society*. New Haven: Yale University Press, 1970.

Democracy and its Critics. New Haven and London: Yale University Press, 1989.

Davidson, Basil, *The Black Man's Burden: Africa and the Curse of the Nation–State*. London: James Curry, 1992.

Davis, Charles, *Religion and the Making of Society: Essays in Social Theology*. Cambridge University Press, 1994.

d'Entreves, A. P., *The Notion of the State: an Introduction to Political Theory*. Oxford: Clarendon Press, 1967.

Dorrien, Gary J., *Reconstructing the Common Good: Theology and the Social Order*. Maryknoll, N.Y.: Orbis, 1990.

Du Toit, André, ed., *Towards Democracy: Building a Culture of Accountability in South Africa*. Cape Town: IDASA, 1991.

Dunn, John, ed., *Democracy: the Unfinished Journey, 508 BC to AD 1993.* Oxford University Press, 1992.

Elshtain, Jean Bethke, *Meditations on Modern Political Thought.* New York: Praeger, 1986.

Everett, William Johnson, *God's Federal Republic: Reconstructing our Governing Symbol.* New York: Paulist Press, 1988.

Fukuyama, Francis, *The End of History and the Last Man.* New York: Free Press, 1992.

Gifford, Paul, *The Christian Churches and Africa's Democratisation.* Leiden: Netherlands; E. J. Brill, 1995.

Gottwald, Norman K., *The Bible and Liberation: Political and Social Hermeneutics.* Maryknoll, N.Y.: Orbis, 1983.

Habermas, Jürgen, *Communication and the Evolution of Society.* Boston: Beacon Press, 1978.

Hauerwas, Stanley, *A Community of Character: Toward a Constructive Christian Social Ethic.* University of Notre Dame Press, 1981.

Held, David, *Models of Democracy.* Cambridge: Polity Press, 1992.

Huntington, Samuel P., *The Third Wave: Democratization in the Late Twentieth Century.* University of Oklahoma Press, 1991.

Lamb, Matthew L., *Solidarity with Victims: Toward a Theology of Social Transformation.* New York: Crossroad, 1982.

Lindsay, Alexander D., *The Churches and Democracy.* London: Epworth, 1934.

Macpherson, C. B., *The Political Theory of Possessive Individualism: Hobbes to Locke.* Oxford: Clarendon Press, 1962.

The Real World of Democracy. Oxford: Clarendon Press, 1966.

Maritain, Jacques, *Christianity and Democracy.* San Francisco: Ignatius Press, 1986.

Micklem, Nathaniel, *The Idea of Liberal Democracy.* London: 1957.

Milbank, John, *Theology and Social Theory: Beyond Secular Reason.* Oxford: Blackwell, 1990.

Nicholls, David, *Deity and Domination Vol. 1: Images of God and the State in the Nineteenth and Twentieth Centuries.* London: Routledge, 1989.

Niebuhr, Reinhold, *The Children of Light and the Children of Darkness: a Vindication of Democracy and a Critique of its Traditional Defense.* New York: Charles Scribner's Sons, 1960.

Niles, D. Preman, ed., *Between the Flood and the Rainbow.* Geneva: WCC, 1992.

Nürnberger, Klaus, ed., *A Democratic Vision for South Africa: Political Realism and Christian Responsibility.* Pietermaritzburg, Encounter Publications, 1991.

Phillips, Anne, *Engendering Democracy.* University Park, PA.: Pennsylvania State University Press, 1991.

Democracy and Difference. Cambridge: Polity Press, 1993.

Preston, Ronald H., *Religion and the Ambiguities of Capitalism*. London: SCM, 1991.

Provost, James and Walf, Knut, eds., *The Tabu of Democracy within the Church*. Concilium, vol. 5, London: SCM, 1992.

Przeworski, Adam, *Democracy and the Market: Political and Economic Reforms in Eastern Europe and Latin America*. Cambridge University Press, 1992.

Rasmussen, Larry L., *Moral Fragments & Moral Community: a Proposal for Church in Society*. Minneapolis: Fortress, 1993.

Rowland, Christopher, *Radical Christianity*. Cambridge: Polity Press, 1988.

Schumpeter, J., *Capitalism, Socialism, and Democracy*. London: Allen and Unwin, 1976.

Skinner, Quentin, *The Foundations of Modern Political Thought*. Volumes 1 and 2. Cambridge University Press, 1978.

Temple, William, *Christianity and Social Order*. London: SPCK, 1976.

Troeltsch, Ernst, *The Social Teaching of the Christian Churches*. Volumes 1 and 2. London: George Allen and Unwin, 1931.

Villa-Vicencio, Charles, *A Theology of Reconstruction: Nation-building and Human Rights*. Cambridge University Press, 1992.

Walsh, Michael, Davies, Brian eds., *Proclaiming Justice and Peace: Documents from John XXIII to John Paul II*. London: Collins, 1984.

West, Cornel, *The American Evasion of Philosophy: A Genealogy of Pragmatism*. University of Wisconsin Press, 1989.

Witte, John ed., *Christianity and Democracy in Global Context*. Boulder: Wedgewood Press 1993.

Wolterstorff, Nicholas, *Until Justice and Peace Embrace*. Grand Rapids: Eerdmans, 1983.

Wuthnow, Robert, *Communities of Discourse: Ideology and Social Structure in the Reformation, the Enlightenment, and European Socialism*. Cambridge, Mass.: Harvard University Press, 1989.

Yoder, John H., *The Priestly Kingdom: Social Ethics as Gospel*. University of Notre Dame Press, 1984.

Index of names

Ambrose of Milan, 60–1
Amin, Idi, 175
Appiah, Kwame, 188
Aquinas, Thomas, 65–6
Aristotle, 17, 64–5, 69, 90, 92
Atherton, John, 271–3
Augustine, 58, 61–2, 65, 236, 239, 245, 250

Babangida, President, 139
Bainton, Roland, 76
Banda, Hastings, 184
Barth, Karl, 9, 116, 126, 195, 242, 255
Basil of Caesarea, 59
Bebbington, David W., 112
Bediako, Kwame, 190
Beker, J. Christiaan, 51
Bellah, Robert, 264
Bellarmine, Robert, 80–1
Benedict of Nursia, 59
Bentham, Jeremy, 97, 264
Berman, Harold, 57, 95, 228
Beto, Frei, 162
Beza, Theodore, 78, 79
Bismark, Otto von, 72, 107, 117, 119, 257
Boesak, Allan, 207
Boff, Leonardo, 240, 252
Bonhoeffer, Dietrich, 9, 121–2, 123, 124–5, 196, 198, 205, 235, 255
Botha, P.W., 34, 35, 207, 208
Bouwsma, William, 78
Bracher, Karl Dieter, 117
Brown, Peter, 245
Bullinger, Heinrich, 89
Bunting, Jabez, 102
Burke, Edmund, 107
Bush, George, 247

Calvin, John, 71, 73, 75–9, 80, 81, 82, 85, 92
Carmichael, Stokely, 141
Carter, President Jimmy, 148
Cartwright, Thomas, 82
Chalmers, Thomas, 104
Chamorro, Violetto, 149
Cheneviére, Marc-Edouard, 76
Chikane, Frank, 211, 214, 222–3
Chiluba, Frederick, 182
Chomsky, Noam, 3
Chopp, Rebecca, 143, 145–6
Cicero, 17, 67
Clark, Kitson, 4
Cleisthenes, 43
Cochrane, Charles Norris, 57, 62
Cone, James, 142–3
Constantine, 52, 58
Cotton, John, 90
Cromwell, Oliver, 86–8

D'Entréves, A. P., 264–5
Davidson, Basil, 188, 260
Davis, Charles, 274
De Klerk, F. W., 35
De Lammenais, Félicité, 109
De Maistre, Joseph, 108
De Mariana, Juan, 81
De Pressensé, Edmond, 110
De Tocqueville, Alexis, 92, 101
Dewey, John, 24, 39
Diamond, Larry, 179
Dibelius, Bishop Otto, 195
Doe, Samuel, 173
Du Montesquieu, Baron, 99
Dunn, John, 4

Eliot, T. S., 126
Elizabeth I, Queen, 84

282

Index of subjects

Standing for the Truth Campaign
(South Africa), 210
Student Non-Violent Co-ordinating
Committee (SNCC), 134
subsidiarity, 62–6
Sudan, 175, 185
suffrage, 19, 20, 28, 102, 106, 117,
140
SWAPO (Namibia), 177
Syllabus of Errors, 109
self-fulfilment, 247
Southern Baptist Convention (USA),
135
Synod of Berlin-Brandenburg, 201

Tanzania, 165, 171, 176
The Social Contract, 98
theocracy, 63, 77, 90, 234, 257
Theologia crucis, 160, 268
third democratic transformation, 2, 5,
9, 194
third way, *Terceristas*, 149, 152, 153,
154, 155
Togo, 180
tolerance, 37, 75, 89, 90, 96, 125, 128,
163, 185, 213, 234, 248, 261
Tory Party (England), 111, 113, 115
totalitarianism, 22, 33, 37, 38, 74, 115,
122, 123, 150, 151, 155, 193, 202,
203, 227, 234, 258, 259
trade unions, 20, 118, 158, 178, 210
trinity, doctrine of, 11, 12, 191, 239,
240, 243, 258
True Whig Party (Liberia), 173
two kingdoms, Lutheran doctrine of,
72, 73, 78, 122, 202, 248

Ubuntu, 191, 219, 242
Uganda, 173, 175, 187
Ujamaa, 176
United Congregational Church of
Southern Africa, 210
United Democratic Front (UDF), 207,
211
United National Independence Party
(UNIP-Zambia), 176
United Nations, 165, 215, 262

United States, 1, 9, 20, 84, 91, 94,
102–6, 126, 131–46, 147, 148, 159,
188, 193, 199, 221, 233, 255, 256;
and Nicaragua, 149–51, 152, 156,
160, 162
UNO (Nicaragua), 150, 151, 158, 159
utopia, utopian vision 7, 31, 49, 53, 86,
99, 145, 159, 162, 230–4, 236–7,
240, 246, 274

values, democratic 8, 69, 113, 145, 170,
189, 218–19, 220, 263, 266
Vatican II, 128, 153, 171, 251, 252, 263,
270, 276
Vatican diplomacy, 175
Via Media, 82–4
Vietnam War, 139, 141, 144, 199
virtues, 61, 62, 164, 260, 271
voluntaryism, 111

Weimar Republic, 35, 117, 118, 119,
120, 121, 122, 125
Whig Party (England), 86, 111
Womens' Rights Convention, Seneca
Falls, 105
women's rights and issues, 16, 20, 27,
28, 31, 50, 51, 52, 103, 104, 105,
106, 117, 132, 133, 143, 144, 145,
158, 166, 174, 185, 210, 213, 219,
220, 243, 250, 251, 276
World Conference on Religion and
Peace, 220
World Council of Churches (WCC) 9,
126, 127, 139, 198, 212, 254, 262;
Amsterdam Assembly, 127; church
and society, 139, 276; justice, peace
and the integrity of creation, 202,
266; life and work, 127; programme
to combat racism, 139; Uppsala
Assembly, 139
World Court, 262
worldview, 29, 58, 62, 202, 230, 237

Zaire, 165, 171, 172, 186
Zambia, 165, 176, 180, 182, 183, 210
Zimbabwe, 171, 172, 181, 207, 209, 210
Zurich, 73, 89

Cambridge Studies in Ideology and Religion